MUSIC THERAPY AND MEDICINE: THEORETICAL AND CLINICAL APPLICATIONS

Music Therapy and Medicine: Theoretical and Clinical Applications

Edited by

Cheryl Dileo
Temple University

American Music Therapy Association, Inc.

Neither the American Music Therapy Association nor its Executive Board is responsible for the conclusions reached or the opinions expressed by the contributors to this book.

The American Music Therapy Association is a non-profit association dedicated to increasing access to quality music therapy services for individuals with disabilities or illnesses or for those who are interested in personal growth and wellness. AMTA provides extensive educational and research information about the music therapy profession. Referrals for qualified music therapists are also provided to consumers and parents. AMTA holds an annual conference every autumn and its eight regions hold conferences every spring.

For up-to-date information, please access the AMTA website at www.musictherapy.org

ISBN: 1–884914–00–4

Published 1999

The American Music Therapy Association, Inc.
8455 Colesville Road, Suite 1000
Silver Spring, MD 20910

Phone: (301) 589-3300
Fax: (301) 589-5175
Email: info@musictherapy.org
Website: www.musictherapy.org

Printed in the United States of America

ACKNOWLEDGMENTS

Perhaps the most gratifying part of editing a book such as this is having the opportunity to acknowledge in writing the individuals who have played significant roles in this project as well as in my life.

First of all, I would like to express my heartfelt appreciation to the contributors of this book: *David Aldridge, Gudrun Aldridge, Joke Bradt, Charles Butler, Jane Edwards, Ellen Griggs-Drane, Roberta Wigle Justice, Roseann Kasayka, Joanne Loewy, David Ramsey, Alan Reitman, Barbara Reuer, Mark Rider, Ruthann Ritchie, Kay Roskam, Bruce Saperston, Benedikte Barth Scheiby, Fred Schwartz, Alan Turry, Ann Turry,* and *Concetta Tomaino* for their enthusiasm, cooperation, support, exceptionally insightful and rapid writing, and important clinical and theoretical offerings to the area of medical music therapy and music medicine. It has been a pleasure and a gift to work with each of them.

I would also like to thank David Smith and the Executive Board of the American Music Therapy Association for commissioning my work as editor, as well as Andrea Farbman and the AMTA office staff for their guidance and direction in organizing the financial and technical aspects of the book. A special thanks to Wordsetters for outstanding editorial and publishing assistance.

I would also like to acknowledge the efforts of Lisa Summer, who assisted in the content area of GIM, and my graduate students, Maria Scutti and Joke Bradt, who helped me with the paperwork, faxes, mailings to authors, and file conversions.

My gratitude also goes to my students, past and present, here and around the world, for teaching me more than they will ever realize.

My appreciation to my mentor, Charles Braswell, is ongoing. He is the individual most responsible for shaping my career as a professional, both through his loving guidance and his example.

Thanks to my dear friends: Ken Bruscia, for his professional and personal support; Julia Marciante, for always being there; Janice Judge and Jason Wong, who personify courage in illness; and Josemiguel Garcia-Cruz for the many "dreams."

My deepest appreciation is expressed to those who share my life and give it meaning: to my unforgettable father, Noble Joseph Dileo, who still lives in my heart and thoughts day by day, for his legacy of love and music; to my mother, Frieda Dileo; to my sisters, Linda Cantrell and Dawn Brooks, for their unfailing encouragement, belief in me, and affection; to my teenage son, Jeffrey Dileo Maranto, the light of my life, for allowing me the space to do this work, for not complaining (more than usual) about my cooking, and for teaching me the virtues of humility and patience; and to my partner, José Ignacio Castaño, for his insistence on my learning WordPerfect 8, for his "cappuccino inspirations," and for his constant and abundant love.

And, as always, I thank my Creator, the source of all my hope and strength.

—Cheryl Dileo

For

José Ignacio "Natxo" Castaño

—who taught my heart to sing

cd

CONTENTS

INTRODUCTION

1

INTRODUCTION TO *MUSIC THERAPY AND MEDICINE*: DEFINITIONS, THERORETICAL ORIENTATIONS AND LEVELS OF PRACTICE

Cheryl Dileo, PhD, MT-BC

MEDICAL APPLICATIONS OF MUSIC

IT EVENTUALLY HAPPENS to every one of us and everyone we love. People get sick, need medical tests, need medical treatment, need to be hospitalized, have accidents, etc. When illness happens, it can cause a crisis and a host of physical, psychological, cognitive, social, and spiritual challenges. Illness or the threat of illness calls upon most or all of the individual's resources for coping. Being sick implies change and adjustment, anxiety, fear, pain, loss, disempowerment, lowered self-esteem, and existential and spiritual questioning.

Many things can help; music is one of them. Knowledge of this fact is growing rapidly in terms of research and clinical information. (Dileo, 1997a; Dileo-Maranto, 1993a, 1993b, 1996a). We already know that music can help patients with a wide variety of medical conditions, or those who are undergoing a wide variety of medical procedures. Some medical specialty areas in which music therapy is used are shown in Figure 1.

We know that music helps ease the anxiety and fear associated with these conditions and procedures. We know that music can help the patient undergo procedures more successfully. We know that music can reduce the perception of pain and help reduce the amount of medicine needed. We know that music can help calm the body's autonomic reactivity and enhance immune response. We know that music can soothe and comfort the individual and reduce the threat of the medical environment. We know that music can help people regain physical functioning better. We know that music provides stimulation within the medical environment and can enhance development. We know that music can help people cope better on many levels. We know that music enhances mood, motivation, and self-expression, and addresses spiritual needs. We know that music can provide an educational tool for health, facilitate decision-making, and increase patient compliance to treatment. We know that music helps create, maintain and enrich social connectedness. We know that music helps people recover from illness better, perhaps even

Neonatology*	Pediatrics*	Physical Rehabilitation*
General Medicine*	Radiology	Pulmonology*
Surgery*	Anesthesiology*	Pain Management*
Intensive Care*	Cardiology*	Obstetrics
Gynecology	Dentistry	Oncology*
Endocrinology	Prevention*	

*included in the current book

Figure 1. Medical Specialty Areas in Which Music Therapy is Used.

contributing to earlier discharges from the hospital. We are beginning to know that music can help prevent illness. And most importantly, we are striving to know how music can help patients more effectively and why. We are seeking to know the clinical approaches used, as well as the underlying theories to these approaches. This is the purpose of this book.

Music Therapy and Music Medicine

Two complementary, yet somewhat different, approaches to the uses of music in medical settings are currently in practice: music therapy and music medicine. Both of these approaches are represented in this book. Both music therapy and music medicine rely on the inherent therapeutic possibilities of music to relieve stress and pain and promote well-being, yet each has essential distinguishing features.

Music medicine is typically used by medical personnel (nonmusic therapists, such as physicians, nurses, dentists and allied health professionals) as an adjunct to various medical treatments or situations. It often represents an attempt to provide a nonpharmacological intervention for stress, anxiety, and/or pain for the medical patient. Examples of music medicine interventions include background music in waiting rooms or other areas of the hospital/treatment environment, musical programs available to the patient prior to surgery or other procedures, and vibroacoustic treatment. Music medicine interventions rely primarily upon receptive music experiences involving prerecorded music (preselected by medical staff or selected by the patient from available programs) (Dileo-Maranto, 1995); music stimuli may include a wide range of music in a variety of genres and styles, low frequency sounds, specially composed music (e.g., womb sounds), or combinations thereof. Sometimes specialized equipment, as in vibroacoustic therapy, is required for administration of the music. The applications of music medicine are indeed broad, and research has supported their effectiveness. Chapters in this book by Schwartz and Ritchie and by Butler provide excellent examples of music medicine.

Music therapy (also referred to in this volume as medical music therapy), on the other hand, in its approach to medical patients always involves a therapeutic process, a music therapist, and a relationship that develops through the music and process (Dileo, 1997a, 1997b, 1997c, 1997d,

1997e, 1998; Dileo-Maranto, 1991, 1992, 1993a, 1993b, 1994, 1995, 1996a, 1996b, 1996c; Wigram & Dileo, 1997). In music medicine, there may certainly be a therapeutic relationship between the patient and the medical staff member(s) involved; however, this relationship does not develop through the music, nor is there a definable process that occurs in relationship to the music.

In music therapy, the gamut of experiences within music are utilized (receptive, improvisation, recreation, activities, combined arts, composition). The focus of music therapy may be broader, involving the whole of the patient on many levels, rather than just the presenting medical condition or reactions to the medical procedure. In music therapy, both the music and therapeutic relationship serve as healing components in treatment. In spite of the fact that there may be emphasis on one, the other, or both during treatment, both are always present (Dileo-Maranto, 1991, 1992). In addition, music therapy may serve as a primary mode of intervention with regard to medical treatment, may be considered supportive to medical treatment, or may work in an equal partnership with medical treatment (Dileo-Maranto, 1991, 1992) (Table 1).

Chapters by Justice and Kasayka, Saperston, Edwards, Aldridge and Aldridge, Scheiby, Rider, Tomaino, Ramsey, Griggs-Drane, Reuer and Roskam, Dileo, Turry and Turry, Dileo and Bradt, and Loewy, in the present volume, provide examples of medical music therapy. Further, these chapters are organized in the text according to the type of music experiences used: receptive, improvisational, re-creative, songs, or combined approaches.

Both music medicine and music therapy approaches are considered important and necessary for the medical patient, and collaborative approaches between medical personnel and music therapists often provide valuable and rich opportunities for research and clinical practice.

Performing Arts Medicine

As music therapy and music medicine represent two subfields in the broad interface between music and medicine, a third possibility is included in this volume: performing arts medicine. This subfield refers to the study and treatment of the performance-related medical and psychological problems of musicians (as well as other performing artists) (Dileo-Maranto, 1991, 1992, 1994). Music therapy is emerging as one possibility for treatment of the problems of musicians, particularly those related to performance-anxiety (Dileo-Maranto, 1994; Habboushe & Dileo-Maranto, 1991). In this book, Reitman provides an excellent description of a music therapy process with this population.

Theoretical Orientations Within Medical Music Therapy

An important purpose of this book is to illuminate the various theoretical approaches that may underlie clinical practice in music therapy with medical patients. As seen in Figure 1, music therapists employed in medical settings often work with a wide range of clinical problems and patient needs. It is not surprising, therefore, that they base what they do upon different theoretical models, and often upon several theoretical models. What is surprising, however, is the breadth of these models. Figure 2 provides an overview and a rather loose classification of the various theoretical models described in this book. It can be accurately assumed that this classification

Table 1
Music Therapy and Music Medicine Characteristics

	Music Therapy	Music Medicine
Music	Yes	Yes
Self-selected/Pre-selected Music	Not Usually	Yes
RelationshipThrough Music	Yes	No
Music Therapist	Yes	No
Assessment Process	Yes	Sometimes
Evaluation	Yes	Sometimes
Goals	Yes	Not Usually
Process	Yes	No
Self-help	No	Sometimes
Types of Music Experiences		
· Receptive	Yes	Yes
· Improvisation	Yes	No
· Recreative	Yes	No
· Composition	Yes	No
· Activity	Yes	No
· Combined Arts	Yes	No

does not fully embrace all of the orientations that are currently being used in practice and, thus, one cannot consider this list as all-inclusive. In addition, new theoretical models for the role of music therapy in medicine are currently being developed, as presented by Rider and by Aldridge and Aldridge.

Although various psychological theories may be employed, the distinction between medical music therapy practice and music psychotherapy is intentionally not made for several reasons. Current research points to the previously artificial divisions between mind, body, the social environment, and spirit, emphasizing the interrelatedness of these parts of the person in etiology, assessment, and treatment. Because of this, it is not possible to isolate the effects of therapy in any of these areas. For example, music psychotherapy can be undertaken with a medical patient to improve his psychological adjustment, but it is becoming increasingly clear that this may and will influence his or her medical condition. The reverse is also true. It may be possible to delineate primary and secondary goals of therapy, for example, as being primarily psychological and secondarily physical, but it is not possible to say that one music therapy strategy addresses physical needs, whereas another addresses social, psychological, and/or spiritual needs. The individual cannot be compartmentalized, and neither can prevention or treatment.

Medical Butler & Lehikoinen Griggs-Drane Schwartz & Ritchie	***Developmental*** Loewy Schwartz & Ritchie	***Psychological*** Edwards (stress)
Behavioral/Cognitive Saperston Reitman	***Gestalt*** Loewy	***Psychoanalytic*** Scheiby Loewy
Behavioral Medicine (Mind-Body Model) Aldridge & Aldridge Justice & Kasayka Loewy Reuer & Roskam Dileo & Bradt Dileo	***Transpersonal/ Spiritual*** Aldridge & Aldridge Justice & Kasayka Turry & Turry Dileo	***Existential*** Aldridge & Aldridge Dileo
Humanistic Tomaino Turry & Turry Dileo	***Anthroposophic*** Turry & Turry	***Communication Theory*** Ramsey
Neurological Tomaino	***Physics*** Rider Dileo & Bradt Butler & Lehikoinen	***Wellness*** Reuer & Roskam
Homeodynamic Rider		

Figure 2. Theoretical Orientations in Medical Music Therapy.

Levels of Medical Music Therapy Practice

When one examines the breadth of theoretical orientations and approaches to medical music therapy clinical practice, as well as the variety of clinical needs addressed in patients, various levels of practice become apparent. Organizing them into some coherent frame of reference is another issue! Realizing that it is not possible to construct a "levels" framework upon which all practitioners would agree, it is nevertheless necessary to begin the process as a starting point for further discussion.

Criteria for designating various levels of practice may and should include the following:

- clinical needs of patient;
- level of training, experience, and qualifications of the therapist and autonomy in designating and implementing therapeutic goals;
- depth of intended goal of music therapy intervention;
- the function of music therapy with regard to medical treatment (supportive, primary, equal).

With these criteria in mind, a levels model is presented for a specific therapeutic goal, e.g., pain management. This model can be either refined or generalized to include various other clinical goals.

Three levels of music therapy work are defined: (1) supportive, (2) specific, and (3) comprehensive (Dileo-Maranto, 1993c, 1993d). Criteria for this classification, as well as examples of music therapy interventions, are shown for each level in Figure 3.

1. Supportive Level

Needs of Client:	Temporary relief from pain
Level of Therapist:	Beginning, intermediate
Depth:	Distraction, provision of coping skills
Function:	Supportive of medical intervention
Common Music Therapy Interventions:	Music and biofeedback, music-based relaxation strategies, vibroacoustic therapy, re-creative techniques

2. Specific Level

Needs of Client:	Understanding of pain
Level of Therapist:	Intermediate, experienced, graduate studies
Depth:	Dialogue with or confrontation of pain
Function:	Equal with medical intervention
Common Music Therapy Interventions:	Improvisation, music and imagery techniques

3. Comprehensive Level

Needs of Client:	Resolution of pain
Level of Therapist:	Advanced, experienced, graduate/specialized training
Depth:	Resonance by therapist with pain
Function:	Primary
Common Music Therapy Interventions:	Entrainment, guided imagery and music

Figure 3. Levels of Music Therapy Practice in Pain Management.

CONCLUSIONS

It is hoped that this brief introduction to medical music therapy, music medicine, and performing arts medicine will help the reader identify these various approaches in clinical practice. It is also hoped that the emphasis on theory and practice in this book will ultimately enrich the practice of medical music therapy. Each reader will evaluate what has been written, agreeing or disagreeing with various orientations and clinical styles. This process is considered very important in formulating and refining one's own beliefs, perspectives, theoretical orientations, and unique way of working.

Medical music therapy is certainly coming of age, and the present volume is only one testament to all that is possible. As said in the beginning of the chapter, illness will eventually cause a crisis in all of our lives. Music therapy can help.

REFERENCES

Dileo, C. (1997a). *Receptive strategies in music therapy.* Paper presented at the Polymedia Music as a Tool for Well-Being and Preventive Health Care Mini-Symposium, Hamburg, Germany.

Dileo, C. (1997b). Reflections on medical music therapy: Biopsychosocial perspectives of the treatment process. In J. Loewy (Ed.), *Music therapy and pediatric pain.* Cherry Hill, NJ: Jeffrey Books.

Dileo, C. (1997c). *The process of medical music therapy.* Paper presented at the annual conference of the National Association for Music Therapy, Los Angeles.

Dileo, C. (1997d). The context of music and medicine. In T. Wigram and C. Dileo (Eds.), *Music vibration and health.* Cherry Hill, NJ: Jeffrey Books.

Dileo, C. (1997e). El proceso musical en Pacientes Medicos. In P. del Campo (Ed.), *La musical como proceso humano.* Salamanca: Amaru Ediciones.

Dileo, C. (1998). *The process of medical music therapy.* Paper presented at the Mid-Atlantic Regional Conference of the American Music Therapy Association, Cherry Hill, NJ.

Dileo-Maranto, C. (1991). A classification model for music and medicine. In C. Dileo-Maranto (Ed.), *Applications of music in medicine*. Washington, DC: National Association for Music Therapy.

Dileo-Maranto, C. (1992). A comprehensive definition of music therapy with an integrative model for music medicine. In R. Spintge & R. Droh (Eds.), *Musicmedicine.* St. Louis: MMB.

Dileo-Maranto, C. (1993a). Music therapy and stress management. In P. Lehrer and R. Woolfolk (Eds.), *Principles and practice of stress management.* New York: Guilford.

Dileo-Maranto, C. (1993b). Applications of music in medicine. In M. Heal and T. Wigram (Eds.), *Music therapy in health and education*. London: Jessica Kingsley.

Dileo-Maranto, C. (1993c). Music therapy clinical practice: A global perspective and classification system. In C. Dileo-Maranto, *Music therapy: International perspectives.* Pipersville, PA: Jeffrey Books.

Dileo-Maranto, C. (1993d). Music therapy in the United States of America. In C. Dileo-Maranto (Ed.), *Music therapy: International perspectives*. Pipersville, PA: Jeffrey Books.

Dileo-Maranto, C. (1994). *The professionalization of musicmedicine and music therapy.* Paper presented at the V International MusicMedicine Symposium, San Antonio, TX.

Dileo-Maranto, C. (1995). *Music and the mind-body connection.* Paper presented at the Centennial Conference of the University of Melbourne, Melbourne, Australia.

Dileo-Maranto, C. (1996a). Research in music and medicine: The state of the art. In M. A. Froehlich (Ed.), *Music therapy for hospitalized children: A creative arts child-life approach.* Cherry Hill, NJ: Jeffrey Books.

Dileo-Maranto, C. (1996b). *New directions and research in music therapy and medicine.* Paper presented at the World Congress of Music Therapy, Hamburg, Germany.

Dileo-Maranto, C. (1996c). Music medicine for patients undergoing colonoscopy procedures and music therapy for oncology patients: Clinical descriptions and distinctions in practice. Paper presented at the VI International MusicMedicine Symposium, San Antonio, TX.

Habboushe, F., & Dileo-Maranto, C. (1991). An overview of medical and psychological problems of musicians. In C. Dileo-Maranto (Ed.), *Applications of music in medicine.* Washington, DC: National Association for Music Therapy.

Wigram, T., & Dileo, C. (1997). Clinical and ethical considerations. In T. Wigram and C. Dileo (Eds.), *Music vibration and health.* Cherry Hill, NJ: Jeffrey Books.

PART I: RECEPTIVE APPROACHES

2

Music Listening in Neonatal Intensive Care Units

Fred J. Schwartz, MD
Ruthann Ritchie, MT-BC

Clinical Needs

THE HOSPITAL CARE of premature, low birth weight infants requires large resources in technology and personnel. The economic cost of care in the United States for Neonatal Intensive Care Units (NICU) and Intermediate ICU averages between $1,000 and $2,000 per day or over $3.5 billion a year. The added costs of special education and continued cost of medical care for these children are larger than the initial costs for their NICU care (Lewit, Baker, Corman & Shiono, 1995). Many of these babies suffer hearing and visual disabilities, mental retardation, cerebral palsy, or learning disabilities.

Over the last two decades there has been a marked increase in the population of low and very low birth weight infants. These infants are deprived of their normal intrauterine environment, and they are susceptible to the effects of stress in the NICU. These adverse effects are reflected by heart rate variations, increasing oxygen consumption and decreased blood oxygen levels, as well as marked blood pressure fluctuations, failure to thrive, and increased levels of agitation. The NICU infant cannot always communicate the feeling of pain, yet when pain is sensed, this sets off a stress reaction, which includes an increase in stress hormone levels (Arnand & Hickey, 1987).

While it is felt that sensory stimulation is necessary for optimal neurological development, the sights and sounds of the modern NICU provide an inappropriate sensory environment for the premature infant (Collins, 1996). An infant in the NICU is exposed to average ambient noise levels ranging from 50 to 88 dB, with peak levels of over 100 dB from sources such as ventilators, monitor alarms, incubator fans and motors, conversations, radios, telephones, water faucets, and cabinet doors (Lynam, 1995). The act of closing an incubator porthole can reach over 110 dB, or the equivalent of a riveting machine. Loud noise and abrupt peaks in sound levels can be highly arousing for the medically fragile, premature baby. Subsequently, conditions such as hypoxemia, blood pressure instability, increased apnea, bradycardia, altered cerebral blood flow, and a predisposition for intraventricular hemorrhage can occur (Lynam, 1995). Besides causing distress, these sounds can inhibit sleep-wake cycles and prevent descent into REM sleep states necessary for maturation and weight gain.

Since the 1980s, a number of studies have looked at the institution of developmental care in the NICU (Als, Lawhon, Duffy, McNulty, Gibes-Grossman, & Blickman, 1994; Petryshen, Stevens, Hawkins, & Stewart, 1997). This approach recognizes the importance of the environment and the appropriate level of stimulation necessary both to foster brain growth and to integrate physiological and behavioral processes. Developmental care incorporates light and noise management, positioning/bundling, use of pacifiers, kangaroo care (consisting of skin contact with mother or caregiver), and "clustering" of stimulative procedures, allowing for delineation of awake and restful state cycles. Some of the very significant benefits of developmental care are improved clinical outcomes as well as faster weight gain, earlier discharge from the hospital, and significant decreases in the cost of hospitalization. The inclusion of music and other sounds is a natural extension to the practice of developmental care.

To understand what is an appropriate environment to create for the premature baby, one can look back at the environment that the premature baby abruptly loses. The intrauterine environment plays an essential role in the growth and development of the fetus. The whole "nature versus nurture" controversy has ignored the influence of the womb on intelligence and personality. Most previous studies have looked at identical twins in examining genetic and environmental effects on intelligence. The assumptions in these studies were that identical twins that are separated in infancy share only genetic effects on their intelligence. This approach ignored the mutual environment these twins shared in the womb. A meta-analysis of 212 studies spanning the last 70 years showed that the womb accounts for 20% of the shared IQ component of these identical twins separated at birth (Devlin, Daniels, & Roeder, 1997). This explains the striking correlation between the IQs of twins, especially those of adult twins raised apart. The explanation for this is that a significant amount of learning takes place in the uterus. There is no doubt that intrauterine auditory stimuli contribute a large part to this environment.

Intrauterine Hearing and Learning

Ultrasound studies have shown that at 16 weeks gestation the fetus can respond to outside sound (Hepper & Shahidullah, 1994; Shahidullah & Hepper, 1992). Hearing is the first sense to develop and the last to deteriorate in the life cycle. Babies learn to adapt to their mother's breathing, her movements, and her voice as she speaks or sings. The sounds of the blood flow through the placenta can be heard at a very loud level in the womb. For the lower sound frequencies below 500 Hz, the fetus hears mean sound levels between 70 and 80 dB (Gerhardt & Abrams, 1996). The fetus hears the mother's heartbeat about 26 million times. This rhythm protects us, and throughout our lives it will attract us as one of the most important components of music, because it symbolizes primary security and dependable return (Decker-Voigt & Maetzel, 1997).

Evidence points to the fact that learning extends back into the prenatal period, and that the sounds and rhythms in the womb may contain information important to the development of the fetal brain (Devlin et al., 1997; Shetler, 1989). The newborn can differentiate a recording of his or her own mother's prenatal womb sounds from a recording of another mother (Righetti, 1996). The newborn can also differentiate emotional content in the recording of his prenatal womb sounds and respond with changes in movement and heart rate (Righetti, 1996).

There is a vast amount of potential information available to the fetus that can be given in the playing of just one musical note or in singing or talking a single syllable. The content of this sound is full of informational and emotional content (Schwartz, 1997). The fetus and newborn have an innate capacity to perceive this information at a very deep, profound level. To label an interaction with a newborn as infantile is to ignore the genuine receptivity of the newborn, who is already prewired for the reception of love, nurturing, and emotional wisdom. These communicative processes, which take place before and after birth, contribute to the promotion of the child's physical development, behavioral characteristics, and level of intelligence (Lipton, 1998).

The synaptic network in the fetal brain, as well as in the infant brain, undergoes learning-dependent reorganization. This process involves synaptic pruning, the regression of neural circuits, as well as the synaptic sprouting of the developing brain. There is a substantial reduction in neurons and synaptic connections that occurs during the last trimester, as well as a more modest reduction during childhood. This is consistent with the observation of psychologists that infants and children may have enhanced behavioral abilities that diminish later in life (Johnston, 1995). Since fetal hearing is probably the major component of this learning-dependent synaptic pruning and sprouting, the fetus is participating in a second and third trimester auditory amphitheater that is perhaps more important than any other classroom. It is apparent that we have only begun to explore the connection between sound and neurobiological development in the fetus and newborn.

Music in the NICU

Some of the hindrances to growth and earlier discharge from the NICU are decreased blood oxygen availability and increased oxygen consumption from stress. The increased stress response also consumes precious calories. The use of music in the NICU has been shown to decrease the stress response and increase oxygen levels. Womb sound music has been shown to be helpful in the care of mechanically ventilated, agitated premature babies with low oxygen levels. Significant increases in oxygen saturation as well as decreased levels of agitation have been found with the use of music (Collins & Kuck, 1991). Another study has shown that when lullaby music was played in the neonatal intensive care unit (NICU), there were fewer episodes of oxygen desaturation (Caine, 1991).

There is no doubt that some of the high decibel sounds from alarms and equipment in the NICU are harmful to the neonate. In one study, premature babies were insulated from their audio environment with earmuffs (Zahr & Traversay, 1995). They had higher oxygen saturations and more time in the sleep state compared to a control group. Several studies using music with premature babies in the NICU have shown a 3 to 5 day earlier discharge from the NICU (Figures 1, 2 and 3; Caine, 1991; Coleman, Pratt, Stoddar, Gerstmann, & Abel, 1998; Standley, 1996). Other studies have shown a doubled daily weight gain when premature babies in the NICU were exposed to music therapy (Figure 2).

A gender difference as far as music benefits has also been observed in most studies, with the benefits of music predominantly benefiting the female babies (Standley, 1998a). This can probably be explained by the fact that newborn girls have more sensitive hearing than boys at birth (Cassidy & Ditty, 1998a).

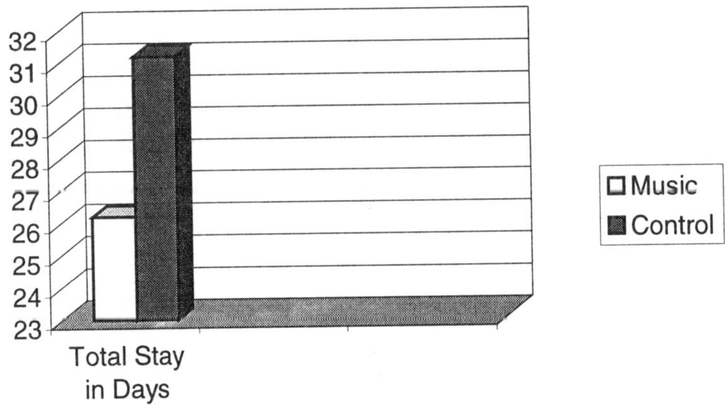

Figure 1. Vocal lullabies decrease length of hospital stay in NICU patients. (Modified from Caine, 1991)

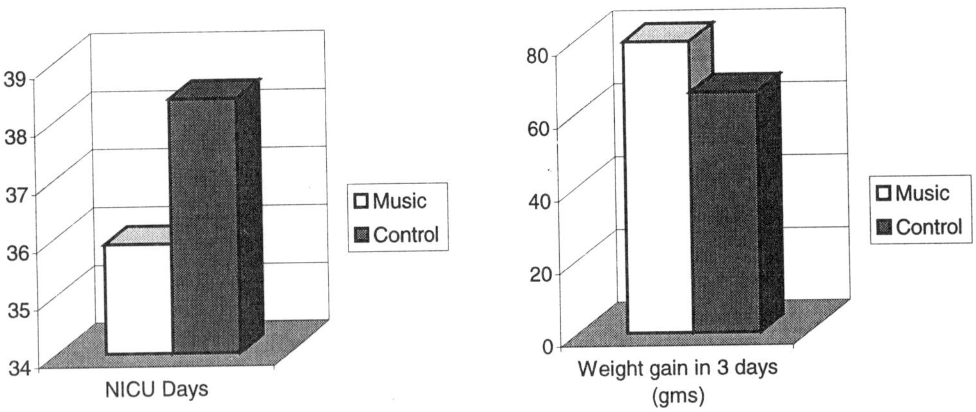

Figure 2. Vocal lullaby music increases weight gain and average 3-day earlier discharge from NICU. (Modified from Coleman et al., 1998)

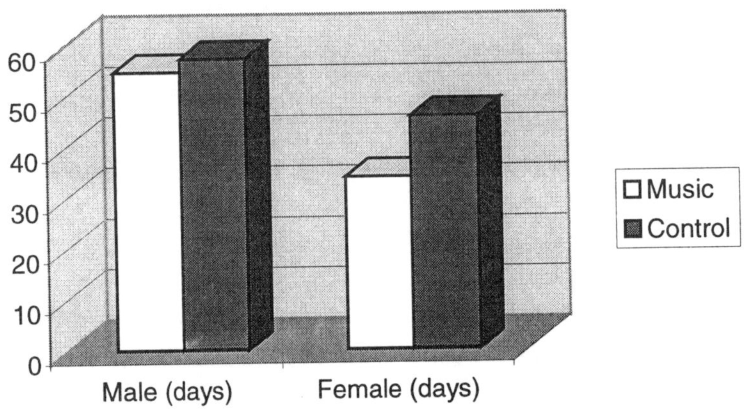

Figure 3. Music and multimodal stimulation decreases hospital stay. (Modified from Standley, 1996)

After music was introduced in our NICU at Piedmont Hospital in early 1998, we noticed a trend for faster growth of head circumference (HC) in the premature babies exposed to music (Schwartz, Ritchie, Sacks, & Phillips, 1998). In a post hoc analysis, this effect of music on HC growth was found to be significant as well in Dr. Jayne Standley's study on the effect of music and multimodal stimulation in the NICU (Standley, 1998b).

It seems logical that the early loss of the intrauterine sound environment would affect brain maturation in the premature baby. Previous work on prenatal intrauterine sound stimulation has shown increases in newborn head circumference and developmental abilities (Logan, 1991). Head circumference is a reliable indicator of brain size in the first 2 years of life (Bray, Shields, Wolcott, & Madsen, 1969; Sheth, Mullett, Bodensteiner, & Hobbs, 1995). We know that malnutrition during infancy leads to reduced head circumferences and IQs later in life (Winick, 1969). There is a definite negative effect on cognitive abilities in the very low birth weight baby (<1.5 kg.) with subnormal head growth in whom catch-up growth does not occur. Decreased head circumference at age 8 months is a strong predictor of decreased intellectual capacity at 8 years of age (Hack, Breslau, Weissman, Aram, Klein, & Borawski, 1991). Thus, low birth weight babies who do not catch up in their HC growth have decreased cognitive abilities later on.

Since it appears that we can foster increased brain growth along with increased synaptic connections in premature babies with music stimulation, the implications are that we can use music to decrease the developmental delays that are common in premature babies. One study found that by exposing premature babies to a recording of the baby's own mother's voice in the hospital, the results at age 5 months showed a significant enhancement in verbal and motor development (Nöcker-Ribaupierre, 1995, 1999). At age 20 months, there remained a trend for these infants to maintain these leads in verbal and motor development despite a small sample size (24 patients control, 24 patients audio stimulation). At age 6, there was still a trend for better verbal skills in the stimulated group.

It becomes clear that there is indeed an effect of music and sound on brain development which extends as far back as the fetal period. This is a natural extension of the "Mozart Effect" in preschool children, which showed that music training can enhance language development, spatial and mathematical abilities (Rauscher et al., 1997), as well as work that showed exposure to Mozart increased spatial IQ in college students (Rauscher, Shaw, & Ky, 1995).

The newborn baby, and especially the premature baby, has a distinct framework of experience with sounds and music. We know that newborns prefer female voices to male voices and prefer their own mother's voice to other women's voices. Some of the most commonly used audio stimulation in the NICU has included lullabies, classical and womb sound music, as well as mother's spoken voice and singing. Previous studies on the use of music with premature and term babies have mostly looked at the benefits of lullabies, classical and womb sound music (Cassidy & Ditty, 1998b). Musical selections for fragile, premature babies must be carefully considered. The emphasis must be given to simplicity, as well as to gentle rhythms, flowing and lyrical melodies, simple harmonies, and a soft tone color. Transient changes in amplitude must be avoided, as well as abrupt tempo changes. Complexity of sound timbre and color should be avoided as well as complex combinations of different instruments. However, the premature baby responds to the quality and precision of musical expression and has the capability of responding to a beautiful recording which expresses love and wisdom.

What tradition is as old, or as universal, as that of singing lullabies to our babies? All families within all cultures from the beginning of time have "lulled" their young ones to sleep with song (Boyd, 1994). The word *lullaby* itself comes from two roots buried deep in the history of the English language. *Lulla* means to soothe and is still used today in the verb "to lull." It may have had its origin in onomatopoeia, because it is easy to imagine a parent improvising a melody for a distressed child, or a sleepy one, uttering no more words than "la-la-la." *Bye* is an old word meaning "sleep," and the word may actually have originated as a contraction of the saying "god be with ye" (Daiken, 1959).

Lullabies may be particularly effective, because, in general, they combine the benefits of the female voice in a simply orchestrated format. All lullabies have the same characteristics: they are slow (about 60–82 beats per minute—similar to a normal, resting adult heartbeat). They are regular, monotonous, and repetitive; there are no exciting disruptions in rhythm and/or melody; and they are most effective when sung in a low voice. Research has shown that high pitches tend to create tension, or excitement, while lower pitches tend to promote relaxation. All of these characteristics contribute to a baby's sense of security, safety, and strength.

Establishing a NICU Music Program

It is important to recognize that a music system should be designed so that it can be used efficiently, with a minimum use of personnel time, and a minimal need for upkeep of the components of the system. It would be optimal to include a music therapist in both the design and the use of the music system. However, it is recognized that playing music 24 hours a day necessitates educating the NICU personnel in the intricacies of using music with this population. Neonatal nurses are extremely busy, and if they will be responsible for deciding on music times, it is best incorporated into their daily flowsheets, along with the charting for therapies and medications. Since the nurses are naturally somewhat preoccupied in responding to critical situations, incorporating a simple box to check if music was played during the shift with room for specific comments will remind the neonatal nurse to think about music time. Initially, some of the neonatal nurses may not be sensitive to the benefits of NICU music, but with time, most become very aware of the many benefits that the infants receive.

Another option is to involve the NICU physical therapist or occupational therapist in the music treatments, which often makes them advocates. It is helpful to put up a small poster at each bedside (perhaps attached to the CD player) with a succinct summary of the benefits of NICU music therapy. This helps to remind the nurses to play the music and to develop interest from the parents of these babies.

Our neonatal music system at Piedmont Hospital in Atlanta, Georgia, has a dedicated CD music system at all 16 patient locations. The CD players, which sit on small wall-mounted brackets, have CD carousels which accept our five common CDs. These are arranged in the same order in each unit so the nurses know which CD they are playing at a given time. In addition, there is an individual slot for an extra CD if the parents wish their child to hear music that he or she had perhaps been exposed to prenatally.

The CD players have a headphone output with a separate volume control. We use a small headphone plug to minijack adapter so we can plug in a self-amplified computer speaker. The adapter also converts the stereo signal to a mono signal, because we use only one of the two computer speakers. We have found that an inexpensive computer speaker system delivers clear sound and can be cleaned easily. The speaker sits between 3 and 10 inches from the baby's ear in the incubator or isolette. Sound levels are intermittently measured at the baby's ear with a battery operated digital sound level meter, so that approximate mean sound levels are 75 dB with peak levels of 80 dB. If sound levels are adjusted according to a baby's response to the music, they are only decreased from these levels. In our unit we typically expose the smallest, most premature babies to womb sound music, and then advance to lullabies and simply orchestrated classical music. Some of the most unstable premature babies do not respond well to any kind of stimulation, including music. We are careful to monitor these babies' behavioral and physiologic responses to music, and occasionally music is not initially played, or is played at low volume, depending on the response.

In our unit, the neonatal nurses choose the timing, frequency, and duration of music interventions, as well as which music selection is played. The following are some guidelines that the nurses use for the music interventions:

NICU Music Guidelines for Desirable Behavioral Changes

- Consider the behavioral state when music is played.
- Try not to disrupt the sleep state.
- Use music to help change the behavioral state from agitation or fussiness and move towards one of quiet alertness or sleep state.
- Play the music for the transition into minimal stimulation time.

NICU Music Guidelines for Desirable Physiologic Changes

- Increase in oxygen saturation
- Decrease in heart rate
- Mild decrease in blood pressure

The following are some of the titles that have been used in NICU music studies. Please note that studies have not been done to compare the relative effectiveness of any of these titles.

Lullabies

A Child's Celebration of Lullaby (Music for Little People)
A Child's Gift of Lullabies (Someday Baby)
Dream a Little Dream (Transitions Music)
Lullaby Berceuse (Music for Little People)
Lullaby Magic (BMG/Discovery Music)
Lullaby Magic 2 (BMG/Discovery Music)
MusicBabies (MMB Music)
The Rock-A-Bye Collection (Someday Baby)

Classical Music

Adagio-Karajan (PolyGram Records)
Mozart for Babies (Perleberg Musik)
Perchance to Dream, Carol Rosenberger (Delos International)

Womb Sound and Heart Beat Music

Baby Go To Sleep 1 (Audio-Therapy Innovations)
Baby Go To Sleep 2 (Audio-Therapy Innovations)
Transitions 1 (Transitions Music)
Transitions 2 Music to Help Baby Sleep (Transitions Music)
Womb Sound Classics for the New Arrival (Perleberg Musik)

Baby's Mother's Voice

Spoken word and singing

SUMMARY

With a relatively small expenditure for music in our neonatal ICUs, we can decrease the time in the NICU by over 3 days and save between $2,000 and $6,000 (U.S.) for every premature baby. The initial cost of music system hardware for each NICU patient area is recovered with a corresponding decrease in medical cost of care within several weeks. Not only are there medical and economic advantages from this type of intervention, but also immediate health benefits which enhance survival. There is no doubt that music transfers love and other emotions as well as wisdom, and this conveys long-term developmental benefits that will allow our little patients to approach their full potential as human beings.

REFERENCES

Als, H. A., Lawhon, G., Duffy, F. H., McNulty, G. B., Gibes-Grossman, R., & Blickman, J. G. (1994). Individualized developmental care for the very low birth-weight preterm infant. *Journal of the American Medical Association, 272*(11), 853–858.

Arnand, K. J., & Hickey, P. R. (1987). Pain and its effects in the human neonate and fetus. *New England Journal of Medicine, 317*, 1322–1329.

Audio-Therapy Innovations, Inc.; 800-537-7748. http://win-edge.com/BabyGoTo Sleep.shtml.

BMG/Discovery Music. http://get music.com.

Boyd, B. (1994). *Lullabies from around the world.* Milwaukee, WI: Hal Leonard Publishing.

Bray, P. F., Shields, W. D., Wolcott, G. J., & Madsen, J. A. (1969). Occipitofrontal head circumference: An accurate measure of intracranial volume. *Journal of Pediatrics, 75*(2), 303–305.

Caine, J. (1991). The effects of music on the selected stress behaviors, weight, caloric and formula intake, and length of hospital stay of premature and low birth-weight neonates in a newborn intensive care unit. *Journal of Music Therapy, 28*, 88–100.

Cassidy, J. W., & Ditty, K. M. (1998a, November). *Gender differences among newborns on a transient otoacoustic emissions test for hearing.* Paper presented at the annual conference of the American Music Therapy Association, Cleveland, OH.

Cassidy, J. W., & Ditty, K. M. (1998b). Presentation of aural stimuli to newborns and premature infants: An audiological perspective. *Journal of Music Therapy, 35*(2), 70–87.

Coleman, J. M., Pratt, R. R., Stoddar, R. A., Gerstmann, D. R, & Abel, H. (1998). The effects of male and female singing and speaking voices on selected physiological and behavioral measures of premature infants in the intensive care unit. *International Journal of Arts Medicine, 5*(8), 4–11.

Collins, S. K. (1996). Music therapy and nursing in the neonatal intensive care unit. In M. R. Froehlich (Ed.), *Music therapy with hospitalized children: A creative arts child life approach* (pp. 73–76). Cherry Hill, NJ: Jeffrey Books.

Collins, S. K. & Kuck, K. (1991). Music therapy in the neonatal intensive care unit. *Neonatal Network, 9*(6), 23–26.

Daiken, L. (1959). *The lullabye book.* London: Adlard.

Decker-Voigt, H. H., & Maetzel, F. K. (1997). *Cardiovascular complaints music and health. Energon: The scientific-medical music program* [Book and CDs]. Hamburg, Germany: PolyGram GmbH.

Delos International. 1645 North Vine St., Suite 340, Hollywood, CA 90028; 800-364-0645. http://www.delosmus.com/.

Devlin, B., Daniels, M., & Roeder, K. (1997). The heritability of IQ. *Nature, 388,* 468–471.

Gerhardt, K. J., & Abrams, R. M. (1996). Fetal hearing: Characterization of the stimulus and response. *Seminars in Perinatology, 20*(1), 11–20.

Hack, M., Breslau, N., Weissman, B., Aram, D., Klein, M., & Borawski, E. (1991). Effect of very low birth-weight and subnormal head size on cognitive abilities at school age. *The New England Journal of Medicine, 325*(4), 231–237.

Hepper, P. G., & Shahidullah, B. S. (1994). Development of fetal hearing. *Archives of Disease in Childhood, 71,* F81–F87.

Johnston, M. V. (1995). Neurotransmitters and vulnerability of the developing brain. *Brain and Development, 17,* 301–306

Lewit, E. M., Baker, L. S., Corman, H., & Shiono, P. H. (1995). The direct cost of low birth-weight. *The Future of Children, 5*(1), 35–56.

Lipton, B. H. (1998). Nature, nurture, and the power of love. *Journal of Prenatal and Perinatal Psychology and Health, 13*(1), 3–10.

Logan, B. (1991). Infant outcomes of a prenatal stimulation pilot study. *Prenatal and Perinatal Psychology Journal, 6*(1), 7–31.

Lynam, L. (1995, September-October). Developmental care in the intensive care nursery: Putting prevention into practice. *Neonatal Intensive Care,* 37–41.

MMB Music, Inc., 3526 Washington Ave., Contemporary Arts Building, St. Louis, MO 63103-1019.

Music for Little People, P.O. Box 1460, Redway, CA 95601; 1-800-346-4445. http://www.mflp.com.

Nöcker-Ribaupierre, M. (1995). *Auditive Stimulation nach Fruhgeburt Ein Beitrag zu Musiktherapie.* Stuttgart: G. Fischer.

Nöcker-Ribaupierre, M. (1999). Premature birth and music therapy. In T. Wigram & J. DeBacker (Eds.), *Clinical application of music therapy in developmental disability, pediatrics and neurology.* London: Jessica Kingsley.

Perleberg Musik. Gewerbestrasse 13, 44866 Bochum, Germany; Fax 49 2327 292 155. http://www.perleberg.de.

Petryshen, P., Stevens, B., Hawkins, J., & Stewart, M. (1997). Comparing nursing costs for preterm infants receiving conventional vs. developmental care. *Nursing Economics 15*(3), 138–150.

PolyGram Records, New York, NY. http://www.polygram-us.com/.

Rauscher, F. H., Shaw, G. L., & Ky, K. N. (1995). Listening to Mozart enhances spatial-temporal reasoning: Towards a neurophysiological basis. *Neuroscience Letter 185*(1), 44–47.

Rauscher, F. H., Shaw, G. L., Levine, L. J., Wright, E. L., Dennis, W. R., & Newcomb, R. L. (1997). Music training causes long-term enhancement of preschool children's spatial-temporal reasoning. *Neurological Research, 19*(1), 218.

Righetti, P. L. (1996). The emotional experience of the fetus: A preliminary report. *Pre- and Perinatal Psychology Journal, 11*(1), 55–65.

Schwartz, F. J. (1997). Perinatal stress reduction, music, and medical cost savings. *Journal of Prenatal and Perinatal Psychology and Health, 12*(1), 19–29.

Schwartz, F. J., Ritchie, R., Sacks, L., & Phillips, C. (1998, July). *Perinatal stress reduction, music, and medical cost savings.* Paper presented at the VII International Music and Medicine Symposium, Melbourne, Australia.

Shahidullah, S., & Hepper, P. G. (1992). Hearing in the fetus: Prenatal detection of deafness. *International Journal of Prenatal and Perinatal Studies, 4*(3/4), 235–240.

Sheth, R. D., Mullett, M. D., Bodensteiner, J. B., & Hobbs, G. R. (1995). Longitudinal head growth in developmentally normal preterm infants. *Archives of Pediatric Adolescent Medicine 149,* 1358–1361.

Shetler, D. J. (1989). The inquiry into prenatal musical experience: A report of The Eastman Project 1980–1987. *Pre- and Perinatal Psychology Journal, 3*(3), 171–189.

Someday Baby, 800-965-2229. http://www.lullabyes.com/.

Standley, J. M. (1996, October). *The effect of music and multimodal stimulation on physiologic and developmental responses of premature infants in neonatal intensive care.* Presented at the VI International Society of Music in Medicine Symposium, San Antonio, TX.

Standley, J. M. (1998a, July). *The effect of contingent music to increase non-nutritive sucking of premature infants.* Presented at the VII International Society of Music in Medicine Symposium, Melbourne, Australia.

Standley, J. M. (1998b, November). *Effect of music intervention on head circumference of premature infants: A post-hoc analysis of music research in neonatal intensive care.* Paper presented at the annual conference of American Music Therapy Association. Cleveland, OH.

Transitions Music, 1930 Monroe Drive, Atlanta, Georgia 30324; 1-800-492-9885. http://www.transitionsmusic.com.

Winick, M. (1969). Malnutrition and brain development. *Journal of Pediatrics, 74*(5), 667–679.

Zahr, L. K., & Traversay, J. D. (1995). Premature infant responses to noise reduction by earmuffs: Effects on behavioral and physiologic measures. *Journal of Perinatology, 15*(6), 448–455.

3

Guided Imagery and Music With Medical Patients

Roberta Wigle Justice, MM, MT-BC
Roseann E. Kasayka, DA, MT-BC

Clinical Needs

AS WESTERN MEDICINE moves from the Cartesian paradigm of mind-body split in treatment towards a quantum paradigm of holistic approaches to wellness, traditional assumptions about the relationship between mind and body must be recognized and challenged. Some of these assumptions are: (a) in disease there is an absence of connection between the physical illness and the mind, (b) consciousness and volition reside exclusively in the central nervous system, and (c) the body is essentially responsive only to the cognitions and emotions of the brain and does not respond to other aspects of the person (Tart, 1975). In the holistic approach, there is the belief in a mind/body/spirit interrelationship, with all aspects of the person acting as connected channels for energy flow (Erlandson, 1998). This belief system includes the assumption that things that are not necessarily quantifiable in the laboratory, such as transpersonal phenomena, affect the functioning of the body and mind. In this belief system, healing is as valid a concept as diagnosis and curing. All of these three concepts function together in treatment.

The transpersonal realm of experience includes aspects of "becoming, unitive consciousness, self actualization, transcendence of the self and individual synergy" (Lewis, 1999). The application of this in medicine addresses those needs of people with disease processes through other than ordinary states of consciousness. The intangible processes of hope, peace, unity, acceptance, and healing can be directly accessed through these levels of consciousness. Specifically, medical patients' needs include decreasing pain perception, decreasing anxiety, connecting with images of hope, and accessing inner strengths and inner wholeness (H. B. Logan, personal communication, March 21, 1999).

THEORETICAL APPROACH

The term *transpersonal* implies “extending beyond the personal or individual” (*Webster's Seventh New Collegiate Dictionary,* 1963). All individuals relate to experiences of ordinary or normal consciousness, i.e., things experienced through the physical, such as perceptions, or through the sequential thinking processes of the intellect (“rational, logical” thinking). Transpersonal therapies, on the other hand, function on levels of consciousness defined as “other than ordinary” or “altered” (Tart, 1975) and frequently deal with experiences not commonly explored in other psychological frameworks. These experiences are often of a religious or spiritual nature.

Transpersonal psychology emerged as a discipline in the late 1960s. Sometimes called “the fourth force,” it evolved from humanistic psychology. Behavioristic psychology and classical analytic psychology are its more distant ancestors. The roots of transpersonal theory are found in the writing of William James, Carl Jung, and Abraham Maslow.

The goal of transpersonal psychology is to explore and explain the development of the whole human person, attempting to make sense of and integrate those experiences that are religious and/or spiritual. While not overly related to structured religious tradition, transpersonal work is spiritual work, i.e., that which is done in the mystical or ecstatic realm. It is work that frequently involves healing and is often done in altered states of consciousness.

Wilber (1975, 1980) has defined nine levels in his “spectrum of consciousness.” These levels move from subconsciousness (instinctual, impulsive, id-ish) to self-consciousness (egoic, conceptual, syntaxical) to superconsciousness (transcendent, transpersonal, trans-temporal) (Lewis, 1999). Within the level of superconsciousness, experiences can include those involving symbolic visions; higher presences; spirit guides; connections with God; and oneness with all beings, a higher power, or the universe. In transpersonal psychology, each of these phenomena is held as authentic and capable of being explored.

The basis for transpersonal work, as seen in Guided Imagery and Music, is contained in Abraham Maslow's exploration of the phenomenon of peak experiences (Maslow, 1968). He identified characteristics of highest happiness and fulfillment in himself and in the people he studied. These characteristics include: (a) perceptions which can be relatively ego-transcending, self forgetful, or egoless; (b) emotional reactions of special wonder, awe, humility, and surrender; (c) views of the world as a single, rich, live unity; (d) fusion, transcendence or resolution of dichotomies, conflicts and polarities; and (e) a loss of fear, anxiety, inhibition, defense, and control. The positive after-effects of peak experiences have been identified as: (a) the removal of symptoms; (b) shifts in the person's way of viewing him or herself from ill to healthy; (c) changes in the individual's view of other persons and his/her relations to them in many ways; (d) temporary or permanent shifts in the individual's view of the world or aspects of it; and (e) feelings that life is worth living, in spite of its adversities and because of the meaningfulness of what has been experienced. (Kasayka, 1988; Lewis, 1999).

Transpersonal work leading to or including peak experiences, then, has a place in medicine as a way of connecting with those positive feelings that support and encourage health of body, mind, and spirit. The Bonny Method of Guided Imagery and Music (GIM) has been shown to facilitate this type of work. Listening to music in altered states of consciousness can elicit insightful experiences, summon healing forces and new ways of looking at problems, impart a sense of unity among people and things, and create a sensitivity for the divine (Bonny & Savary, 1973). Grocke (1999) has identified "pivotal" moments in GIM during which clients experience life-changing insights into their own processes. Lewis (1999) has introduced guidelines for categorizing phenomena experienced in GIM sessions, which include levels of transpersonal experiences, and has also described evidence of such experiences in sessions from 30 different subjects.

Clinical Approach

The Bonny Method of Guided Imagery and Music is a process focusing on the conscious use of imagery arising in response to a formalized program of relaxation and classical music. In its traditional form, GIM is practiced in a dyad, with dialogue between a client/traveler and therapist/guide. Modifications and adaptations have been developed for group work with several populations, including medical patients.

A GIM session is traditionally described as being comprised of four segments. The first segment is a period of verbal discussion around clients' issues, themes, topics, and goals, and may include art work, creative writing, musical improvisation or movement.

The second segment is a period of relaxation/induction without music and structured to meet the immediate needs of the client. This section helps the client to move from an ordinary waking state of consciousness to a more deeply relaxed or altered state of consciousness. The induction generally includes a focus image to stimulate the beginning of the imagery process. This image may or may not be visual in nature and is also designed to meet the client's current needs.

The third segment begins with the music program chosen by the GIM therapist. There are a variety of standard GIM programs, which are usually 30–45 minutes in length. The programs consist of selections of Western art music from the Baroque period through the 20th century. These pieces have the qualities that fit Bonny's "affective contour" (Bonny, 1978) and that also have the potential to elicit generalized emotional responses in the listener. Examples of music programs include (but are not limited to) those designed to facilitate internal exploration; sustain intense affect, such as grief or anger; and provide support and comfort.

During the third segment, the client, while in a relaxed or altered state of consciousness, verbalizes his/her responses to the chosen music. The therapist uses interventions designed to support and validate the client's experiences and help the client connect as fully as possible with the music and the experiences. These experiences may include visual images, kinesthetic experiences, energy experiences, emotions, thoughts, and/or memories. The client may shift from one form of experience to another, sometimes experiencing two or more forms simultaneously, and may undergo shifts to deeper or lighter states of consciousness in response to the music. The therapist makes a written transcript of the sequence of the client's responses, including visual images, emotions, kinesthetic experiences reported, and affective changes visually observed. It is in this section that experiences of a transpersonal nature can occur, which can include body/space enlargement, a sense of union with the music/divine/universe/all people, transcendence of time and space, deeply felt positive moods, a great sense of awe or reverence, instant insight, ineffable feelings of beauty or emotion, a sense of healing, or deep peace (Kasayka, 1999). Several of these experiences are the same as those described by Maslow in his peak and plateau experiences which bring about positive life changes.

At the completion of the music, the therapist helps the client bring the experience to a close and become reoriented to a normal waking state of consciousness. Processing of the material elicited during the music is done verbally and/or through the use of art media. Insight can occur during the processing time, or later on as the client reflects on, writes about, or talks about the experience. Usually GIM is practiced in a series of sessions, with sessions becoming "chapters" in a personal life story; the material from one session often accents and interlaces with material from previous sessions. In fact, peak experiences in GIM, as in music itself, are peak *because* of what has led up to them and what follows them.

Each person's process is individual, unfolding according to his or her own intuitive wisdom in response to the music. Each person's series is different due to his or her own unique needs and goals. However, some generalities may be seen. At the beginning of a series of sessions, the client explores the process, his/her own psyche and subconscious, and begins to develop an individual style of "traveling" or responding to the music. At some point, the client uses the music to move more deeply inward and work on issues of personal meaning. This can be done in visual imagery, or in emotional or kinesthetic responses to the music, but is often accomplished in a combination of these responses. This deeper work might be accompanied or followed by a memory. It is often after this depth work, which usually involves some sort of struggle or experiencing of difficult emotions, that resolving, peaceful, healing, or mystical experiences occur; these experiences can be transpersonal in nature. This may happen in the same session or in successive sessions. Often at the completion of a GIM series, clients report having a more positive outlook on life, feel that things have "shifted" inside, feel stronger, know better their direction in life, are more at peace with themselves and the world, and/or are better able to handle life's stresses. This shift is consistent both with Maslow's description of the characteristics of peak experiences as well as the body of literature on mysticism.

In GIM with clients having medical illnesses, sessions may range from the typical format to specially adapted formats. When using a typical dyad format, specific inductions may be developed by the therapist alone or jointly with the client to represent the client's illness, and the session may begin with the client's letting the music help him/her explore the image. Unlike some of the improvisational models of music-mediated healing imagery, the client goes into the music without a consciously preconceived idea of how, or even if, the image needs to change. The ensuing personal process unfolds to the music, as in any other GIM session, without cognitive interpretation of "how the problem needs to be solved." By allowing themselves to let the music connect with the subconscious, clients can access their own internal, intuitive wisdom concerning what, if anything, needs to happen with the image. Examples of responses to this approach include one man's changing of a pain image through a sense of cooling, a feeling of water cleansing the area, and a color change in the image, with a subsequent decrease in pain. These image changes occurred spontaneously in response to the music, and not through the conscious choice of the client. Another example is a woman's color/shape image of pain becoming a humanoid entity with which she could nonverbally interact. Through various changes and mutations, the image led her to an awareness about the need for acceptance in herself. A third example is of a cardiac patient who focused initially on the image of her damaged heart. Over a period of several sessions that involved unfolding layers of "heart" work (including relationship issues), her heart image transformed to one of peacefulness and calm, with accompanying deep feelings. She was subsequently free from symptoms for several years.

A final example involves a woman with uterine cancer. Initially she imaged a white light moving through the affected area, gently probing and seeking out the cancer cells to bring them to the light. After several sessions, the image of the white light spontaneously changed to an image of clear, pure water. This water flowed through and washed clean the entire abdominal area. The transformation of the image brought with it a sense of acceptance. When surgery finally took place, the physician reported far less cancer than was originally suspected. Continued use of the same music during and after the surgery helped to make the time in the recovery room and the actual length of the hospital stay shorter.

Specific adaptations to the typical GIM process for medical patients have been described by several practitioners (H. B. Logan, personal communication, March 21, 1999; D. Pienta, personal communication, March 18, 1999). Persons with medical problems may already be in weakened, fragile, or altered states of consciousness depending on the intensity and stage of their illness and/or the treatment they are receiving. Medications also affect the state of consciousness and the level of energy available for work. Many times a single session instead of a series of sessions is all that is possible to provide. In these situations, the relaxation portion of the session may be lengthened and deepened, with the inductions gentle, supportive, and holding. The focus may be placed on the symptoms themselves, being in a safe place, healing colors, or facilitating feelings of inner strengths and wholeness.

The music used in these situations is often 6–15 minutes, shorter than a normal 30–45 minute session. The music chosen is what is referred to in GIM language as a "small container," more singly structured, more repetitive, individual melodies (as opposed to counterpoint), with overall fewer ambiguities, as this requires less energy from the client for attention and response, and supports the singular intent of the deepening of relaxation. This allows for maintaining focus on the induction, whether it be an image or feeling, and for a deepening into this space. This also limits (but does not prohibit) the amount of movement away from this focus. Selections from recordings by Daniel Kobialka fit this description, as do some shorter pieces on the "Music for Imagination" recordings from Barcelona Press. The GIM therapist must choose the music to best fit the needs of the client at the time. The most powerful images for an individual, including images of healing, symbols and feelings of peace, and voyages to inner places of wholeness, are those that come from the individual directly in response to the music (Achterburg, 1985).

The processing of the session may include verbal reinforcement of the experiences and deep feelings that occurred during the session. Drawing may be used to concretize or bring to waking consciousness the experience, and to provide a visual stimulus for recalling healing colors, shapes, and symbols of safe, relaxing places. Patients have taped such drawings on the walls and ceilings near their beds and focused on them with or without music during painful times, or when trying to go to sleep. If necessary to maintain a sterile environment, the drawings may be laminated so they may be disinfected during cleaning. When a person has transcended pain and illness and reached a place of deep, inner peace in a session, the drawings reflecting this are often abstract, with clear colors and radiating or balanced forms. The structured format used in mandala work (i.e., a blank circle placed in the center of a sheet of paper) is often chosen by the patients for drawing, rather than a totally blank sheet of paper.

Group GIM work with medical patients may involve other specific adaptations. Groups may sit rather than lie down for the experience. Relaxations are generally shorter for groups than for individuals. Types and qualities of inductions depend on the strengths and needs of the group members. For groups of medically fragile or weak individuals, inductions are used to elicit relaxing, comforting images similar to those described for medically weakened individuals. The inductions are more specific and focused than in general GIM work. For groups in early stages of illness or groups of survivors, inductions may be more generic, as their purpose is for more personal psychodynamic work. In work with people living with multiple sclerosis, L. D. Mitran (personal communication, March 25, 1999) has found that short relaxations with a focus on the body are helpful.

Music for groups with medical conditions is shorter than that used in adapted GIM sessions for individuals, and generally is less than 10 minutes in length. The musical container varies depending on the strengths/needs of the group members. Groups with good ego strengths, as in clients with early stage illnesses or survivors of illness, may need a short segment of music with greater complexity than groups of medically weakened or fragile people. The purpose for the session and the strength of the group members determine the amount of complexity and ambiguity in the music chosen by the GIM therapist.

The processing of GIM experiences in medical groups is similar to that which is done with individuals or in other types of groups. Drawing, again, may be used to concretize the images or feelings. Verbal sharing and explaining the drawing helps group members relate with each others' experiences, and this group work provides a social support which helps counteract feelings of isolation and depression. The function of the GIM therapist is to facilitate this process, deepen the experiences, and help individuals gain insight into their own experiences. Witnessing the responses and process of others gives individuals new options and choices for themselves when facing challenges related to their own illness.

ROLES OF MUSIC AND THE THERAPEUTIC RELATIONSHIP

GIM is a receptive music therapy technique in which the music is used and viewed as a co-therapist. Kasayka (1988) describes GIM as an inherently musical process, one in which music is both a tool for therapeutic intervention as well as the matrix for it. In the GIM process, the client and the therapist exist simultaneously in a musical space, sharing and receiving the sound. The therapist chooses the music to best fit the emotional, physical, and psychological needs of the client (or group) for each session. This is to establish a musical space (also called container) that will furnish a "best-fit" balance of musical ambiguity and variety with structure and support. The therapist must consider the complexity of melodic, harmonic, and rhythmic structure in the music being selected for the session, as well as its tempo, dynamics, and timbre.

The music is both a catalyst for and container of the ensuing process. By listening to the music in an altered or relaxed state of consciousness, the client's responses (in the form of images, emotions, memories, and subconscious) material come from inner spaces. Theoretically, this material can come from as many potential sources as the physical body, all levels of the mind, the spirit, the collective consciousness, and the collective unconscious. The music guides the client to his/her own best answer to whatever problem is present. Kasayka (1988) states: "As the therapist chooses music that is appropriate to the client's energy and issues, the dialogue between the client's inner resources and motivations and the external factors in the field, namely the music and therapist, ensues. The language of this dialogue is the imagery."

The therapist in GIM is in the same receptive musical space as the client. The therapist shares in the responses of the client to the music and facilitates the process by knowing the music well enough to engage the client with it as appropriate. The therapist is also familiar with a range of potential responses to the music and sensitive to what changes are occurring in the client, through physical sensations, emotions, and imagery movement. The therapist must be aware of his/her counter-transferences to the client and his/her own issues, as well as how to work with these in the imagery. For example, in imagery dealing with symbolism of symptoms of an illness, it is important for the therapist to recognize that acceptance of the client's symptom is as powerful and valuable as any attempt to eliminate it (which may be the therapist's own bias). This supports the client in pursuing the solution that is true for him or her.

By being connected to the music and the musical space, the energy of the therapist is focused on holding the client in that space and channeling the music to the client. This is done verbally as well as nonverbally through mental concentration and physical touch where appropriate. By trusting the music and the internal wisdom of the client to find the best solution for the problem, the GIM therapist is a supportive witness to the individual's power to transcend the confines of normal waking consciousness and intellectual thought, and reach planes of energy where true healing can take place.

References

Achterburg, J. (1985). *Imagery in healing.* Boston: Shambhala Press.

Bonny, H. L. (1978). *The role of taped music programs in the GIM process.* Baltimore, MD: ICM Books.

Bonny, H. L., & Savary, L. M. (1973). *Music and your mind.* Barrytown, NY: Station Hill Press.

Erlandson, E. E. (1998, October). *Integrated therapies: A new view of health and wholeness.* Paper at St. Joseph Mercy Hospital, Ypsilanti, MI.

Grocke, D. E. (1999). *Understanding pivotal moments in guided imagery and music therapy: Perspectives from clients and therapists.* Unpublished doctoral dissertation, University of Melbourne, Parkville, Victoria, Australia.

Kasayka, R. E. (1988). *To meet and match the moment of hope: Transpersonal elements of the guided imagery and music experience.* Unpublished manuscript.

Kasayka, R. E. (1999, February). *Transpersonal experiences in guided imagery and music.* Paper presented at the Bonny Method of Guided Imagery and Music Personal Voyage meeting, Whitehouse, OH.

Lewis, K. A. (1999). *The Bonny method of guided imagery and music: Matrix for transpersonal experience.* Manuscript submitted for publication.

Maslow, A. (1968). *Towards a psychology of being.* New York: D. Van Nostrand.

Tart, C. T. (Ed.). (1975). *Transpersonal psychologies.* New York: Harper & Row.

Webster's Seventh New Collegiate Dictionary. (1963). Springfield, MA: Merriam-Webster.

Wilber, K. (1975). Psychologia perennis: The spectrum of consciousness. *Journal of Transpersonal Psychology, 7*(2), 105–132.

Wilber, K. (1980). *The Atman project.* Wheaton, IL: Quest.

4

Physioacoustic Therapy With Post-Surgical and Critically Ill Patients

Charles Butler, MD, PhD

Clinical Needs

HOW MANY TIMES have I watched physicians walk a little faster past the doors of their patients with inoperable/incurable cancer? Why do they interpret terminal disease as a personal failure that their egos do not allow them to face? What effect does this have on the dying person in the bed who calls them "Doctor"? A human being at end-life is not a failure, but someone who has a real need not to be abandoned. Or imagine the families who "protect" their loved ones by having caregivers lie to them about the true nature of their conditions, when the loved ones well understand their frailty and the limited time given to them. Is it so hard to realize that a dying human being does not want to be lied to? He or she wants only to be loved. Many good doctors, nurses, and families understand this. Too many do not.

With modern medicine cutting back on hospital and physician reimbursement, physicians see more patients to maintain their income. Fewer nurses are assigned to hospital floors. Many of the nurses now must serve as administrators overseeing less skilled, less well trained, and lower paid personnel who serve as the direct caregivers to the critically ill. As this trend continues, there will be more, not fewer, instances of patients on a ventilator after open heart surgery . . . scared to death, intubated, unable to speak . . . hearing nurse and physician discuss unintelligible but frightening plans for their care.

Postsurgical and critically ill patients often suffer from anxiety, pain, sleep deprivation, and uncertainty about their overall well-being (Burke, 1997). Particularly nagging can be problems such as back pain and skin breakdown in those patients spending much time in bed. It is into this environment that the music therapist must bring calmness, humanity, security, and a sense of participation to the stressed victims of modern medicine. If therapists can decrease the pain or soothe the aching soul, they can fill the void created by the current needs of the system. But, music therapists also face challenges. They enter an arena of cost-cutting with an armamentarium of skills, which include the benefits of music, improvisation, personalization, and transference. To help the patient survive in this difficult environment, physioacoustics can provide the music therapist with a powerful tool to bring about physiologic changes based on the use of sound. It can provide those who master it with a new skill that will increase their value to the medical team, and, most of all, to the patient. Similar needs may be found in the normal population, who may likewise find benefit in this technology. However, failure to address these problems expeditiously in the normal population will be followed by much less dire consequences than in those who are critically ill.

Physioacoustics is a new therapeutic science. It allows us to cause various desirable physiologic and psychological effects in human beings by exposing them to what amounts to ordinary sound. Researchers in physioacoustics use pure sine waves in the frequency range of 27 to 113 Hz to achieve their goals. To put this in perspective, the lowest key on a piano is 18.5 Hz. The only proven side effect of ordinary sound in this range is "noise deafness" if it is turned up too loud.

Researchers in the field have demonstrated highly statistically significant decreases in anxiety, tension, and arousal states, and dramatic increases in relaxation. Psychological testing shows that people who receive physioacoustic treatments feel better about themselves. Physiologically, patients with spasticity demonstrate statistically significant improvement in range of motion. People sleep significantly longer without medication. The FDA listed physioacoustic equipment as a class one medical device. The FDA further allowed the claims of relief of pain, increase of blood circulation, and relaxation.

Physioacoustic treatments generally take 20 minutes. The subject sits in a physioacoustic recliner or lies on a specially designed bed while the selected frequencies or sounds are played through simple speakers (or other more technically advanced transmitters). Sound or sine waves in these bass frequencies are more felt than heard. Specific frequencies can be felt at quite precise locations in the body. A frequency can be selected that will be felt in the exact location of musculoskeletal pain. Stimulation of such sites often produces dramatic relief. This means the therapist can create programs to treat defined problems in a purposeful way. Psychological testing or physical measurement has been used at the end of sessions to assess results. If undisturbed during a session, most subjects will be observed to fall asleep.

THEORETICAL APPROACH

The theoretical approach to physioacoustics may be described as hypothesis based on physical observations. Imagine that we are going to build a bed. This bed will be constructed with several speakers mounted on its underside. Anyone who lies on the bed will also be lying on the padded speakers. Any sound generated by the speakers will not only be heard by the person on the bed, but will also play directly into the body of that person. The speakers will be connected to a generator which will create sounds in pure tones

Sound waves come in three shapes: saw tooth waves (those generated by most musical instruments), square waves (those generated by some musical instruments—usually instruments that are blown into and which have a closed end), and, finally, sine waves. Saw tooth wave sound and square wave sound generate many resonances, that is, secondary sounds. If we use them, it would make it difficult to associate any particular tone or tones with an observed physiologic effect. Furthermore, pure saw tooth or square wave tones are very unpleasant to most subjects who experience them.

Sine waves, so named because they have a smoothly curved form, are much more pleasant to sensation. More importantly, because of their smooth configuration, they do not generate resonance frequencies. This means that any physiologic effect seen in the client resting upon the bed can be attributed to the particular frequency sine wave to which the body is exposed. As we tune the sine wave generator slowly from 20 to 70 Hz, the client on the bed will point to specific parts of his body and "feel" the sound there, as if the particular area affected is being massaged. If we expose aching muscles to their own specific frequencies, pain is relieved. Human subjects exposed to low frequency sound in the region of 40 Hz often fall asleep. These are a few of the observations made. How can they be explained?

In the early 1990s, Llinas and Ribary (1993) at New York University discovered that brain cells oscillate at about 40 Hz. Using a 37-channel magnetoencephalograph, they determined that every time a human being focuses on an object, his "attention" generates a "40 Hz" Wave. This wave begins in the thalamus and passes over the cortex in a specific fashion. Learning does not occur unless the subject can generate the "40 Hz response." In patients with Alzheimer's disease, learning does not occur, and there is no "40 Hz response." Similarly, in patients with brain trauma, the "40 Hz response" is disproportionately weaker. In dream sleep (REM sleep), the brain locks into a constant 40 Hz response, which begins when the subject enters REM sleep and terminates with the end of REM sleep.

We hypothesize, then, that we are setting up a resonance frequency response similar to that which occurs between two tuning forks of the same frequency: when one is struck, the other is activated in resonance. Similarly, if we can generate the precise frequency at which a subject's brain resonates, we will be able to induce sleep through a resonance phenomenon. We send 40 Hz, the brain locks into a 40 Hz wave, and sleep ensues. Analogously, researchers reasoned that the establishment of resonance frequencies (either with the muscle fibers themselves or with the fibers of the nerves which innervate them) affected various muscle groups. We refer to this as the "resonance theory."

All of this is slightly simplified. Actually, researchers have observed slight variations in the exact frequency at which particular muscle groups or the nervous system responds. These variations occur in different individuals, or in the same individual at different times. One can think about the normal differences in hydration state that occur in everyone. As muscle and nerve cells take on more or less water, their thickness changes. Their resonance frequency would be anticipated to vary slightly with that thickness change. Physioacoustic programs are designed to scan frequencies within an empirically established range to create an effect. For example, although the "40 Hz response" is used to put people to sleep, in actuality, most individuals' central nervous systems will oscillate between 38 and 42 Hz. Thus, well-written physioacoustic sleep programs will scan within this range to obtain the desired result in the maximum number of clients.

This "resonance theory" is based on the observed facts and can explain all observed phenomena. It is currently the mechanism that we accept to explain the physiologic and psychological benefits obtained by physioacoustics.

CLINICAL APPROACH

With experience, each therapist will individualize his or her approach to the use of low frequency sound with clients. Our approach has been rooted in the belief that open-heart surgery patients will have fewer complications, will cooperate with medical staff to a greater degree, and will progress better if they understand the conditions surrounding them, their possible treatment options, and how they can best contribute to their own recovery.

When patients enter the hospital for elective, open-heart surgery, the need for the procedure, its risks and complications are explained to them. Next follows a discussion of the postoperative phase. If patients are entered in a controlled study of physioacoustics versus pain medicine, discussion must be limited to avoid prejudice in the data. Otherwise, we discuss fully what they can expect. Unless they are unconscious, all patients who undergo major surgery will experience pain. Narcotics suppress pain, but they also suppress consciousness as well as the patient's natural drive to breathe. Overuse of these medications can result in prolonged time on a ventilator which may result in the fatal complications of pneumonia and blood clots. On the other hand, low frequency sound treatments may decrease pain without suppression of consciousness or respiration. These treatments may need to be supplemented from time to time with intravenous narcotic therapy, and the object after surgery is to strike a balance between over sedation and excess pain.

Each patient is given two buttons, either of which may be pushed. One button administers a dose of intravenous morphine; the other button delivers a 20-minute physioacoustic treatment. Patients may initiate either therapy repeatedly without asking the staff. This is important, because it gives patients control over their pain management. It does not create pressure for the patient to meet any perceived false expectations of the staff with regard to pain medicine.

Using this clinical model after open-heart surgery, we discovered to our surprise that most patients activated the physioacoustic program repeatedly. They seemed to use much less pain medication. Many patients stated that they preferred the "sound programs," because they did not like being "sedated." In an initial pilot study of eight patients (Butler & Butler, 1997), we found that patients decreased their time on the ventilator from 17 to 7 hours. They cut their time in the intensive care unit from 36 to 18 hours. Further, patients went home at an average of 5 days after surgery instead of the previously required 9. After this study was published, these findings persisted through several hundred additional patients, further supporting their credence. An unsolicited patient letter read:

> When I was first introduced to the idea of using sound to produce physiological and psychological benefits after surgery, I was skeptical. The physical benefits have been recorded; the psychological benefits are just as important. The feeling of serenity I got from the use of the bed was profound. . . . I was calm and had no worries about my recovery and used little in the way of chemical pain relief. I am a believer now. The bed has definite benefits for a faster recovery." (Patient X, 2-19-95)

Other Applications of Physioacoustics

The literature contains many examples of the effective use of physioacoustic and low frequency sound treatment in other clinical settings (Butler, 1998).

At the Helsinki University Central Hospital, Petri Lehikoinen and Hannu Naukkarinen (Lehikoinen, Naukkarinen, Paakkari, & Saukkonnen, 1990) studied patients suffering from severe anxiety. Each patient received ten 20-minute sessions of physioacoustic therapy. Psychological testing was performed before and after treatment. These tests demonstrated statistically significant decreases in psychosomatic pain, tension, and anxiety.

Lehikoinen (1990) and Wigram (1997a, 1997b) demonstrated significantly improved muscle relaxation and range of motion in patients suffering from spastic disorders. In both studies, a low frequency sound treatment was found to be approximately equivalent to a treatment involving physical therapy.

At the University of Kuopio, Nissenen (Nissenen & Kivinen, 1990) studied 56 patients suffering from high blood pressure. At the end of the study, the group treated with physioacoustics showed a statistically significant decrease in blood pressure.

Wigram (1997c) studied the effects of low frequency sound on "normal" professional people. Psychological testing (UWIST-MACL) demonstrated that low frequency sine wave stimulation caused a statistically significant increase in relaxation.

The Clinical Process

Physioacoustic therapy has many potential applications. In each case, the process may be similar. The therapist visits the patient and assesses his/her needs. In addition to establishing his or her normal treatment plan, the therapist may select an appropriate physioacoustic program for recommendation to the treatment team. This could be a back pain program, relaxation program, sleep program, blood pressure program, etc. Once the selected program has been agreed upon, it is made available to the patient, who may initiate treatments on a demand basis. As the treatment plan progresses, the treatment team assesses the patient's response and adjusts the program accordingly. As the patient gains experience, he or she may be given the freedom to choose the program that feels best and gives the most effective relief to his or her problem.

The two most important determinants of patient outcome in any therapeutic situation are (1) the competence of the practitioner, and (2) the therapeutic relationship between the practitioner and the patient. No new technology will ever replace the first duty of the therapist to establish a relationship of warmth and trust with the patient. Once this is done, the therapist may introduce an ambulatory patient to the physioacoustic recliner or bed. At that time, the therapist may take the opportunity to explain a little about the purpose and use of low frequency sine wave stimulation. The condition and interest of the patient will guide the discussion. The therapist will initially select a program appropriate for the patient's need and invite the patient to initiate the program at a volume that he/she finds comfortable.

Once the volume has been selected, many experienced therapists will encourage their patient to readjust the volume, decreasing it about 20%. This volume correction is made for two reasons. First, from experience, many therapists have noted that patients enjoy the sensation and turn the stimulus up too loud. If this is not corrected at the start of the program, the subject will usually turn down the program himself after about 10 minutes or request that the therapist do so. Some fear that this interruption may interfere with the desired therapeutic effect. Second, to avoid "shocking" the client, most physioacoustic programs are designed to start at a low level of stimulation, build to a crescendo after a "warm-up" period, and gradually decrease the level of stimulation in a "cool down" period. The patient using physioacoustics for the first time will not know this. He or she will have a natural tendency then to set the initial volume too high.

Initially, many therapists also encourage their patients to decrease the volume of the transducer closest to the head. The therapist does this realizing that if the head is stimulated too vigorously, motion sickness may result. If this occurs, the client may develop a dislike for the system and a fear of using it again. This will ultimately eliminate any possible therapeutic benefit.

In the rare circumstance that everything is done correctly but the subject still develops some symptom of motion sickness, three things can be done: (1) the speaker nearest the head should be turned down much further or turned off; (2) a foam rubber pillow can be placed beneath the patient's head, which will absorb the stimulus (conversely, a styrofoam pillow may be used to increase stimulus transmission); and (3) the head of the bed or recliner may be adjusted to a more upright position. These steps will decrease any tendency to develop symptoms.

The therapist should explain to the patient that once familiarity with the system is achieved, the volume might be adjusted as loudly as desired. The patient should also feel comfortable to adjust the intensity of any of the four transducers so that the stimulus level produces maximum enjoyment and pleasure. Most people find physioacoustic treatment extremely enjoyable and experience no problems. However, a cautious beginning may result in a much more desirable end.

A few words should be said about idiosyncratic differences. As always in life, diverse biological organisms may experience the same stimulus differently. The more complex the organism, the harder it becomes to predict the precise result of any intervention. The programs developed for use in the physioacoustic system achieve their desired purpose over 80% of the time. But this point warrants more attention. Let us take, for example, the "warm-up" program, which was developed for and used by many Olympic athletes just before strenuous exercise or competition. The gold, silver, and bronze medalists in ski jumping at Lillehammer used it, as it was designed to warm up the athlete, stimulate circulation, and improve endurance. Some people, however, prefer a particular program to all others and find great benefit from it. One of the developers of the current system liked the "warm-up program." This young lady uses the program before marathon training. However, she also uses the same program to help her relax and even to help her sleep better! Many similar instances could be described. The experienced therapist recognizes that there are many differences between human beings that we do not understand. In humility, the therapist lets the experienced patient choose the program. The operative words here are "experienced patient." The patient who has been encouraged to use physioacoustic equipment on demand and to experiment with various programs at leisure will soon be able to select the program most beneficial to him or her. Often such patients, without the slightest knowledge of the science of sound, will select programs and achieve physiologic goals well beyond the hopes of the treatment team.

EQUIPMENT

A physioacoustic system usually consists of four speakers or transducers that are fitted into either a reclining chair or mattress. The speakers are powered by amplifiers and coupled to a computer unit. The computer unit generates the selected program. Normal electric current powers the computer unit and amplifiers. A transformer between the control unit and chair or mattress reduces the current to about 15 volts before it passes to the speakers. Thus, there is no risk of electric shock from the recliner or mattress.

Physioacoustic programs generate pure sinusoidal sound waves from 27 to 113 Hz. These programs generate pure tones in a range that may be heard on the radio. A person riding on a bus or an airplane would be exposed to the same frequencies, only in much higher intensity. We wouldn't even consider discussing the decibel exposure to these frequencies that occur at a rock concert! On airplanes and buses these bass frequencies are all jumbled together to form noise, so they are not nearly as effective in creating any controlled result. Although not predictable, some effects associated with low frequency noise are recorded in the medical literature. Studies have blamed some late-night automobile accidents on driver fatigue aggravated by low frequency road noise. Some animals, children, and adults have been observed to go to sleep quickly once they are riding airplanes, buses, trains, or cars. To summarize, noise in this range can, on occasion, be observed to cause random physiologic effects, and it is safe for human exposure if it is not too loud. We prefer to target specific predictable effects through program selection. Selecting pure tones in this safe, audible range allows us to create the sought-after physiologic effect.

Physioacoustics differs from ordinary mechanical vibration in the following ways:

1. Ordinary mechanical vibration creates numbness; low frequency sine wave stimulation never causes numbness.
2. Ordinary mechanical vibration, when applied to muscle fibers, will cause the muscle fibers to contract. In the laboratory, this is called the "Tonic Vibration Response." When trying to induce relaxation, it is *never* desirable to cause muscle contraction, and low frequency sine wave stimulation *never* causes muscle contraction.
3. Ordinary mechanical vibration brings on muscle fatigue; physioacoustic stimulation never causes muscle fatigue.
4. Ordinary vibration may relieve pain or a muscle ache for a very short period of time. Soon the relief wears off ("stimulus fatigue") and, exponentially, more energy is required to maintain the result. It is impossible to obtain such a great energy increase. Because of the proprietary rotating, scanning, and pulsating structure of physioacoustic programs, "stimulus fatigue" does not occur.
5. *Mechanical vibration by its nature tends to create harmful infrasonic resonances.* Physioacoustic stimulation does not. Let's take a minute to consider this last point.

Low frequency sound in the range of 27 to 113 Hz is harmless unless turned up too loud. The only known negative side effect is noise deafness. Infrasound—sound waves of frequencies lower than 20 Hz—have been associated with many deleterious side effects in man. For examples, 0.5 Hz can cause profound nausea, 2.0 Hz causes nystagmus, 4.0 Hz causes degradation of skilled use of the hands and eyes, and 6.0 Hz has been associated with vertebral body lesions and back pain. The harmful effects of infrasound have been studied and cataloged by the Swedish Defense

Agency. These are published and available to the public. Physioacoustics does not use infrasound; it uses low frequency sound.

The International Standards Organization (ISO) sets safety standards for human exposure. The system as currently designed has been tested by an independent agency and has been determined safe for human exposure, even if used at maximum amplitude 24 hours per day.

A final word . . . The beneficial effects of low frequency sound treatment in no way interfere with the benefits inherent in music therapy. Physioacoustic programs are specific sequences of tones. They are songs. Simply put, they are a different form of music. Studies have shown the benefits of physioacoustic treatment to be additive to the benefits of music therapy. Physioacoustic programs may be used without music to allow researchers to determine their precise physiologic effect. In real life, the therapist is not worried about "confounding two variables." He or she wants the client to have all the benefits of music and of low frequency sound. Physioacoustics is not a substitute for music. It is not a replacement for the music therapist. It is, rather, another arrow in the quiver of music therapy. It is a powerful therapeutic modality available to the therapist who would master its use and use it to the benefit of the patient.

REFERENCES

Burke, M. A. (1997). Effects of physioacoustic intervention on pain management of postoperative gynecological patients. In T. Wigram & C. Dileo (Eds.), *Music vibration and health* (pp. 107–123). Cherry Hill, NJ: Jeffrey Books.

Butler, C. F. (1998). *Physioacoustics: The sound treatment of pain and stress.* Institute on Stress Management and Pain. Presented at the annual conference of the American Music Therapy Association, Cleveland, Ohio.

Butler, C. F., & Butler, P. J. (1997). Physioacoustic therapy with cardiac surgery patients. In T. Wigram & C. Dileo (Eds.), *Music vibration and health* (pp. 197–207). Cherry Hill, NJ: Jeffrey Books.

Lehikoinen, P. (1990). *The physioacoustic method.* Kalamazoo, MI: Next Wave, Inc. (Unpublished).

Lehikoinen, P., Naukkarinen, H., Paakkari, T., & Saukkonnen, N. (1990). *The physioacoustic method in the treatment of psychic anxiety.* Paper presented at the 5th International Congress of Psychophysiology, Budapest, Hungary.

Llinas, R., & Ribary, U. (1993). Coherent 40-Hz oscillation characterized dreamlike states in humans. *Neurobiology, 90,* 2078–2081.

Nissenen, A., & Kivinen, P. (1990). University of Kuopio Hypertension Study.

Wigram, T. (1997a). The effect of VA therapy on multiply handicapped adults with high muscle tone and spasticity. In T. Wigram & C. Dileo (Eds.), *Music vibration and health* (pp. 57–68). Cherry Hill, NJ: Jeffrey Books.

Wigram, T. (1997b) The effect of vibroacoustic therapy compared with music and movement based physiotherapy on multiply handicapped patients with high muscle tone and spasticity. In T. Wigram & C. Dileo (Eds.), *Music vibration and health* (pp. 69–85). Cherry Hill, NJ: Jeffrey Books.

Wigram, T. (1997c). The measurement of mood and physiological responses to vibroacoustic therapy in non-clinical subjects. In T. Wigram & C. Dileo (Eds.), *Music vibration and health* (pp. 87–98). Cherry Hill, NJ: Jeffrey Books.

Physioacoustic equipment can be obtained through Heritage Medical Products (Kalamazoo, Michigan), Tel: 616-388-6000; Fax: 616-388-4600.

5

MUSIC-BASED INDIVIDUALIZED RELAXATION TRAINING IN MEDICAL SETTINGS

Bruce Saperston, PhD, MT-BC

MEDICAL PATIENTS often experience anxiety due to numerous factors related to medical interventions. A few such factors commonly reported in the literature include those fears about pain, medical interventions, treatment outcomes and limitations imposed by illnesses and disabilities, as well as issues related to hospitalization, such as the unfamiliarity of the environment and feelings of isolation and helplessness (Schwankovsky & Guthrie, 1984; Spintge, 1989). Anxiety can negatively impact treatment and recovery processes by depleting immune responses and resistance to infection, by increasing basal metabolism rates and incidences of cardiac complications, and by increasing the need for higher doses of anesthetics and postoperative pain medications (Spintge, 1989). Comprehensive literature reviews indicate that music and music therapy interventions may be useful in reducing patient anxiety during a variety of medical procedures (Dileo-Maranto, 1993; Standley, 1986).

The purpose of this chapter is to provide a music-based stress reduction model that can be applied to patients manifesting a wide range of diagnoses in a variety of settings, including general hospital, clinic, nursing home, and patient's residence. The music-based individualized relaxation training (MBIRT) method (Saperston, 1989) was originally developed as a means of providing relaxation training for individuals with developmental disabilities and/or behavioral disturbances. As MBIRT provides sequential strategies for addressing the specific needs of individuals regardless of their mental, emotional, and physical levels of functioning, it can be applied widely with medical populations.

Music-based individualized relaxation training is a behavior therapy approach in which one or more elements of music are incorporated in individualized task-specific training strategies designed to elicit and/or shape one or more behaviors identified as necessary in the eventual achievement of a generalized state of relaxation. The approach is "music-based" because music serves a variety of functions during all phases of training. In general, its goals are designed to move the individual from respondent procedures to operant procedures so that relaxation skills can be performed independently. The MBIRT method incorporates applications from the fields of behavioral medicine, behavioral therapy, and music therapy, including progressive relaxation training, biofeedback, entrainment, iso-music, contingent music, interactive music, imagery, and vibroacoustic therapy.

While music was originally applied in MBIRT as a means of assisting individuals with learning and behavioral problems, it also can be applied in helping patients with cognitive deficits caused by medications, brain injuries, disease, pain, and surgical interventions. Several factors make music a particularly powerful and efficient stimulus for such purposes. First, as an auditory stimulus, music pervades the environment and is difficult to ignore (Jaynes, 1976). Second, musical inputs are mediated at the thalamic level of the brain and arouse sensations, emotions, and feelings in individuals with impaired functioning who may not be responsive at a verbal (cortical) level (Weigl, 1959). Third, the temporal aspect of music allows for its precise administration in conjunction with motor responses and physiological fluctuations. The various functions of music in MBIRT can be categorized within three general areas: music as a reinforcing stimulus, music as a structural prompt, and music as an eliciting stimulus.

Music as a Reinforcing Stimulus

Music listening provides an excellent means for initially engaging individuals in relaxation training regardless of their level of cognitive functioning because (a) it is a reinforcing experience for individuals with cognitive deficits (Bellamy & Sontag, 1973; Saperston, 1973; Saperston, Chan, Morphew, & Carsrud, 1980; Underhill & Harris, 1974; Wolfe, 1980); (b) it provides meaning to the activity (e.g., individual participates by listening to music); and (c) considering the requisite behaviors for participating in relaxation training (i.e., lying still, eyes closed, remaining quiet, etc.), it is one of the few experiences that can be presented. Throughout MBIRT, music is used as a contingent reinforcer in developing behaviors consistent with relaxation skills.

Music as a Structural Prompt

"If music is structured in time concurrent with the behavior, it is generally being used as a structural prompt" (Jellison, 1977, p. 253). Research has demonstrated the effectiveness of music as a structural prompt in improving language discrimination and comprehension skills (Harrison & Lecrome, 1966; Madsen & Geringer, 1976), retention abilities (Gfeller, 1983; Isern, 1961; Lathom, 1970), and the rhythmic motor behaviors of various populations (Clark, McCorkle, & Williams, 1981; Staum, 1983).

Music is applied as a structural prompt during MBIRT procedures primarily through the use of instructional song and chanting activities. Instructions to perform relaxation skills (e.g., cues to close eyes and progressively relax specific body parts) and concepts associated with the relaxation process (e.g., "Now I'm going to my special place") are presented through songs to facilitate and improve the comprehension and retention of information. Language cues to "breathe in" and "breathe out" are sung and accompanied by slow rhythmic chord changes as structural prompts to teach the patient rhythmic, diaphragmatic breath control skills. The patient's chanting of short phrases (e.g., "Now I am calm") is utilized (a) to develop breath control and slow respiration by gradually reducing the tempo of the accompanying music, and (b) to focus attention on the relaxation task and/or redirect attention from distracting or anxiety-provoking thoughts.

MUSIC AS AN ELICITING STIMULUS

Five areas of research provide findings germane to the presentation of music as an eliciting stimulus during MBIRT procedures. The first area includes research in which music has been combined with traditional stress-reduction techniques. These studies have demonstrated that music can be effective in facilitating relaxation responses when it is administered in conjunction with biofeedback training (Kibler & Rider, 1983; Scartelli, 1982; Scartelli & Borling, 1986), progressive relaxation training (Kibler & Rider, 1983; Rider, 1985), and guided imagery (Bonny & Savary, 1973; Rider, 1985).

The second area of research includes investigations in which the effects of music on the psychological and physiological responses of subjects were studied. Hanser (1985) has provided a comprehensive review of this research, and the following summarizes findings and ideas reported by her that are of relevance to MBIRT procedures: (a) music is effective in eliciting perceptions of improved states of relaxation as measured by A-State Anxiety Inventory scores and verbal reports, (b) music preference and familiarity with music may be influential factors in a subject's psychological response to music, (c) physiological responses to music have been inconsistent, and (d) there is a lack of correlation between subjects' reported perceptions of more relaxed states and their physiological responses.

The third area to be addressed is that body of knowledge that supports the use of the "iso-moodic" or "iso" principle (Altshuler, 1948). The iso principle involves matching musical stimuli to an individual's existing mood and then changing the musical stimuli in the direction in which the individual's mood is to be influenced. Early research supported this approach with both psychotic and normal subjects (Altshuler, 1948; Orton, 1953). More recent research supports the use of "iso" structured music in altering mood as well as various physiological parameters, including muscle tension (EMG) (Rider, 1985) and systolic blood pressure (Pignatielo, Camp, Elder, & Rasar, 1989).

The fourth area, physiologically interactive music (Saperston, 1995), is a new approach for presenting musical stimuli within the iso model to entrain (synchronize) a specific physiological response. Prior to the development of this model, a few studies had revealed the utility of auditory or musical stimuli in entraining respiration (Hass, Distenfeld, & Axen, 1986; Lovell & Morgan, 1942) and heart rates (Bason & Celler, 1972); however, no studies had been done in which music was systematically manipulated in relation to ongoing physiological responses for the purpose of entraining such responses.

Saperston (1995) has defined this approach as follows:

> Physiologically interactive music is an hypothesized approach in which one or more elements of music (or combinations of the same element of music) are continuously presented in a systematic relationship to an organismic rhythm within the periodicity limits necessary for entraining the organismic rhythm. As the organismic rhythm changes, either in the desired direction (i.e., towards the musical synchronizer) or away from the synchronizer, the musical synchronizer is again presented within the new periodicity limits necessary for entrainment. The process is repeated in a continuous manner.

> The process is "interactive" because of the hypothesized interdependent relationship which is set up between the musical stimuli and the physiological response. An example of this approach would be the use of "physiologically interactive tempi" (PIT) in altering heart rate. First, the tempo of the music is dependent upon the heart rate, as the music is presented at a tempo just under the heart rate. Secondly, if the tempo is within the periodicity limits necessary for entrainment, the heart rate is influenced by the tempo. Thirdly, the tempo is once again influenced by the heart rate, as it is presented just under the new heart rate. (p. 66)

Research demonstrated that synthesized music presented according to the physiologically interactive model resulted in significant decreases ($p < .05$) in the heart rates of normal adult subjects, while the same music presented at a slow tempo (M.M. = 48) and a moderately fast tempo (M.M. = 86) resulted in minimal, nonsignificant heart rate decreases and increases, respectively (Saperston, 1995). The physiologically interactive music was the only music to significantly influence heart rate change, but heart rate decreases were not significantly greater than those in the no-music control group. While further studies are needed to both refine and determine the validity of this model, presenting elements of music in an ongoing manner in conjunction with specific physiological responses may serve to enhance the overall (i.e., physiological as well as psychological) entrainment process.

Therefore, in addition to presenting rhythmic chord changes as a structural prompt to influence diaphragmatic breathing skills as previously described (see music as a structural prompt), the music therapist should maintain an awareness of the individual's physiological responses and, when possible, interact musically by matching and subsequently influencing these responses. For example, tempi may be matched to an individual's respiration rate or heart rate (using visual or auditory feedback from a heart rate monitor).

The fifth manner of employing music as an eliciting stimulus in MBIRT procedures is as a conditioned stimulus that has been repeatedly paired with another relaxation-eliciting stimulus to the extent that eventually the music alone triggers the relaxation response. Examples of relaxation-eliciting stimuli that may be incorporated in such respondent conditioning procedures include various physical therapy modalities, such as heat and hydrotherapy, as well as therapeutic massage.

Some studies suggest that vibroacoustic therapy, a technique in which low frequency sine waves are presented along with prerecorded music, may be useful in reducing physical and psychological measures of stress (Wigram, 1997a, 1997b). In MBIRT, vibroacoustic therapy could be presented initially. The intensity of the low frequency tones would then be faded gradually throughout sessions as the music would become the conditioned stimulus for relaxation. It should be noted that caution should be exercised in providing vibroacoustic therapy to medical patients, as contraindications for this treatment are still being identified. Considerations related to such contraindications have been provided by Wigram and Dileo (1997).

MBIRT Assumptions

MBIRT procedures for presenting music as a stimulus for more relaxed responding are based on assumptions derived from the literature previously reviewed and the author's clinical observations.

1. *The patient's music preferences should be incorporated during procedures.* Music preferences are defined both in terms of Gaston's (1951) definitions for stimulative and sedative music and with regard to styles of music (i.e., rock, country, baroque, etc.). Music preferences are assessed both initially and on an ongoing basis. Two categories of preferred music are determined: the patient's overall preferred music and the patient's preferred music for relaxation.

Procedures for incorporating a patient's music preferences are determined by the type of music the patient prefers. When a patient's preferred relaxation music is stimulative, it is presented early in the session to enhance patient participation, and later in the session as a reinforcer. Procedures for modifying the patient's music preferences (Assumptions 4 and 5) are gradually implemented.

2. *Music that elicits more relaxed physiological responding should be incorporated during procedures.* Training procedures are determined by two factors: (1) whether or not the patient's preferred relaxation music and best physiological music are congruent, and (2) the types of music determined as preferred relaxation music and best physiological music. The objective for each patient is to bring these categories into congruence with sedative music as the patient's preferred relaxation music (see Assumptions 4 and 5). Initially the patient's preferred relaxation music and best physiological music are each employed in developing basic relaxation concepts and skills.

3. *Sedative music is considered the best music for facilitating more relaxed psychological and physiological states when this music is presented in conjunction with the iso principle (e.g., decreasing tempi) and/or physiologically interactive music.* While research findings regarding the effects of sedative music have been inconsistent (Haack, 1980; Hanser, 1985), those studies in which sedative music and/or the iso principle were incorporated with relaxation techniques have consistently demonstrated the effectiveness of such music in enhancing the relaxation response (Kibler & Rider, 1983; Rider, 1985; Scartelli, 1982). The present author has observed that patients who originally achieved lower EMG levels with preferred stimulative music eventually attained considerably lower EMG readings with sedative music.

In addition to facilitating the relaxation response, iso-structured sessions provide an excellent model because musical stimuli of varying tempi and styles can be presented. Therefore, it is possible to include a patient's preferred music and best physiological music during all sessions, while incorporating techniques to modify the patient's responses to different types of music.

4. *The patient's music preferences are based on psychological and physiological factors that can be helpful in interpreting responses to different musical stimuli.* Benenzon's (1981) individual iso's, somewhat redefined, are useful in describing these factors. In behavioral terms, the "group iso" refers to the patient's learning history in which specific types of music have been associated with significant people and events. The "complimentary iso" reflects the patient's current psychological state as determined by environmental events occurring just prior to, during, or shortly after the session. The "universal iso" is redefined to represent the patient's current physiological response to music and previous physiological conditioning experiences that contribute to current response patterns.

Saperston (1989) provided a clinical example in which an individual consistently evidenced lower EMG readings while listening to rock music than while listening to sedative music because rock music matched the individual's group, contemporary, and universal iso's. Rock music served as a distraction from anxiety-provoking thoughts, while sedative music did not elicit his attention.

5. *A patient's music preferences can be modified to facilitate more relaxed responding.* Two approaches can be used in modifying an individual's music preference when their preferred relaxation music is stimulative.

The first approach involves modifying the patient's individual psychological iso's (i.e., contemporary and group) through cognitive restructuring techniques. This process could include either helping the patient redefine particular iso's or expanding the patient's awareness of the types of music that are consistent with his established iso's.

A second approach for modifying a patient's preferred relaxation music entails repetitively pairing closer approximations of the targeted music (i.e., music of slow tempi, etc.) with reinforcing experiences. Improved states of relaxation can be reinforcing to the patient. Some patients, therefore, may learn to associate sedative music with more relaxed states after several iso-structured sessions. Positively reinforcing verbalizations and guided imagery techniques designed to elicit positive associations can also be paired with the targeted music.

As each of the aforementioned approaches requires considerable time, they should be considered only for individuals with long-term treatment needs. In addition, the necessity of modifying an individual's music preferences should be considered on an individual basis.

Medical MBIRT Intervention Procedures

As MBIRT intervention procedures were originally ordered in a hierarchical sequence to meet the needs of individuals with developmental disabilities and/or severe behavioral disorders, it is necessary to provide an adapted model for presenting MBIRT strategies to meet the needs of various medical patients. The four general levels of intervention remain the same and are based on an individual's ability to perform relaxation skills more independently. Level I—The Development of Enabling Behaviors, Level II—The Development of Therapist Directed Relaxation Responses, Level III—The Development of Independent Relaxation Responses, and Level IV—The Development of Transfer and Generalization Skills.

The order in which interventions from these levels are presented will vary depending upon the immediate mental, physical, and emotional status of the patient. For example, a patient may be capable of participating successfully in Level III independent relaxation skill activities prior to surgery to reduce preoperative anxiety. However, the best intervention six hours postsurgically for the same patient might be Level II prerecorded iso-music with periodic rhythmic breathing cues. A board-certified music therapist must carry out MBIRT so that the patient's status and needs can be assessed and appropriate interventions implemented on an ongoing basis. In general, this intervention is one that meets the patient's immediate needs for reducing psychological/physiological tension without imposing additional stress associated with either cognitive or physical tasks (e.g., attending and responding to instructions, tensing muscle groups, etc.).

There are three other important reasons why only a board-certified music therapist should administer MBIRT procedures. First, music can be an extremely potent stimulus for eliciting emotional responses or retrieving repressed information from individuals in particularly vulnerable psychological states (such as medical patients). The professional music therapist understands psychosocial factors related to the patient's condition and possesses the counseling skills for assisting the patient. Second, the development of a therapeutic relationship between the therapist and patient is critical to the success of this program. Third, the board-certified music therapist has the knowledge and skills to present the different types of musical stimuli required in this approach.

The following summarizes the four general levels of MBIRT intervention.

Level I—The Development of Enabling Behaviors

Level I procedures were originally developed specifically for individuals with severe behavioral disorders and may not be required frequently in medical settings. Level I strategies are designed to teach patients to perform and maintain behavior considered as prerequisite for relaxation training. Criterion for Level I is attained when the patient is able to recline or lie down while remaining still (i.e., exhibiting minimal movements) and keeping his or her eyes closed for approximately 15 minutes while listening to music. The therapist's discretion is used in formulating more specific operational definitions for objectives presented in this overview paper. Interfering behaviors symptomatic of anxiety (e.g., bruxism, fidgeting, etc.) are also targeted for elimination and/or reduction during Level I procedures. Level I strategies are not intended to facilitate relaxed responding, although this may occur. The basic premise of these procedures is that the patient must learn to control overt responses before physiological control skills can be developed. Respondent conditioning techniques (i.e., iso-music, heat treatment, vibroacoustic therapy, etc.) may be implemented.

Other primary objectives common to both Level I and Level II procedures are the development of therapist-patient rapport and the establishment of the session as a reinforcing experience.

Level II—The Development of Therapist-Directed Relaxation Responses

Criterion for Level II is achieved when the patient can remain still with eyes closed and perform muscle relaxation (progressive relaxation training or autogenic methods) and diaphragmatic breath control skills with the assistance of musical structural prompts (i.e., instructional songs, chants, interactive music). Initial therapist-directed sessions may be comprised of only musical stimuli (e.g., iso-music, interactive music, therapist singing general cues to relax without specific instructions) and/or musical stimuli paired with other relaxation eliciting stimuli (e.g., vibroacoustic therapy, massage, etc.). Throughout subsequent sessions, the therapist gradually introduces cues to periodically take slow deep breaths (sung or spoken) accompanied by musical structural prompts (chord changes to match breaths). The therapist also gradually introduces cues to relax specific muscle groups. Music listening segments between these instructional cues should be comprised of iso- or interactive music.

The therapist may use live music or prerecorded tapes during Level II sessions and should note the following in preparing prerecorded tapes. First, it is important that prerecorded materials be individualized to the extent that patients are never instructed to perform muscle relaxation on a portion of their bodies that would be contraindicated due to their medical condition. Second, MBIRT basic assumptions regarding the use of the patient's preferred music should be followed. Third, in programming prerecorded tapes for hospital/clinic use, the therapist or patient must own the original recordings in order to be in compliance with copyright law. If the therapist prerecords tapes for the patient's home use, the patient must own the original recordings. Fourth, the therapist will find it helpful to have a collection of preprogrammed iso-music tapes in a variety of styles for use in the hospital/clinic setting. Familiarity with these tapes would enable the therapist to begin the listening presentation at different points in the tape to more accurately match the patient's mood/physiological state at the onset of the session.

The following is a model of a Level II session:

- Preferred music listening to establish mood.
- Instructional song with introductory message (e.g., "Time to relax") followed by cues for controlled breathing (e.g., "breathe in," "breathe out").
- Muscle relaxation song for lower body parts.
- Chanting to focus attention and decrease respiration (e.g., tempi decreased).
- Interactive music.
- Muscle relaxation song for trunk and arms.
- Chant or interactive music at slower tempo for controlled breathing.
- Muscle relaxation song for neck, face, and head.
- Improvised or prerecorded music at successively slower tempi for listening.
- Reinstatement of breath control concept song or chant, if needed.
- During music listening the therapist may implement one or more of the following:
    - Guided imagery to elicit positive associations and/or relaxation;
    - Biofeedback training utilizing various modes of feedback (e.g., verbal coaching, clicks, etc.);
    - Improvised interactive music.
- Patient is gradually and carefully returned to an alert state.

During Level II procedures, the patient begins to become aware of feelings associated with more relaxed responding through periodic participation in respondent conditioning procedures and biofeedback training. Techniques for modifying music preferences may be begun during Level II programming.

Level III—The Development of Independent Relaxation Responses

During Level III procedures structured music prompts are slowly faded and replaced with verbal instructions accompanied by background music. Respondent techniques are gradually replaced by operant methods including increased durations of biofeedback training.

Criterion for Level III is attained when the patient (a) demonstrates the ability of correctly performing relaxation skills when instructions are presented verbally, and (b) demonstrates the ability of achieving a more relaxed physiological state while performing relaxation procedures.

Level IV—The Development of Transfer and Generalization Skills

During this level, patients learn to recognize when they need to reduce stress and to use relaxation skills in other settings (e.g., home, work, etc.).

The four levels of MBIRT intervention provide the music therapist with options for presenting music-based strategies relevant to meeting the diverse needs of medical patients. In addition to the patient's psychological and physical status, the duration and type of medical treatment will often dictate the most appropriate MBIRT applications. Patients receiving short-term medical treatment may derive the greatest benefits from the therapist-directed strategies, whereas patients involved in long-term treatment would have both the time and need for developing Level III and IV skills.

REFERENCES

Altshuler, I. M. (1948). A psychiatrist's experience with music as a therapeutic agent. In D. M. Schullian & M. Shoen (Eds.), *Music and medicine*. Freeport, NY: Book for Libraries Press.

Bason, P. T. & Celler, B. G. (1972) Control of the heart rate by external stimuli. *Nature, 238*, 279–280.

Bellamy, T., & Sontag, E. (1973). Use of group contingent music to increase assembly line production rates of retarded students in a simulated sheltered workshop. *Journal of Music Therapy, 10*, 125–136.

Benenzon, R. (1981). *Music therapy manual* (Grabia, Trans.). Springfield, IL: Charles C. Thomas.

Bonny, H. L., & Savary, L. (1973). *Music and your mind.* New York: Harper and Row.

Clark, M., McCorkle, R. R., & Williams, S. B. (1981). Music therapy-assisted labor and delivery. *Journal of Music Therapy, 18*, 88–100.

Dileo-Maranto, C. (1993). Music therapy and stress management. In P. M. Lehrer & R. L. Woolfolk (Eds.), *Principles and practice of stress management* (2nd ed., pp. 407–442). New York: Guilford Press.

Gaston, E. T. (1951). Dynamic music factors in mood change. *Music Educators Journal, 37*, 42–44.

Gfeller, K. E. (1983). Music mnemonics as an aid to retention with normal and learning disabled students. *Journal of Music Therapy, 20*, 179–189.

Haack, P. (1980). The behaviors of music listeners. In D. Hodges (Ed.), *Handbook of music psychology* (pp. 141–182). Washington, DC: National Association for Music Therapy.

Hanser, S. B. (1985). Music therapy and stress reduction research. *Journal of Music Therapy*, 22, 193–206.

Harrison, W., & Lecrome, H. (1966). The effect of music and exercise upon the self-help skills of non-verbal retardates. *American Journal of Mental Deficiency, 71*, 279–282.

Hass, F., Distenfeld, S., & Axen, K. (1986). Effects of perceived musical rhythm on respiratory pattern. *Applied Physiology, 62*, 1185–1191.

Isern, B. (1961). Summary, conclusions, and implications: The influence of music upon the memory of mentally retarded children. *Proceedings of the National Association for Music Therapy*, 10, 149–153.

Jaynes, J. (1976). *The origin of consciousness in the breakdown of the bicameral mind.* Boston: Houghton-Mifflin.

Jellison, J. A. (1977). Music instructional programs for the severely handicapped. In E. Sontag, J. Smith, & N. Certo (Eds.), *Educational programming for the severely and profoundly handicapped* (pp. 250–252). Reston, VA: Council for Exceptional Children.

Kibler, V. E., & Rider, M. S. (1983). The effect of progressive muscle relaxation and music on stress as measured by finger temperature response. *Journal of Clinical Psychology, 39*(2), 213–215.

Lathom, W. B. (1970). *Retarded children's retention of songs, stories and poems.* Unpublished doctoral dissertation, The University of Kansas, Lawrence.

Lovell, G., & Morgan, J. (1942). Physiological and motor responses to a regularly recurring sound: A study in monotony. *Experimental Psychology, 30*, 435–451.

Madsen, C. K., & Geringer, J. M. (1976). Choice of televised music lessons versus free play in relationship to academic improvement. *Journal of Music Therapy, 13*(4), 154–162.

Orton, M. R. (1953). *Application of the iso-moodic principle in the use of music with psychotic and "normal" subjects.* Unpublished master's thesis, The University of Kansas, Lawrence.

Pignatiello, M., Camp, C. J., Elder, S. T., & Rasar, L. A. (1989). A psychophysiological comparison of the Velton and Musical Mood Induction Techniques. *Music Therapy, 26*, 140–154.

Rider, M. S. (1985). Entrainment mechanisms are involved in pain reduction, muscle relaxation, and music-mediated imagery. *Journal of Music Therapy, 22*, 183–192.

Saperston, B. (1973). The use of music in establishing communication with an autistic mentally retarded child. *Journal of Music Therapy, 10*, 184–188.

Saperston, B. (1989). Music-based individualized relaxation training (MBIRT): A stress-reduction approach for the behaviorally disburbed mentally retarded. *Music Therapy Perspectives, 6*, 26–33.

Saperston, B. (1995). The effects of consistent tempi and physiologically interactive tempi on heart rate and EMG responses. In T. Wigram, B. M. Saperston, and R. West (Eds.), *The art and science of music therapy: A handbook.* Switzerland: Harwood Academic.

Saperston, B. M., Chan, R., Morphew, C., & Carsrud, K. B. (1980). Music listening versus juice as a reinforcement for learning in profoundly mentally retarded individuals. *Journal of Music Therapy, 17*, 174–183.

Scartelli, J. P. (1982). The effect of sedative music on electromyographic biofeedback assisted relaxation training of spastic cerebral palsied adults. *Journal of Music Therapy, 19*, 210–218.

Scartelli, J. P., & Borling, J. E. (1986). The effects of sequenced versus simultaneous EMG biofeedback and sedative music on frontalis relaxation training. *Journal of Music Therapy, 23*, 157–165.

Schwankovsky L. M., & Guthrie, P. T. (1984). Music therapy for other health impaired children: Monograph 3. In W. B. Lathom & C. T. Eagle, Jr. (Eds.), *Music therapy for handicapped children* (Vol, 3, pp. 119–173). Lawrence, KS: AMS.

Spintge, R. (1989). The anxiolytic effects of music. In M. H. M. Lee (Ed.), *Rehabilitation, music and human well-being* (pp. 82–97). St. Louis: MMB Music.

Standley, J. M. (1986). Music research in medical/dental treatment: Meta-analysis and clinical applications. *Journal of Music Therapy, 23*(2), 56–122.

Staum, M. J. (1983). Music and rhythmic stimuli in the rehabilitation of gait disorders. *Journal of Music Therapy, 20*, 69–87.

Underhill, K. K., & Harris, L. M. (1974). The effect of contingent music on establishing imitation in behaviorally disturbed retarded children. *Journal of Music Therapy, 11*, 156–166.

Weigl, V. (1959). Functional music. A therapeutic tool in working with the mentally retarded. *American Journal of Mental Deficiency, 63*, 672–678.

Wigram, T. (1997a). The effect of VA therapy on multiply handicapped adults with high muscle tone and spasticity. In T. Wigram & C. Dileo (Eds.), *Music vibration and health* (pp. 57–68). Cherry Hill, NJ: Jeffrey Books.

Wigram, T. (1997b). The measurement of mood and physiological responses to vibroacoustic therapy in non-clinical subjects. In T. Wigram & C. Dileo (Eds.), *Music vibration and health* (pp. 87–97). Cherry Hill, NJ: Jeffrey Books.

Wigram, T. & Dileo, C. (1997). Clinical and ethical considerations. In T. Wigram & C. Dileo (Eds.), *Music vibration and health* (pp. 225–234). Cherry Hill, NJ: Jeffrey Books.

Wolfe, D. E. (1980). The effect of automated interrupted music on head posturing of cerebral palsied individuals. *Journal of Music Therapy, 17*, 184–206.

6

Performing Arts Medicine: Music Therapy to Treat Anxiety in Musicians

Alan D. Reitman, PhD, MT-BC

MUSIC PERFORMANCE ANXIETY (MPA) has been defined as "the experience of persistent, distressful apprehension about and/or actual impairment of, performance skills in a public context, to a degree unwarranted given the musician's aptitude, training, and level of preparation" (Salmon, 1990, p. 3). Musicians may experience cognitive, behavioral, and physiological symptoms of MPA in advance of, during, or after a particular performance. Left unattended, these anxiety-related symptoms may interact with each other in a manner that can wreak havoc on a musician's lifestyle, affecting mental and physical health as well as musical performance (Dileo-Maranto, 1996). Music performance anxiety may also bring about a change in the musician's attitude toward, and relationship with, music itself. The purpose of this chapter is to present a model of treatment for MPA that incorporates music therapy techniques with clinically demonstrated, nonpharmacological anxiety reduction techniques. This model of therapy has proven useful in ameliorating the symptoms associated with MPA (Reitman, 1997) and may provide a means of reparation for the musician's relationship with music as well.

As alluded to above, anxiety may greatly impair the quality of a musician's performance and have serious consequences on his or her career. Surveys of professional musicians indicate that while 96% of musicians may experience performance-related stress, 24% of professional musicians experience marked stress while performing, and 16% rate performance anxiety as a severe problem, markedly affecting their careers (Bartel & Thompson, 1995; Fishbein, Middlestadt, Ottati, Strauss, & Ellis, 1988; James, 1984). Similar results have been noted for student and faculty musicians, with students reporting a greater incidence of performance anxiety (Wesner, Noyes, & Davis, 1990). The above surveys assessed actively performing musicians and did not indicate the percentage of musicians who may have left their careers due to performance anxiety. Therefore, the number of musicians who may have been impaired by performance anxiety may be even higher than the surveys suggest.

Musicians have been found to be among the top five occupational groups seeking treatment in mental health centers in a single state, with an admission rate of 19.14 per 1000 (Colligan, Smith, & Hurrell, 1977). Musicians frequently perform under highly demanding circumstances which may include high levels of stress that are associated with and contribute to biomedical and psychosocial conditions (Fishbein et al., 1988). Factors attributed to this stress include the demand for perfection, public access to recordings of prior performances, and professional competition (Lehrer, 1987).

Continued performance despite the presence of MPA may exacerbate performance-related medical conditions, such as overuse syndrome and neural impingement (Fishbein et al., 1988; Lockwood, 1989). Repeated exposure to stress has been associated with other physical ailments, including hypertension, headaches, peptic ulcers, arthritis, colitis, diarrhea, asthma, cardiac arrhythmias, sexual problems, circulatory problems (cold hands and feet), muscle tension, and cancer (Davis, Eshelman, & McKay, 1982). Long continued exposure to the same stressor, such as prolonged autonomic arousal associated with MPA, may result in physiological decompensation and exhaustion of the body's capacity to resist and adapt (Selye, 1978). Musicians may have a 5% greater morbidity rate from coronary disease than the general public (Tucker, Faulkner, & Horvath, 1971). Excessive sympathetic activation has been linked to the release of free fatty acids in the bloodstream, increasing the risk of coronary artery disease (James, 1984).

Musicians with music performance anxiety may address these stressors/symptoms by avoiding performance-related activities, taking medication without prescription (such as beta-blockers), or resorting to drug or alcohol use. Fishbein et al. (1988) found that a majority of the respondents who reported use of beta-blocking medication also reported occasional nonprescribed use. Another study revealed that 51% of 146 musicians reported drinking an alcoholic beverage before performing on stage (Steptoe & Fidler, 1987).

THREE SYSTEMS THEORY OF ANXIETY

Empirical research during the past two decades suggests that anxiety may involve the coordination of several response systems, as well as personality factors (Lang, 1968; Lang, Miller, & Levin, 1988; Spielberger, 1972). Based on an extensive literature review, as well as his own research, Lang (1971) proposed a three-systems model of anxiety. This theory conceptualizes anxiety in terms of three relatively independent but highly interactive response systems including (a) *physiological responses,* which are associated with increases in sympathetic nervous system arousal; (b) *cognitive responses,* which include verbal reports of anxiety, fear, panic, and related complaints of worry, obsessions, inability to concentrate, and similar thoughts; and (c) *behavioral responses,* which consist of the observable acts of anxiety and fear, avoidance, escape, hypervigilance, dysfunctional mobility, compulsive mannerisms, and deficits in attention, performance, and control.

Although described as separate entities, these systems are interrelated. Findings suggest that cognitions may mediate other anxiety response systems. Cognitions were found to be highly correlated with physiological and behavioral manifestations of anxiety (Lehrer & Woolfolk, 1982). Physiological and behavioral manifestations proved to be more weakly correlated.

Physiological Symptoms of MPA

Physiological symptoms of music performance anxiety can be attributed to sympathetic nervous system arousal, as first described by Cannon's (1929) "fight or flight" response. These symptoms, inclusive of rapid heartbeat, trembling, increased muscle tension, dry mouth, shortness of breath, nausea, and dizziness, often result in impairment of functioning (Wesner, Noyes, & Davis, 1990). In addition to these symptoms, Wesner et al. (1990) found that performing musicians also identified poor concentration, sweating, flushing, and quavering voice as significant symptoms of music performance anxiety. Research has demonstrated that the debilitating effects of these symptoms may be instrument-specific in musicians, suggesting that these responses may be learned or conditioned (e.g., dry mouth in woodwind players, trembling hands in violinists) (Wolfe, 1989).

It is important to note, however, that heightened arousal is not the same as anxiety, wherein the musician may have apprehension or dread that closely resembles fear (Kaplan, Sadock, & Grebb, 1994; Leary, 1990). Heightened arousal has been found to facilitate the performance of musicians who interpret it as exhilarating rather than threatening (Hamann & Sobaje, 1983). The effects of physiological arousal act in accordance with the Yerkes-Dodson law which maintains that while a moderate amount of arousal is necessary for optimal performance, both hypo- and hyper-aroused states tend to result in the impairment of functioning (Yerkes & Dodson, 1908). Hence, low-arousal states may be as debilitating to performance as high arousal states, resulting in a lackluster musical performance.

Cognitive Symptoms of MPA

While physiological symptoms may be debilitating to musical performers, cognitive processes are integral to their interpretation as anxiety-provoking stimuli (Salmon, 1990; Steptoe, 1989). In fact, cognitive symptoms of anxiety may be persistent and perhaps more debilitating than physiological symptoms. Clark and Agras (1991) found that musicians taking beta-blocking medications reported a decrease in physiological symptomatology, while still experiencing cognitive symptoms of anxiety.

The cognitive distortions most frequently associated with MPA include: (a) *fear of threat related to one's personal construct of the world*—including one's own reaction to loss of control, e.g., over performance environment, reactions of others, or what one's body might do; (b) *catastrophizing*—dwelling on the most extreme negative consequence possible, even in circumstances where little danger is actually imminent (Freeman, Pretzer, Fleming, & Simon, 1990); (c) *negative self statements*—related to one's anticipated self-efficacy within a performance context (Bandura, 1977); and (d) *worry*—the mental activity involved in contemplating the unpleasantness of possible unfortunate events (Lehrer, Goldman, & Strommen, 1990).

Research examining the cognitive strategies used by performing musicians has found worry to be significantly correlated to MPA (Lehrer et al., 1990). Musicians identified as having intense MPA reported either catastrophic cognitions (e.g., "I'm almost sure to make a dreadful mistake, and that will ruin everything"; "I think I'm going to faint"), or a blasé attitude ("It's just another concert . . .") (Steptoe & Fidler, 1987). Those with moderate levels of anxiety were more likely to realistically appraise the situation.

Behavioral Symptoms of MPA

Behavioral symptoms of anxiety may arise in anticipation of, in conjunction with, or in response to cognitive appraisal (Leary, 1990). These symptoms may include "technical problems that detract from performance; interpersonal problems with teachers, friends, managers, and stage hands; and a tendency for people to avoid doing the things that make them anxious, such as practicing and creating performance opportunities for themselves" (Lehrer, 1987, p. 148).

Observable signs of MPA include the following:

1. Feet and legs: Paces, shuffles, shifts weight, has trembling knees, taps toe or foot.
2. Body: Sways body, breathes heavily.
3. Arms and hands: Makes extraneous arm or hand movements, clutches instrument, touches stand, touches self (lips, face, hand on hips, adjusts clothes).
4. Face: Appears deadpan, is pale, blushes, moistens lips, swallows, clears throat, perspires, moves head, winks, bats eyes.
5. Instrumental behavior: Adjusts mouthpiece, clears spit valve, manipulates slide or valves, adjusts or inspects instrument.
6. Vocalization: Hums, whistles, counts, jokes. (Wardle, 1975, p. 199)

Coping Systematic Desensitization

One of the most effective treatment protocols for musicians with performance anxiety is a cognitive-behavioral technique known as systematic desensitization (SD) (Appel, 1976; Bryson, 1980; McCune, 1983). This procedure involves training the client in deep muscle relaxation, constructing a hierarchy of anxiety provoking scenes, and having the client imagine each of the scenes while in a relaxed state. Following the imaginal exposure, in-vivo ("real life") exposure is sometimes added as a fourth step (Levin & Gross, 1985). While the theoretical mechanisms for its effectiveness remain unclear, research over the past two decades suggests that SD works through a combination of processes, including "(a) enhancing imagery, enabling the client to process anxious stimuli more completely; and (b) reducing arousal to allow more rapid habituation" (Williams & Chambless 1994, p. 367).

As noted above, traditional systematic desensitization was conceptualized as involving the participant in a passive deconditioning process, wherein relaxation reciprocally inhibited the anxiety reaction. Goldfried (1971) developed a variant of SD that made use of a mediational or coping model.

Coping may be defined as the efforts made by people to avert or reduce the impact of potentially stressful events (Lazarus & Folkman, 1984). Within the coping paradigm, the subject identifies physiological, psychological, and behavioral indicators of stress, and actively intervenes to reduce them. In this manner, the participant develops a skill that may generalize beyond the target stressor itself. Coping systematic desensitization (CSD) has been found as effective as SD in reducing anxiety and lends itself to both individual and group training.

Rationale for Music-Assisted Coping Systematic Desensitization

While systematic desensitization has proven effective for musicians, coping systematic desensitization results in a generalizable skill that may afford musicians a sense of mastery over their anxiety that traditional SD may not. This would seem particularly relevant for anxious musicians who work in a variety of performance venues and must contend with many situations affected by performance-related stress (e.g., the effects of performance anxiety on relationships).

There is evidence to suggest that music-assisted coping systematic desensitization may prove even more beneficial. Research has indicated that responsiveness to music (for all types of listeners) is learned and results from a long-term interaction with the music (Lundin, 1967). Yet, musicians have been found to demonstrate different responses to music listening than nonmusicians, including differential mood responses; significantly different physiological responses, such as electroencephalograph (EEG), surface electromyography (sEMG), galvanic skin response (GSR) (i.e., skin conductance), and respiration; a tendency to listen to music more analytically; and increased tolerance for tension in music (Bartlett, 1996; Dileo-Maranto, 1992; VanderArk & Ely, 1992). A recent study found that musicians who rely predominantly on sound, or "auditives," to interpret their world, were more likely to experience performance anxiety, suggesting that there is a "need to develop auditive-specific interventions, environments, and therapeutic regimes for the treatment of musicians with performance anxiety" (Brodsky, Sloboda, & Waterman, 1994, p. 101).

Music has the potential to induce states of physiological and self-reported relaxation, which may act as a counter-condition to the extreme physiological arousal associated with anxiety (Davis & Thaut, 1989; Fried, 1990a). While not musician-specific, researchers have found music effective in enhancing the anxiety-ameliorating factors associated with relaxation training and systematic desensitization. Both increased relaxation and listening to music have been associated with increases in imagery production and maintenance (Bonny & Savary, 1973; Borkovec & Sides, 1979).

It would seem that the responsiveness of musicians to music may be used to their benefit. For instance, a particularly strong relaxation response to music might prove quite helpful in reducing anxiety in an SD protocol, as musicians may be able to cue a relaxation response by simply recalling the relaxing music. Furthermore, musicians may be more receptive to a music-assisted therapeutic technique because of their life-long relationship with music and a belief system that may support the efficacy of music (Dileo-Maranto, 1992). Finally, music-assisted CSD would provide musicians with a safe, noninvasive, accessible, stigma-free treatment for performance anxiety that might also complement their lifestyles (Dileo-Maranto, 1993).

Ethical Considerations

Music therapists should take the following ethical issues into consideration prior to initiating music-assisted coping systematic desensitization. Therapists must assess for any psychiatric or medical conditions that might contraindicate the treatment (i.e., the client should not be taking anti-anxiety medications, should have no history of panic attacks or psychotic episodes). The music therapist should be trained in relaxation techniques and should be aware of how to manage altered state-related adverse reactions. The therapist should also be experienced in cognitive behavioral techniques, specifically, coping systematic desensitization. Therapists who are novices at these techniques should seek additional training and supervision.

MUSIC-ASSISTED COPING SYSTEMATIC DESENSITIZATION (MACSD) PROCEDURE

The following protocol is designed for treatment of groups of up to six clients at a time. This number is best to allow the time necessary for briefing and debriefing. The entire procedure,. inclusive of the pre-post performances, takes approximately 10 sessions. The treatment sessions should take approximately 75 minutes each. The lights in the treatment room should be on a dimmer, or turned down: The musicians should sit in firmly padded upright chairs (preferably with no arm rests), as relaxation training in the upright position, as opposed to lying down, is more easily generalized to other conditions. Reclining is not recommended as it tends to induce sleep. A good quality stereo system is needed to provide adequate musical support.

In order to record treatment progress, as well as changes in performance anxiety-related symptomatology amongst and between symptom systems, it is useful to conduct a battery of pre/posttreatment music performance anxiety assessments. These assessments should include cognitive, physiological, and behavioral measures, as well as anecdotal accounts related to real-life performances before and after treatment. A one-month follow-up survey may be indicated, due to the time it takes to assimilate treatment-related skills. Cognitive assessment tools may include the Musical Performance Anxiety Questionnaire (MPAQ; Lehrer & Woolfolk, 1982) and/or Performance Anxiety Response Questionnaire (PARQ; Appel, 1976).

Session I

In the first session, it is useful to orient the participants to the treatment. The therapist should allow time for introductions and brief descriptions of how their performance anxiety has affected their performance and their lives. Following the introduction, the therapist should provide a rationale for music-assisted coping systematic desensitization.

When choosing music for music-assisted coping systematic desensitization, the therapist may wish to consider "transcultural" music (Fried, 1990). This type of music (often referred to as "New Age") has no particular cultural or compositional cues for the musicians to interpret in a familiar manner (which might interfere with relaxation and treatment-related imagery). Music with a drone, a melody that is slow-paced to entrain breathing and heart rate, and no sudden shifts in tempo, dynamics, timbre, or harmonies is most useful for this type of training. The therapist wants to provide an "envelope of sound" or psychophysiological interference (Bonny & Savary, 1973). Seven Roach's "Dreaming and Sleep" (1986) is a good example of this type of music, and I have found it particularly suited for MASCD (Reitman, 1997).

In order to determine which relaxing (or "sedative") music will be most appropriate for group treatment, the group should have the opportunity to rate several pieces on a Likert-type scale. Each piece should be at least 2 minutes in length to provide for habituation. This will afford the therapist the opportunity to assess the appropriate music for its relaxing potential and any physical or psychological discomfort that may be brought up by the music.

Once appropriate music has been selected, group members should be assisted in developing a relaxing image or scenes to be used during the desensitization procedure. These scenes should involve a place where the person is alone but feels at peace with him or herself and is very relaxed. Participants should use sensory-related cues to make their relaxing scenes as realistic as possible (e.g., in the case of a beach scene: I can feel the sun on my skin, the breeze in my hair. I can hear the sound of the ocean . . .). The clients should be allowed an opportunity to imagine these scenes in as vivid detail as possible for brief periods of time (e.g., 10–15 seconds) in order to verify their clarity and relaxing potential. Visualizing these scenes will also help to establish the standard for realism necessary to reciprocally inhibit anxiety during the MACSD treatment. Suggested homework involves having the clients review a 15-item music performance-related hierarchy to determine if it adequately represents the sequence of events leading to performance and their relative anxiety-evoking potential (rated by clients on a subjective units of distress ["SUDS"] scale of 1–150) (see Appendix).

Session II

The therapist may begin with a review of the hierarchy homework and any difficulties that may have arisen, and then work with the clients to create a group fear hierarchy for use in treatment. If differences of 30 SUDS exist between group members' reactions to a particular image, the image can be replaced with one that elicits the required amount of anxiety, but with less discrepancy.

Next, the rationale for progressive relaxation training, which should be in an abbreviated form, is reviewed. The progressive relaxation training begins by creating the appropriate environment (i.e., making sure the therapist's voice can be heard by all group members over the music, the lights dimmed, the room quieted, etc.), by playing the music, and by providing instructions for the relaxation training. The initial progressive relaxation instructions should include gentle tensing and relaxing of various muscle groups. It is important to use consistent wording, such as "say the word *relax* to yourself and let go," so that the word *relax* itself eventually provides a cue for relaxation to take place.

The therapist should regard the music as a co-therapist, working with the phrasing of the music when providing relaxation instructions, and trying to time the beginning of each spoken phrase with the beginning of a musical phrase. It is useful to allow a musical phrase or two to pass by with no instructions in order to let the music assist relaxation. Breathing with the melody lines may help the therapist to determine the length, pacing, and affective tone of his or her phrasing. After the group has become deeply relaxed, it can be suggested that group members recall their relaxing images in as much detail as possible to associate the feeling of relaxation with their images.

Following the relaxation training, an inquiry should be made as to the relative efficacy of the relaxation training technique and the vividness/relaxing quality of the relaxation images. Homework includes practicing the initial relaxation technique at least two times a day for 5–7 days between sessions. Clients should receive tape-recorded music-assisted relaxation instructions to assist with home practice. In order to maintain an ongoing evaluation of the effectiveness of treatment, it is helpful for clients to maintain a relaxation log to document home training-related experiences.

Session III

The therapist begins with a review of the homework and related experiences, and participants are asked to complete any of the remaining fear hierarchy scenes. Clients may now be trained in progressive relaxation that involves simply scanning and letting go of the tension in each muscle group (with no actual tensing and releasing). This should be followed, once again, by an induction into the musicians' personal relaxing images.

At this point, several factors are converging to assist the musician in achieving relaxation. These include increased trust in the process (a result of previous and ongoing sharing of personal and treatment-related experiences), the increased ability to detect and release excess physiological tension, and the increased ability to recall and sustain relaxing imagery. The effects of the music are also usually observable at this time. Musicians should relax quickly and deeply and report the ability to recall feelings of relaxation simply by imagining the music. This is often surprising to musicians, who are often resistant to using music for relaxation purposes (perhaps because they tend to theoretically analyze or critique it). This simple shift in relationship to music can be marked for musicians, as it allows them to take advantage of their art and their profound reactions to it in a manner that is healing for them. The therapist needs to be aware of this shift and validate/support this awareness as it arises in the group.

Music-assisted coping systematic desensitization to the hierarchy images should begin at this point. The therapist reminds the musicians that, should they experience any undue tension or discomfort, they may stop the proceedings by shifting to their relaxing image or simply opening their eyes. Prior to invoking the hierarchy images (and throughout the presentation of hierarchy images), the therapist should always visually scan the musicians for tension and help them relax it away further if necessary. This scanning can also assist the therapist in providing feedback for the musicians in the follow-up discussion (e.g., Were you aware of any excess tension in your neck? You seemed to become tense each time I mentioned . . .), and revising the hierarchy if necessary.

Desensitization should commence with the instruction to "allow your mind's eye to turn off your relaxing image and turn on the image of the first scene in your hierarchy," repeated at least twice to allow for the shift in imagery to take place. Events that have been identified via the performance-related hierarchy are then verbally described by the therapist, beginning with the event that is lowest in rated distress and progressing gradually upward on the hierarchy. All verbal instructions, including hierarchy-related events, should be paced with the phrasing of the music. The musicians are asked to imagine these events as realistically and with as much sensorial detail as possible. The therapist's description of the events, as well, should be quite vivid to stimulate the imaginal process of the participants. Once the description of the image is complete, the therapist should instruct the musicians to relax away any tension that may have arisen in this image. The therapist may want to add instructions to use the music to help relax away tension. In this manner, the music, which is usually easily recalled by the musician, becomes a cue for the relaxation response in later anxiety-provoking circumstances.

After each hierarchy scene has been imagined and some time has passed to allow for relaxation to occur in response to the image, the musicians are invited to return to their personally relaxing image. The therapist should, once more, provide instructions at least twice for the musicians to shift their imagery in order for a complete change of scenes to take place. Once the therapist has assisted the musicians in entering back into their relaxing scenes (complete with another scanning for and relaxing away of muscle tension), the therapist assesses for undue tension in response to the hierarchy image. This is done by asking anyone who experienced any tension in relation to the preceding hierarchy image to raise an index finger. It is also important to conduct a visual scan in case someone is clearly tense but not aware of his or her response. Should anyone have experienced tension that he or she was not able to relax away, the scene is imaged again. Once all participants indicate no tension in response to a particular hierarchy image, the therapist proceeds to the next image. Desensitization should be followed by a postsession interview and assignment to practice both progressive relaxation procedures once a day for the next 5–7 days.

Session IV

This session begins with a review of relaxation practice, followed by "brief" relaxation training, which consists of simply scanning the muscle groups for excess tension, saying the word *relax* to oneself, and letting go. This technique provides a simple way of generalizing learned relaxation skills into the musicians' daily environment, as briefs can be done within a minute, several times a day. Musicians can be encouraged to use this technique prior to and following practice sessions. This also helps prevent tension levels from creeping up during the day. After group members are guided through brief relaxation training, MACSD may proceed. MACSD should commence with the hierarchy item preceding the last one from the previous session. This should ensure successful coping-relaxation to the first image. The therapist can provide a follow-up to the session with a postsession interview and a homework assignment to practice the second progressive relaxation training technique two times a day, and brief relaxation four to five times a day, for at least 5 of the next 7 days.

Session V–VII

These sessions involve continued MACSD training (as above). At the onset of the sessions, the therapist reviews self-monitoring homework. Homework involves having participants practice up to 15 brief relaxations per day and incorporating the relaxation training procedures into real-life situations that paralleled the images they had created for the hierarchy (e.g., playing the piece in front of friends).

An issue that tends to emerge at this stage of training is the generalizability, or lack thereof, of the relaxation/coping into "real-life" situations. The musicians may experience frustration as they try to relax in former anxiety-provoking situations, only to find that they become more anxious or too relaxed. The therapist needs to be alert to these situations, as they are a natural part of desensitization training. Initial increases in anxiety are to be expected, as the musicians face their fears. Novice trainees may, in fact, experience performance anxiety of their "relaxation" experiences if are expecting too much of themselves. These expectations may coax them to move along their home practice hierarchy far too quickly.

At this point, the musicians may be starting to experience and explore playing their instrument in a new manner. Their relationships to their instrument, music making, and music listening are changing as they progress through treatment. This is a particularly threatening time for the musicians. The therapist needs to encourage and support discussions of these shifts in awareness. The therapist may note that these changes may evoke apprehension at first, and even create more performance-related mistakes, as musicians literally relearn how to approach and perform on their instrument/voice. However, as the musicians begin to find the balance of arousal that helps to facilitate their performance and practice in these newly achieved states, they will soon exhibit more control over their anxiety levels and more ability to focus their attention on and enjoy the process of music making.

Countertransference issues, such as the need to perform successfully as a therapist, the need to protect the musicians from anxiety, or the exacerbation of one's own tension anxiety, need to be monitored by the therapist. The music involved in the treatment may be useful for the therapist as well, as he or she may use it to remain relaxed and focused throughout the process. However, the therapist needs to be alert to the aforementioned issues and take measures to maintain his or her ability to provide effective support.

At this point, the music is being gradually faded from the musicians' home training, as no tape is required to practice brief relaxation. The music is still present in the group sessions, however. This fading period helps to assure that generalization of music-assisted training is taking place, as the musician may wish to recall or "audiate" the music to cue a relaxation response. Some musicians may report that they do not become as relaxed with brief relaxation training as with music-assisted training. In such cases, the therapist may choose to have the musicians practice the music-assisted training once a day, along with several brief training exercises, for another week or so. Another useful option is to have them listen to the music as they do their briefs. The goal, however, is to gradually fade the music from the relaxation training. This also helps reduce satiation to the music, which might otherwise occur.

Session VIII

Initially, the therapist reviews home monitoring and commences MACSD with any remaining scenes. It is helpful to end the session with a brief relaxation and visualization of personally relaxing images. Once again, it is important to emphasize that this type of training often involves a period of readjustment, wherein musicians relearn how to play/perform on their instruments. Therefore, success may not be immediate but may occur after successive practice and generalization of skills in actual performance conditions.

Posttest: In addition to symptom surveys, the therapist may have the participants fill out post-treatment Likert-type scales related to the overall effectiveness of treatment.

Analysis of the Therapeutic Relationship with Regard to MACSD

From a clinical perspective, the music-assisted coping systematic desensitization procedure creates numerous avenues for developing the therapeutic relationship. Consistent with a three-systems theory approach, numerous psychophysiological systems may be assessed and actively addressed via MACSD. However, this treatment approach goes beyond the three systems theory to address musician-specific concerns. Individual concerns and reactions are taken into consideration in every phase of the process, including pre- and posttreatment assessments, choosing the relaxation music, reacting to the relaxation procedures, creating the hierarchies, and developing individually relaxing imagery. Each of these areas helps to guide the treatment procedure via providing important ongoing clinical information. In this manner, the therapist may individually tailor the treatment, even though it may take place within a group setting.

Although the group MACSD procedure may seem prescriptive, it addresses many areas of the musicians' experience, allowing the therapist to foster individual experiences (as above) as well as facilitate a supportive group dynamic. For example, simply talking about their experiences with music performance anxiety helps to build rapport and trust between clients and serves to de-stigmatize both MPA and the treatment procedure itself. During the treatment process, the musicians re-explore how their mind-body connection functions in performance. Through reviewing homework together, they share their struggles to re-adjust their thinking and playing so as to decrease their fear and improve their relationship with their music and their audiences. Participants address their past fears in a manner that validates each step they take in this process (whether it be forward or temporarily backward).

In addition to the great potential for therapeutic intervention afforded by the MACSD procedure, the music therapist has the luxury and benefit of working with music. Far from being ancillary to the process, the music clearly functions as a co-therapist in this procedure. The therapist uses the music to pace the wording of the relaxation and desensitization scripts. In this manner, the music assists the therapist in providing an appropriate fear-reducing environment for the participants. It also keeps the therapist relaxed during the procedure, which may invite a variety of countertransference issues, not the least of which is becoming anxious him/herself!

Through the process of developing relationships within the therapy context and trusting the music as a healing medium, musicians may begin to expand and redevelop their relationship with music. Trusting the music to help them overcome anxiety invites musicians to consider/rediscover music's inherent healing potential and their responsiveness to it. Their re-exploration of personal responsiveness to the relaxation music is often broadened to include the re-exploration of their responsiveness to music in their current repertoire, as well as throughout their lives. Guiding the musician through this process can be extremely rewarding for the therapist, as the musician moves beyond a delimited world view to a world of infinite exciting possibilities. From this personal exploration and reconstruction, the musician moves into the performance context with a renewed sense of self-confidence and confidence in the music itself.

REFERENCES

Appel, S. (1976). Modifying solo performance anxiety in adult pianists. *Journal of Music Therapy, 13*(1), 2–16.

Bandura, A. (1977). Self-efficacy: Toward a unifying theory of behavior therapy. *Psychological Review, 84,* 191–215.

Bartel, L. R., & Thompson, E. G. (1995). Coping with performance stress: A study of professional orchestra musicians in Canada. *Quarterly Journal of Music Teaching and Learning, 5,* 70–78.

Bartlett, D. L. (1996). Physiological responses to music and sound stimuli. In D. A. Hodges (Ed.), *Handbook of music psychology* (pp. 323–383). San Antonio, TX: IMR.

Bonny, H. L., & Savary, L. M. (1973). *Music and your mind.* New York: Harper & Row.

Borkovec T. D., & Sides, J. K. (1979). The contribution of relaxation and expectancy to fear reduction via graded, imaginal exposure to the feared stimuli. *Behavioral Research Therapy, 17,* 529–540.

Brodsky, W., Sloboda, J. A., & Waterman, M. G. (1994). An exploratory investigation into auditory style as a correlate and predictor of music performance anxiety. *Medical Problems of Performing Artists, 9,* 101–112.

Bryson, E. L. (1980). *Reducing performance anxiety in pianists and vocalists.* Unpublished master's thesis, Appalachian State University, Boone, NC.

Cannon, W. B. (1929). *Bodily changes in pain, hunger, fear, and rage: An account of recent researches into the function of emotional excitement.* New York: Appleton-Century.

Clark, D. B., & Agras, S. W. (1991). The assessment and treatment of performance anxiety in musicians. *American Journal of Psychiatry, 148*(5), 598–605.

Colligan, M. J., Smith, M. J., & Hurrell, J. J. (1977). Occupational incidence rates of mental health disorders. *Journal of Human Stress 3,* 34–49.

Davis, M., Eshelman, E. R., & McKay, M. (1982). *The relaxation and stress reduction workbook.* California: New Harbinger.

Davis, W. B., & Thaut, M. H. (1989). The influence of preferred relaxing music on measures of state anxiety, relaxation, and physiological responses. *Journal of Music Therapy, 26*(4), 169–187.

Dileo-Maranto, C. (1992). Music therapy in the treatment of performance anxiety in musicians. In R. Spingte & R. Droh (Eds.), *Music medicine* (pp. 273–283). St. Louis: MMB.

Dileo-Maranto, C. (1993). Music therapy and stress management. In P. M. Lehrer & R. L. Woolfolk (Eds.), *Principles and practices of stress management* (2nd ed., pp. 407–433). New York: Guilford Press.

Dileo-Maranto, C. (1996). Biopsychosocial aspects of music performance: Performing arts health. In R. R. Pratt & R. Spingte (Eds.), *Music medicine* (Vol. 2, pp. 262–274). St. Louis: MMB.

Fishbein, M., Middlestadt, S. E., Ottati, V., Strauss, S., & Ellis, A. (1988). Medical problems among ICSOM musicians: Overview of a national survey. *Medical Problems of Performing Artists, 3,* 1–8.

Freeman, A., Pretzer, J., Fleming, B., & Simon, K. M. (1990). *Clinical applications of cognitive therapy.* New York: Plenum.

Fried, R. (1990). Integrating music in breathing training and relaxation: I. Background, rationale, and relevant elements. *Biofeedback and Self Regulation, 15*(2), 161–169.

Goldfried, M. R. (1971). Systematic desensitization as training in self-control. *Journal of Consulting and Clinical Psychology, 37*(2), 228–234.

Hamann, D. L., & Sobaje, M. (1983). Anxiety and the college musician: A study of performance conditions and subject variables. *Psychology of Music, 11,* 37–50.

Kaplan, H. I., Sadock, B. J., & Grebb, J. A. (1994). *Synopsis of psychiatry* (7th ed.). Baltimore: Williams & Wilkins.

James, I. (1984, November). How players show stress symptoms. *Classical Music, 17*(3), 7.

Lang, P. J. (1968). Fear reduction and behavior: Problems in treating a construct. In J. M. Shlien (Ed.), *Research in psychotherapy* (Vol. 3). Washington DC: APA.

Lang, P. J. (1971). The application of psychophysiological methods to the study of psychotherapy and behavior modification. In A. Bergin & S. Garfield (Eds.), *Handbook of psychotherapy and behavior change.* New York: Wiley.

Lang, P. J., Miller, G. A., & Levin, D. (1988). Anxiety and fear. In R. J. Davidson, G. E. Schwartz, & D. Shapiro (Eds.), *Consciousness and self-regulation* (pp. 123–151). New York: Plenum.

Lazarus, R. S., & Folkman, S. (1984). *Stress, appraisal, and coping.* New York: Springer.

Leary, M. R. (1990). Anxiety, cognition, and behavior: In search of a broader perspective. *Journal of Social Behavior and Personality, 5*(2), 39–44.

Lehrer, P. M. (1987). A review of the approaches to the management of tension and stage fright in music performance. *Journal of Research in Music Education, 55*(5), 143–152.

Lehrer, P. M., Goldman, N., & Strommen, E. (1990). A principle components assessment of performance anxiety amongst musicians. *Medical Problems of Performing Artists, 5,* 12–18.

Lehrer, P. M., & Woolfolk, R. L. (1982). Self-report assessment of anxiety: Somatic, cognitive, and behavioral modalities. *Behavioral Assessment, 4,* 167–177.

Levin, R. B., & Gross, A. M. (1985). The role of relaxation in systematic desensitization. *Behavior Research Therapy, 23*(2), 187–196.

Lockwood, A. H. (1989). Medical problems of musicians. *The New England Journal of Medicine, 320*(4), 221–227.

Lundin, R. W. (1967). *An objective psychology of music* (2nd ed.). New York: Ronald Press.

McCune, B. A. (1983). Functional performance anxiety modification in adult pianists (Doctoral dissertation, Columbia University Teachers College, 1982). *Dissertation Abstracts International, 43/10,* 3254A.

Reitman, A. (1997). The effects of music-assisted coping systematic desensitization on music performance anxiety: A three systems model approach (Doctoral dissertation, Temple University, 1997). *Dissertation Abstracts International, 58/6,* 3334B.

Roach, S. (1986). Dreaming and sleep. On *Quiet Music 3* [Cassette]. West Germany: Fortune Records.

Salmon, P. (1990). A psychological perspective on musical performance anxiety: A review of the literature. *Medical Problems of Performing Artists, 4*(2), 77–80.

Selye, H. (1978). *The stress of life.* New York: McGraw Hill.

Spielberger, C. D. (1972). Anxiety as an emotional state. In C. D. Spielberger (Ed.), *Anxiety: Current trends in theory and research* (Vol. 1). New York: Academic Press.

Steptoe, A. (1989). Stress, coping, and stage fright in professional musicians. *Psychology of Music, 17,* 3–11.

Steptoe, A., & Fidler, H. (1987). Stage fright in orchestral musicians: A study of cognitive and behavioral strategies in performance anxiety. *British Journal of Psychology, 78,* 241–249.

Tucker, A., Faulkner, M. E., & Horvath, S. M. (1971). Electrocardiography and lung function in instrumental brass players. *Archives of Environmental Health, 23,* 327–334.

VanderArk, S. D., & Ely, D. (1992). Biochemical and galvanic skin responses to music stimuli by college students in biology and music. *Perceptual and Motor Skills, 74,* 1078–1090.

Wardle, A. (1975). Behavior modification by reciprocal inhibition of music performance anxiety. In C. Madsen (Ed.), *Research in music behavior.* New York: Teachers College Press.

Wesner, R. B., Noyes, R., & Davis, T. (1990). The occurrence of performance anxiety among musicians. *Journal of Affective Disorders, 18,* 177–185.

Williams, K. E., & Chambless, D. L. (1994). Behavioral therapies. In B. B. Wolman & G. Stricker (Eds.), *Anxiety and related disorders* (pp. 358–375). New York: Wiley.

Wolfe, M. (1989). Correlates of adaptive and maladaptive musical performance anxiety. *Medical Problems of Performing Artists, 4,* 49–56.

Yerkes, R. M., & Dodson, J. D. (1908). The relation of strength of stimulus to rapidity of habit formation. *The Journal of Comparative Neurology and Psychology, 18,* 459–482.

The author would like to thank his loving companion, Michelle Hintz, for her patience, support and editorial assistance in the preparation of this chapter.

APPENDIX

MUSICIANS' PERFORMANCE SUDS HIERARCHY

This checklist is composed of 15 scenes related to the performance experience and your feelings of confidence as a performer. Each item should be evaluated according to your past experience in recitals, exams, and other solo performances. Based on your first impression, please rate each scene from the least (1) to the most anxiety arousing (150). Try to use all 150 points. Add any items you would suggest at the bottom of the list.

Image	**Rating 1–150**
1) Practicing a solo alone two days before the performance	______
2) Practicing a solo two weeks before the performance	______
3) Waiting for the results after the performance	______
4) First notification of the performance	______
5) Performing the piece for your teacher during a private lesson	______
6) Playing the solo for friends	______
7) Traveling to the site of the performance	______
8) During dress rehearsal	______
9) Looking at the audience	______
10) Five minutes before a performance	______
11) Approaching a difficult passage	______
12) Waiting while others perform first	______
13) Walking into the performance room	______
14) Initial moments of the performance	______
15) During the performance	______

MUSICIANS' PERFORMANCE SUDS HIERARCHY

Additional Fear Situations Pertaining to Solo Performance

Image	**Rating 1–150**
16)	______
17)	______
18)	______

7

ANXIETY MANAGEMENT IN PEDIATRIC MUSIC THERAPY

Jane Edwards, M.Mus., RMT

CLINICAL NEEDS

IT IS UNDISPUTED that many children find being in the hospital a stressful experience (Bossert, 1994), but the view that hospitalization per se is stressful for all children is arguably too general to be of much use in practice. Therefore, some researchers have sought to delimit the requirements or "tasks" of hospitalization. Aldwin (1994) cited seven "major adaptive tasks," originally proposed by Moos and Schaefer (1984), as important in management of the psychological components of illness. The first three are described as "illness-related tasks" and include: (1) dealing with the psychological consequences of the illness, including symptoms, pain, and disability; (2) dealing with the treatment and hospital environment; and (3) developing and maintaining good relations with health care workers. The following four are considered "general tasks": (4) maintaining some sort of emotional equilibrium; (5) maintaining a sense of self including competence and mastery; (6) maintaining good relations with family and friends; and (7) preparing for future exigencies (Aldwin, 1994, p. 160).

For children in a hospital, as well as for their family members, each of the "illness-related tasks" needs to be navigated and accomplished during admission or in-patient visits, and as will be seen in this chapter, music therapy can facilitate their realization. For example, to facilitate psychological adjustment to hospitalization, children can be encouraged through music therapy to express and reflect upon their experiences of illness and injury through song writing, metaphoric play, or song choice. In addition, music therapy support during treatment procedures can be provided through playing live music or providing taped music developed in consultation with the patient. Children can also use aspects of music therapy sessions to relate to other clinical staff in a nontreatment relationship.

With reference to the "general" tasks of hospitalization, the music therapist can provide opportunities for the child to recall positive experiences and interact with family members and friends. Music therapy aims to help the child express and receive support for his or her feelings and reactions, thus contributing to the child's coping with the overall experience of hospitalization. A child's anticipation of what life will be like when he or she returns home from the hospital can also be explored. Reactions to current experiences can be supported and validated. It is understood that this support assists children in managing their reactions within the hospital context, thereby improving overall coping.

THEORETICAL APPROACH

Stress as a notion or concept has a range of uses and definitions. In the field of health, the management of a patient's anxiety reactions to stress is important in the delivery of quality care. The study of children's experience of and reactions to stress has, however, been described as a "thicket" with "an unusually rich growth of tangled thoughts and thorny assumptions" (Rutter, 1981, p. 323). The application of a stress model, therefore, needs to be undertaken carefully and thoughtfully by the pediatric music therapist, paying attention to definitions and controversies in the literature.

Two significant approaches to the issue of psychological stress derive from the work of Lazarus and Folkman (1984) and Aldwin (1994). Lazarus and Folkman (1984) defined psychological stress as "a relationship between the person and the environment that is appraised by the person as taxing or exceeding his or her resources and endangering his or her well-being" (p. 21). They proposed that appraisal, i.e., the individual's interpretation of the meaning or perceived threat of the experience, is fundamental to his or her stress response. External criteria concerning the magnitude or significance of the event are not necessarily useful reference points by which to understand an individual's stress response.

Aldwin (1994) proposed a transactional approach to modeling the processes and interactions which create the stress response. The fundamental tenet of this approach is that stress reactions and the consequent requirements to achieve coping should be seen as complex, multidimensional, and multifaceted (transactionism), rather than as simple causal relational models (reductionism). Aldwin suggested that three important dimensions of stress experience are: (1) the strain experienced, which has emotional and physiological dimensions; (2) the stressor, including the type of stress and its temporal dimensions; and (3) the transaction between these dimensions, including the person's cognitive appraisal of the stress and the perceived intensity of the stress, all of which contribute to responses. That is, "the person, the situation and coping mutually affect each other in a process that evolves over time" (Aldwin, 1994, p. 85).

This transition in thinking observed in the stress literature is reflected in theoretical developments in music therapy. For example, Davis and Thaut (1989) discuss the need for a broader view in the study of music responses. Specifically, it may not be possible to attribute these responses to a single, causal stimulus, either within the music or between the music and the individual. Rather, responses should be conceptualized as complex, idiosyncratic, and possibly inconsistent, impacted by a range of individual, unique factors.

Pediatric music therapy is, in general, informed from an expressive arts perspective with the paramount notion that music is readily able to be used by children to play, to express feelings, and to interact with others. Within a psychological stress model, these opportunities are intended to lessen the feelings of threat and harm that can arise in an unfamiliar environment. Additionally, the music therapist can use sessions to assist in identifying children's appraisal of their situation. Opportunities for song writing, for example, can help identify core issues and experiences of the patient (Edwards, 1998; Hadley, 1996; Robb, 1996). A child's appraisal of his or her circumstances may also be evaluated through singing interactive songs that request statements about feelings. Opportunities to improvise music and discuss any ideas or issues emerging from the improvisation can provide a means for self-expression and an opportunity for the therapist to discern themes important to the child.

The pediatric music therapist working within the psychological stress model considers the ways in which a child's current experience may be impacted by previous experiences with illness and hospitalization, developmental stage, family support, relationships to staff, comprehension of the reason for hospitalization, and tolerance for treatment interventions. Many children have an existing relationship to music, usually positive, and are able to indicate their preferences and interests; these are significant considerations in designing music therapy interventions to minimize anxiety and maximize coping.

With regard to children in pain, it is understood that psychological distress and pain are not always able to be clearly distinguished (Maron & Bush, 1991). Therefore, when appropriate medication has been provided to a child during a treatment procedure, the use of music therapy to manage anxiety is part of a comprehensive approach to assist the child in coping.

Client-Therapist Relationship

The music therapy relationship is conceptualized as one of trust and support in which a child has opportunities to maximize coping skills in relation to the demands of hospitalization and treatments. It is proposed that the role of the therapist, as a person not associated directly with medical treatment or procedures, along with the familiar medium of music, provides a calming and sympathetic presence (Chetta, 1981; Edwards, 1995; Loveszy, 1991). Froehlich (1984), for example, advocated that the relationship had the qualities of being "comforting, nonthreatening and not associated with medical procedures" (p. 5).

The child patient may already have positive, well established musical associations, linking certain songs to family members, as well as connecting previous music experiences with fun and play. These existing positive associations with music can be used by the therapist to establish positive rapport with a child relatively quickly when using familiar and preferred musical material.

Music Therapy for Anxiety Management

The use of music has been described in the management of anxiety prior to surgery (Aldridge, 1993; Robb, Nichols, Rutan, Bishop, & Parker, 1995) and in relation to isolation for infection control (Brodsky, 1989). Specific applications of techniques have been described to achieve expressive therapy goals, including writing songs (Edwards, 1998; Hadley, 1996; Robb, 1996) and listening to familiar music played live by the therapist (Malone, 1996).

There is evidence that music therapy is an effective intervention in the management of stress in both general and illness-related domains for children in the hospital. Music therapy sessions can address children's needs for comfort, support, and self-expression (Dun, 1993; Robb, 1996). Music therapy reduces distressed behaviors during treatment procedures, such as injections (Malone, 1996), and can provide support and distraction in burn treatment procedures (Barker, 1991; Edwards, 1995).

Music therapy sessions at bedside can include fun and play at developmentally appropriate levels. Children's anxieties can be addressed through music provided to facilitate self-expression, such as song-writing opportunities, music choice, instrument play, improvisation, story telling through improvised song, and the singing of known song material. Children are encouraged to participate at the level they wish, and sometimes a nod or shake of the head may be the level of communication with which children feel comfortable. Family members can be included in these sessions, and children may want to take charge, letting everyone know which instruments and songs are to be played.

Singing known songs and music listening are well documented strategies for use in distracting children from pain during procedures, and research has indicated benefits even when music listening opportunities are supplied by nonmusic therapists (e.g., Fowler-Kerry & Ramsay-Lander, 1990). Children are encouraged to use music to place pain at "the periphery of awareness" (McCaffery & Wong, 1993, pp. 312–313). Staff can suggest to children that they focus on the music or can encourage them to slow and deepen their breathing. Once breathing has slowed, the therapist can turn the music on. Alternatively, if the music therapist is present, he or she can begin playing at the rate of the patient's breathing and gradually slow the tempo.

For the pediatric music therapist working toward anxiety management goals during procedures, dimensions of the child's experience can be addressed in the music therapy process, including control, choice, and self-expression. While not all aspects of treatment situations can be controlled by children, a music therapist can help them request or plan the songs that will be sung during a procedure. The music therapist can work with the child to reduce behavioral distress or can assist parents to be involved in a supportive role during treatments. Children's emotional reactions and experiences can be expressed and "held" during music therapy sessions.

Two cautions must be kept in mind in the use of techniques that seek to focus a child's attention away from the pain experienced during procedures. The first is that distraction is most appropriately conceptualized as a coping strategy. That is, pain may become more tolerable, but may not become less severe in intensity (McCaffery & Wong, 1993). In addition, clinicians may observe the child to become cooperative, and this behavior could be erroneously interpreted as a reduction in pain rather than an improvement in coping, resulting in the inappropriate withdrawal of pain medication (McCaffery & Wong, 1993). Some children will not be able to use music listening without the presence of the music therapist; other children, however, may benefit from programmed taped music, developed in consultation with the music therapist, but used without the therapist present.

Based on the experience of this author, several approaches, as described below, may be helpful to beginning practitioners.

Music Relaxation as a Procedural Preparation Technique

The pediatric music therapist can use music and relaxation or music play as a preparation for procedures. Malone (1996) demonstrated the efficacy of using familiar song material sung live by the therapist before, during, and after venipuncture to achieve reduction in behavioral distress. Robb et al. (1995) examined the effects of music-assisted relaxation as a preparation for skin graft surgery.

Techniques include the use of breathing exercises with children, teaching them to take deep, slow breaths and then asking them to focus on quiet music provided through headphones, free field, or live by the therapist. Older children can practice using this music before procedures with the general guideline that they should practice their breathing first and then turn on the music. Suggestions given by the music therapist such as "other children in this hospital have used this music and they have told me it has helped them" can be used occasionally.

Music Provided During a Procedure

The use of music during procedures can be conceptualized as offering either relaxation or focusing opportunities toward anxiety-reduction goals. Music therapists need to consider whether pharmacological goals fall into pain or anxiety-reduction domains and to adjust their techniques accordingly, even as the approaches taken by music therapists described here represent primarily anxiety-reduction efforts. That is, although pain and anxiety cannot be usefully distinguished in the child patient, as stated earlier, often the efforts of the clinical team can be usefully categorized as pain reduction or anxiety reduction.

When the primary goal of the pharmacological and verbal support provided to the child is to reduce pain perception, distraction through music therapy intervention is indicated. This involves any musical intervention that provides an opportunity for the child to focus on a stimulus other than the pain. The therapist may consider standing where the child can see him or her and may use familiar song material, parodies, or improvisations on these to provide support and focus. In addition, encouraging children to watch the therapist or the instrument and suggesting that they listen to the music are appropriate supportive strategies. If the child says "I don't want to" or "No," this can be incorporated into the music and validated, rather than negated. If at any time the child does not want the music to continue, this should be respected.

When the child's pharmacological and related treatment goals primarily involve the reduction of anxiety, the music therapist should consider playing music with limited evocative potential, either live or prerecorded at a low volume. The therapist should consider using music that has a predictable harmonic structure; limited use of lyrics; step-wise melodies; and regular, predictable harmonic resolutions. If the music is used over many sessions, the therapist may consider possible habituation issues, wherein the potency of the stimulus can be reduced through overexposure. In this case, some changes in music selection in consultation with the patient may be indicated.

As a general principle, I have used the phrase "nice slow breathing" as the main verbal intervention in an anxiety-reducing approach, and "watch me/the guitar and listen to the song I'm going to sing" as the main verbal intervention in a focusing approach. Many times, however, it is appropriate to begin playing without providing these verbal cues for children. The experienced pediatric music therapist understands that it is not possible to simply apply techniques such as these with every patient in the same way. Children have to be approached based on their individual needs and preferences.

Clinicians also need to be aware that the behavior of a child in one procedure may not be predictive of behavior in subsequent treatments. Daveson (1999), for example, proposed that children undergo stages in coping with debridement procedures: (a) fear, (b) emotional expression, and (c) resistance. In each of these stages, Daveson suggests that the therapist use music interaction in ways relevant to the manifest behaviors. In essence, the music therapist develops a relationship with the child, which may change over time, and through which the needs of the child, in relation to anxiety and distress, can be accommodated.

Other interventions are also possible in the procedural context. Children, for example, may have a favorite instrument they wish to have close to them during the procedure. Ways to incorporate the instrument may be explored by the music therapist (e.g., as a projective device with younger children— "Look at the bear tambourine—What would he like Jane to sing now?").

The relationship between the therapist, the music, and the patient can minimize the patient's fear during procedures. Further, sessions outside of procedures can be used to facilitate opportunities for emotional expression. Resistive behaviors can be responded to in a range of ways, including participation through choice of songs or directions to the therapist about how the patient would like him or her to sing.

Summary and Conclusion

Children's anxiety reactions to the stress of hospitalization can be managed successfully through music therapy. Children can be assisted in each of the "tasks" of coping with the illness and/or injury. They can be supported to manage psychological aspects of symptoms and pain through music listening or through live music provided by the therapist. Children can successfully relate to the treatment and the hospital environment when they have opportunities to express feelings and to interact positively with health care workers.

The opportunities provided for self-expression through music therapy sessions can contribute to the maintenance of emotional equilibrium and to feelings of competence and mastery; the therapist provides choices in sessions and facilitates positive experiences through music. Family and friends can join in sessions if they are present or can be sung/talked about in music therapy time. Children can be assisted to think about life outside the hospital and to express feelings about their future life, where appropriate.

A psychological stress model takes into consideration these various "tasks" of children in relation to the management of self within the hospital context. This model may be useful for practitioners to consider in pediatric music therapy work. Developmental and physiological theories are also useful informants when anxiety management is the clinical goal. Music is an appropriate therapeutic approach to the child's needs, as it provides a familiar and accessible tool to be used flexibly by the therapist. Music is offered live by the therapist or through taped listening experiences.

Children regularly respond positively when offered participation in music therapy sessions and when provided with music as a psychological support during treatments. Opportunities abound in current pediatric music therapy practice, and developments are promising with many avenues for further exploration, research, and development.

References

Aldridge, K. (1993). The use of music to relieve pre-operational anxiety in children attending day surgery. *The Australian Journal of Music Therapy, 4,* 19–35.

Aldwin, C. (1994). *Stress, coping and development: An integrative perspective*. New York: Guilford Press.

Barker, L. (1991). The use of music and relaxation techniques to reduce pain of burn patients during daily debridement. In C. Dileo-Maranto (Ed.), *Applications of music in medicine.* Washington, DC: National Association for Music Therapy.

Bossert, E. (1994). Stress appraisals of hospitalized school-age children. *Children's Health Care, 23*(1), 33–49.

Brodsky, W. (1989). Music therapy as an intervention for children with cancer in isolation rooms. *Music Therapy, 8*(1), 17–34.

Chetta, H. (1981). The effect of music and desensitization on preoperative anxiety in children. *Journal of Music Therapy, 18,* 74–87.

Daveson, B. A. (1999). A model of response: Coping mechanisms and music therapy techniques during debridement. *Music Therapy Perspectives, 17*(2).

Davis, W. B., & Thaut, M. H. (1989). The influence of preferred relaxing music on measures of state anxiety, relaxation and physiological responses. *Journal of Music Therapy, 26*(4), 168–187.

Dun, B. (1993). Music therapy at Royal Children's Hospital Melbourne. In A. Lem (Ed)., *Music therapy collection.* Canberra: Ausdance.

Edwards, J. (1995). "You are singing beautifully": Music therapy and the debridement bath. *The Arts in Psychotherapy, 22*(1), 53–55.

Edwards, J. (1998). Music therapy for children with severe burn injury. *Music Therapy Perspectives, 16*(2), 20–25.

Fowler-Kerry, S., & Ramsay-Lander, J. (1990). Utilizing cognitive strategies to relieve pain in young children. In D. C. Tyler & E. J. Krane (Eds.), *Advances in pain research and therapy.* New York: Raven Press.

Froehlich, M. (1984). A comparison of the effect of music therapy and medical play therapy on the verbalization behavior of pediatric patients. *Journal of Music Therapy, 21,* 2–15.

Hadley, S. (1996). A rationale for the use of songs with children undergoing bone marrow transplantation. *The Australian Journal of Music Therapy, 7,* 16–27.

Lazarus, R. S., & Folkman, S. (1984). *Stress, appraisal and coping.* New York: Springer.

Loveszy, R. (1991). The use of Latin music, puppetry, and visualisation in reducing the physical and emotional pain of a child with severe burns. In K. Bruscia (Ed.), *Case studies in music therapy.* Phoenixville, PA: Barcelona.

Malone, A. (1996). The effects of live music on the distress of pediatric patients receiving intravenous starts, venipunctures, injections and heel sticks. *Journal of Music Therapy, 33*(1), 19–33.

Maron, M., & Bush, J. P. (1991). Burn injury and treatment pain. In J. P. Bush & S. W. Harkins (Eds.), *Children in pain: Clinical and research issues from a developmental perspective.* New York: Springer-Verlag.

McCaffery, M., & Wong, D. (1993). Nursing interventions for pain control in children. In N. L. Schecter, C. B. Berde, & M. Yaster (Eds.), *Pain in infants, children, and adolescents.* Baltimore: Williams & Wilkins.

Moos, R. H., & Schaefer, J. A. (1984). The crisis of physical illness. In R. Moos (Ed.), *Coping with physical illness.* New York: Plenum.

Robb, S. (1996). Techniques in song writing: Restoring emotional and physical well being in adolescents who have been traumatically injured. *Music Therapy Perspectives, 14*(1), 30–37.

Robb, S., Nichols, R., Rutan, R. Bishop, B., & Parker, J. (1995). The effects of music assisted relaxation on preoperative anxiety. *Journal of Music Therapy, 32*(1), 2–22.

Rutter, M. (1981). Stress, coping and development: Some issues and some questions. *Journal of Child Psychology and Psychiatry*, *22*(4), 323–356.

PART II: IMPROVISATIONAL AND RE-CREATIVE APPROACHES

LIFE AS JAZZ: HOPE, MEANING AND MUSIC THERAPY IN THE TREATMENT OF LIFE-THREATENING ILLNESS[1]

David Aldridge, PhD
Gudrun Aldridge, PhD

> What strikes me is the fact that in our society, art has become something which is related only to objects and not to individuals, or to life. That art is something which is specialized or done by experts who are artists. But couldn't everyone's life become a work of art? Why should the lamp or the house be an art object, but not our life? (Michel Foucault in *Rabinow,* 1986, p. 50)

IN THE FOLLOWING PAGES, we want to propose that creatively improvising music is one way to develop individual responses to life-threatening illness. Bernie Siegel (1995) has raised the importance of the metaphors we adopt in describing the relationship between mind and body, and the images we assume in guiding our treatment initiatives. What we are proposing here is a musical metaphor for understanding the human being. Our preference for a musical metaphor rests on the many dimensions of music: it can be understood horizontally (it occurs in time), vertically (it can include the component of harmony, several voices performing together), and dynamically. While music can be an individual activity, it also occurs as an activity with others. Above all, it is cultural—sounds are recognized as music through cultural attribution.

In our modern culture, we often use a mechanical metaphor for the body. When a person is ill, then we take the body for repair, and with the appropriate treatment it is fixed. We could say the same about a computer hardware model that must be rewired or a software model that must be reprogrammed. What we are proposing is something quite different. We are not built like mechanisms, but we are composed like pieces of music. We are in the world as intentional biological, psychological, social organisms who are constantly improvising (and being improvised) to meet the internal and external demands of our daily lives. (For immunologists this should not sound like such a strange idea.) Each of us has a theme that is our identity; a repertoire of being

[1]A version of this article was previously published and is reprinted from *Advances in Mind-Body Medicine*, *14*(4), pp. 271–282, copyright 1998, The Fetzer Institute.

by which we move in the world, one that is continually being improvised upon as we adapt to life's challenges. In music therapy, our task is to facilitate that improvisation by extending the repertoires of our individual identities so as to meet overwhelming challenges or even to develop new repertoires when a life has been decisively interrupted by misfortune.

Our very human being is symphonic, co-ordinated not like a mechanism, but rather like a piece of chamber music co-ordinates its various instrumental voices. There are distinct and separate voices that we can discern, but the whole must be co-ordinated. It is in its wholeness that the "music" that is our being has its identity (Aldridge, 1993a; Aldridge, 1993b).

What links the performance of music and the performance of health is the element of participation. The semiologist Nattiez (1990) labels the aspect of performance a "poietic process," the aspect of listening and making sense an "esthetic process," and the reality of the work itself a material object, "the trace," as he calls it. We can see the same dimensions in health. There is the poietic, active process of becoming healthy—what we perform to become healthy; the esthetic process of understanding of our health by listening to our bodies; and the material traces that these activities leave in our bodies. The body, like a musical work, is the material "trace" of our health activity. For many clinicians, the task is to read this bodily "score" from signs and symptoms. For practitioners of a more psychological bent, what our patients do and say comprise the performance that we "read" and perceive. In creative music therapy, the music that is performed is the trace of a relationship, the relationship between patient and therapist.

In this paper, we want to make the case for music therapy having a significant role to play in the treatment of patients whose existence is threatened. Not only is music therapy an existential form of therapy that accepts people as they are, and offers them an opportunity to define themselves as they wish to be, it is also primarily concerned with aesthetic issues of form and existential notions of *potential* rather than with concepts of pathology. Rather than the Cartesian "cogito ergo sum"—I think, therefore I am, we propose "argo ergo sum"—I perform, therefore I am. This perspective reminds us that our identity, even at the cellular level of the immune system, is an active system that is being improvised anew each moment to meet life's contingencies. This is not to say that nothing remains the same. We have our personality as a recurring theme. We remain recognizable. But we must accept that everything can change. Change in the face of challenge is the biological imperative. Improvising to express ourselves anew is the existential imperative.

With people who suffer from life-threatening illnesses, the end stage of our therapeutic endeavor is usually that the patient will die. This brute fact raises important questions about the nature and goals of therapy, with important implications for establishing the criteria for measuring or assessing the efficacy of our therapeutic endeavors. Many of the concerns we need to attend to, particularly with the dying, are not amenable to operational definition and are thereby elusive to measurement (Feifel, 1990). However, they are amenable to artistic expression in that they can be written as poetry, acted as drama, moved as dance, drawn, sculpted and painted as art, told as stories, and—in the form I concentrate on here—played as music.

To explore our argument, we first consider the different features of the life-threatening illnesses of AIDS and breast cancer, and the role of music therapy in each of them.

AIDS and Music Therapy: Maintaining Integrity and Hope in the Immunologically Challenged

The immune system is the biochemical part of our identity. It is both a system of reaction and a proactive system. Its actions are projected into the future to develop, restore and maintain our physiological identity based on the experiences of today and yesterday. Immunological reactions are not only effects caused by aggressive stimuli; they are also meaningful memories of our physiological make up. The immune system is the major integrative network within our bodies that facilitates our biological adaptation (Wiedermann & Wiedermann, 1988).

For the HIV infected patient the task is one of maintaining an identity whose source is partially and perpetually self-corrupted (in that the DNA material of some cells is changed). In itself this situation calls for both an acceptance of self and the effort to create a new self. It also calls for a massive new alignment of bodily immune regulation.

Positive emotions are known to be beneficial for the immune system. It is possible to go further and say that the positive qualitative aspects of life—hope, joy, beauty and unconditional love, among them—are also vital and beneficial in therapy. This is precisely the ground on which the creative arts can fulfill their own nature. With the arts, patients can explore and express their beings in a context that is creative and not limited by the infection that they suffer. When patients express and explore their beings, we would expect that although physical parameters may fluctuate or deteriorate, life-quality measures or existential indicators would show improvement.

Let us focus on hope, a special factor in enhancing the quality of life. Hope has been identified as a multifaceted phenomenon that is a valuable human response even in the face of a severe reduction in the chances of survival. Like prayer (Saudia et al., 1991), it is a coping strategy used by those confronted with a chronic illness. In a study of 30 terminally ill adults, Herth (1990) explored the meaning of hope, and identified strategies that patients used to foster it. Herth defined hope as an "inner power directed toward enrichment of 'being.'" Overall, levels of hope among his subjects were high and were found to remain stable over time. Herth identified seven hope-fostering categories—interpersonal connectedness, attainable aims, a spiritual base, personal attributes, light-heartedness, uplifting memories and affirmation of worth; and three hope-hindering categories—abandonment and isolation, uncontrollable pain and discomfort, devaluation of personhood.

Hope involves an expectation that goes beyond visible facts and can be seen as a motivating force to achieve inner goals. In the course of a life-threatening illness, goals change. Among AIDS patients, with the progression of physical deterioration, the future is defined less in terms of time and more in terms of the meaning attached to life events with meaningful others. In later stages there is a shift towards less concrete goals and a refocussing of the self to include the inner peace and serenity necessary for dying (Herth, 1990). In this context, in particular, music therapy, with its ability to offer an experience of time that is qualitatively rich, and not chronologically determined, is a valuable intervention. Music therapy can offer hope in situations of seeming hopelessness and is, in this sense, a means of transcendence. The idea of transcendence, the ability to extend the self beyond the immediate context to achieve new perspectives, is important in the last phases of life where dying patients are encouraged to maintain a sense of well-being in the face of imminent biological and social loss. We shall return to this issue.

Breast Cancer and Music Therapy: Meeting the Relational and Emotional Needs of the Patient

We now turn to the potentially life-threatening disease of breast cancer and discuss the implications that music therapy has for its treatment.

From the literature we know that it is important for patients with breast cancer to be able to express their feelings. We also know that melody in our modern culture is an important form of expression. If expression is important for breast cancer patients, and melody is an important form of musical expression, then it makes sense to develop the melody-playing abilities of patients in music therapy (Aldridge, 1996). The further additional point we know is that the cancer sufferer often faces psychological challenges that can exacerbate the course of the illness. Our thesis is that by adopting an expressive medium that does not expect an immediate lexical response—feelings do not have to be identified or named—we have the chance to use it to bring powerful emotions into an expressive form. These forms can be made new, are dynamic and have the potential to be positive and life-enhancing.

To experience breast-cancer in our society, in which the female breast is a part of the cultural code for femininity and sexuality, is a very deep trauma (Wear, 1993). In facing this potentially fatal disease, a woman faces the loss of a precious part of her body that is deeply embedded in her sexuality and femininity.

Of the varying events that are feared most in breast cancer are mutilation or amputation of the breast, the pain of that amputation, the uncertainty about the success of treatment, the possibility of the disease's recurrence, a deterioration of the patient's current health condition, and death. Fundamental questions emerge about how to deal with the body after amputation, how to deal with the emotional suffering that then ensues, how to cope with the image that remains of an altered body, and how to handle the consequent social and professional problems (reorganizing life at home with the family; communicating with family, friends, and acquaintances; dealing with possible financial difficulties). There is also a problem of how to deal with the distance that other people place between the sufferer and themselves, and the distance the sufferer may feel towards her own body. To be faced with such issues causes deep and significant feelings "that cannot be medicalized into neat stage theories or normalized by upbeat assurances" (Wear, 1993, p. 82). One aim of therapy is to facilitate the expression of feelings associated with these events and to bring them into a form that can be managed.

Further, at a time of increasing personal uncertainty, questions about guilt and one's own abnormal behavior occur. Things that one is afraid of, or that are felt as an insult or viewed with repulsion, may easily be linked to the disease. Wilkinson and Kitzinger (1993) see it as no coincidence that breast cancer is often viewed within a moral context. Our society has a general tendency to place an individual's behavior or attitudes within a moral secular view that presumably illuminates the merit or deficiency of the person. When this moral perspective is transferred to the body and health concerns, opinions identify "inharmonious" individuals as susceptible to diseases. In this way, the illness of breast cancer is sometimes viewed as a kind of moral judgment about the degree of control an individual has over her life.

As in the recognition of being HIV-positive, the diagnosis of cancer can precipitate a state of profound anxiety that is associated with increased sensitivity to emotional hurt, vulnerability, hopelessness, thoughts about death and uncertainty about the future (Wong & Bramwell, 1992).

This mental state may itself contribute to the progressive development of cancer. Spiegel (1991) shows that the suppression of, and the inability to express, anger is in some ways associated with the appearance of cancer (though he does not argue that cancer can be caused by the inability to express anger). Further, there are indicators in the literature suggesting that survival and disease progression can be influenced by psychosocial interventions.

Carter (1994) points out that in this area of work, social stigma and discrimination confront many women who return to work after breast cancer treatment. These attitudes can undermine the women's efforts to reconstruct a positive sense of self.

In a post-operative study of breast cancer, Carter and Carter (1993) report that the women were not adequately prepared for their postoperative life since many of them continued to experience physical symptoms and depression as long as four years after treatment. Patients described their postoperative experiences as a survival process, one of "going through." Each phase of the process was experienced as a temporal phenomenon, having a past, a present, and an anticipated future, a process of moving from something to something else. Each phase contained an element of pessimism.

Thus, we can take from the literature the fact that psychological and social factors are important aspects of patient care and have a crucial influence on the postoperative phase. Current medical treatment for breast cancer is a radical one (amputation, radiation/chemotherapy), yet it is not sufficient to provide patients with the most possible healing chances. Medical treatment alone cannot be content with surgery and radiation, but has to include and offer psychosocial interventions that enable women to find a way to handle their disease and the very consequences of medical intervention.

Creative music therapy can be a valuable contribution to meet the different needs of different patients. Playing and creating music enables a breast cancer patient to become aware of her feelings, provides possibilities to achieve a new intimacy with her body, and creates an inner dialogue to reinforce, and activate, interpersonal communication (Aldridge, 1996).

Anxiety and depression are often cited as the predominant affective patterns that emerge in facing cancer. Patients are forced by their disease to learn how to deal with their own emotional reactions. Some may succeed better than others, depending upon their nature. Music, while having everything to do with emotion, has nothing to do with the labels "anxiety"or "depression." Music therapy, thus, has the effect of offering patients space and possibilities to express themselves directly out of their difficult individual situations, without normative expectations and without the fear of judgment that they are doing everything wrong. (It is presumed here that therapists are basing their reactions on acceptance and not moral judgements.)

Having the ability to play in a creative way what one feels provides a chance for breast cancer patients to achieve a sense of a new identity. The act of performing musically as an active manifestation of self may itself contribute to mood improvement and reduce negative feelings like despair, depression, loneliness and anxiety. As we noted earlier, even if there is a deterioration of physical parameters, the process engaged by playing as one feels could reasonably lead to an improvement of life quality.

In her study of hospitalized cancer patients, Bailey (1983) emphasizes the pervasive influence of music on mood improvement. In this respect music therapy should be used as a form of creative intervention not only after a breast is removed surgically and during the postoperative phase but also during other stages of the disease. Music therapy as a receptive measure proves effective in many ways. Not only does it provide patients with distraction, it can also reduce nausea and vomiting, promote relaxation and bring overall relief. In a study of the effects of music therapy on anticipatory anxiety among women receiving chemotherapy for breast cancer, Jacobsen and colleagues (1993) describe the musically attained relief of such anxiety before a second treatment of chemotherapy.

Being actively involved in musical improvisation means that women make decisions regarding that improvisation. The patient in this way becomes an active partner in health care rather than a passive recipient of that care. The woman has the opportunity to exert influence on her own playing and take responsibility for her actions, thereby influencing her fate.

In all, melodic improvisation promotes the important aspect of expressivity. Through melody the patient can find a way to put her feelings and musical intuition into a musical activity that she directs and creates. Her creative energy is dynamically challenged and brought into an expressive form that makes sense to her. For breast cancer patients, faced with expressing overwhelming feelings and challenged with adjusting to a new, radically altered future, the process of bringing their feelings into conscious form without any immediate verbal label may be a valuable step on the road to recovery. As one woman remarked after a music therapy session where she had developed a melody of her own and integrated it into a complete improvisation, "That was like a walk through the streets of Paris" (Aldridge, 1996).

Simply exhorting women to express themselves, when that is the very problem itself, is futile. Encouraging the expression of anger may indeed be carthartic, but in the longer term may not be subtle enough, or positive enough for prolonged recovery. Music therapy offers the means to expression that has no value labels. Each woman is inspired to create her own expressions in her own time. She is given the opportunity to accept herself in a spontaneous authentic way. She creates an identity that has an aesthetic and is recognized as such in a therapeutic relationship. The woman performs; she is not judged. Her inner realities are experienced as beautiful.

Spirituality and Music Therapy

> Our spirit is the real part of us, our body its garment. A man would not find peace at the tailor's because his coat comes from there: neither can the spirit obtain true happiness from the earth just because his body belongs to earth . . . Behind us all is one spirit and one life. How then can we be happy if our neighbor is not also happy? (Khan, 1979, p. 123)

Active, creative music therapy is an intervention that offers a chance for clients to use their own creativity and creative strength to cope with their crises and maintain coherence as they move through their illnesses. In this sense, music therapy can make a valuable contribution to the improvement of the quality of life at all stages of a disease. It is possible to find a different musical form appropriate to the varying stages of the disease, whether it be for recovery or the accompaniment to dying.

However, when we speak of accompanying the dying or of promoting hope with the living, we should realize that we are entering a realm of spiritual considerations. Palliative care has a tradition of breadth in its understanding of health care needs, and throughout the palliative care literature we regularly find mention of the spiritual needs of patients. It is these needs that we want to elaborate upon here, taking one step further the link of hope to working creatively with music.

The Crises We Face

What we are proposing is that in working with the dying and the chronically ill, we need to consider that which helps us to transcend our daily lives. Note that we do not separate practitioners and patients, for we all surely face the great questions of life: "What is the meaning of life? What is the nature of suffering? Why me? What can I do?" Even though this fact is often forgotten, we are all facing death, and in doing so, we are all asked the question of how to live.

When we look at our lives from this perspective of how to live, then we are faced with a crisis. We are using crisis here in a broad sense, to mean a judgment or discernment. Indeed, the difficulty faced in caring for dying patients is that, while the problem appears to that of chronic illness, in reality the challenges are acute and appear as a series of crises. Each crisis with a dying patients is a matter of identity: "Who am I ? What will become of me?"

We now have two large questions, one concerned with existence and one with identity, and these questions have been the fundamental questions of all spiritual traditions. The practical ramifications of these questions are related to how we care for each other, and how we recognize each other's quality as a person. To answer these questions, we need to be alive to a new consciousness.

The main emphasis of spirituality has always been that it will help us to achieve a new consciousness by transcending the moment. So, too, with the concept of hope; there is the expectation of a leap forward. In music therapy, this transcending, expectant leap is made through the creative act.

Creativity occurs in realizing an idea as created form. In the same way that the thoughts and ideas presented here realize their architecture in words; in the same way that the architecture of the cathedral is realized in stone, so the architecture of music is realized in sounds. Using sound, we can be the architects of hope. By transcending the moment of suffering, a new consciousness is created, realized concretely in the performance of music. We play what we are. There is no precocious need to identify this explicitly as an emotional experience; all we need to do is savor the experience in the moment itself.

As we explained at the outset, our proposal regarding the relationship between music and its benefit for clinical practice rests on the proposition that our human identity is like the identity of a piece of music continually being composed in the moment. In contrast to a mechanistic metaphor of humanity, which sees the body as an entity to be repaired, this view sees each being as vital and open to creation. We are improvised as a fresh identity according to every one of life's contingencies. We are each a song that is continually being sung.

Music therapy is an activity which promotes the expression of this song. People are given the opportunity to creatively define themselves as they wish to be. What this may be, what a person will become and how a personal future is defined—a future that admittedly is restricted and often tragically curtailed—will emerge in the joint therapeutic endeavor between therapist and patient (Aldridge, 1991c). All this understood, it is still possible to realize ourselves in the moment not solely as a body restricted by infirmity, but as a soul realizable in the music.

In writing this way, we want to acknowledge the importance of suffering. Illness can be seen as a step on life's way that brings us in contact with whom we really are. The positive aspect of suffering has been neglected in our modern scientific culture such that we, as practitioners and patients, often search for immediate relief. While the management of cancer pain has been a major contribution of the hospice movement, the understanding of suffering is still elusive in the literature. We are not suggesting that we actively seek out suffering, or deny that pain is debilitating. We would simply remind us that part of the human condition is indeed to suffer. In seeking to relieve suffering we can still value the opportunity it brings to learn. It may well be that the difficulties reported in effectively relieving pain are the result of the failure to identify suffering.

We have all been asked the ultimate question of what meaning and purpose our lives would have had if we were to die now. Most of our activities cut us off from this brutal confrontation, except in the field in which we health professionals work. While the management of pain is often a scientific and technical task, the relief of suffering is an existential task. In the major spiritual traditions suffering has always had the potential to transform the individual. As Tournier (1981) reminds us, it is love which has the power to change the sign of suffering from negative to positive.

Music Therapy and the Creative Act

> Each individual composes the music of his own life. If he injures another he breaks the harmony, and there is discord in the melody of life. (Khan, 1983, p. 65)

Music therapy—with its ability to offer an experience of time that is qualitatively rich, and not chronologically determined—is a valuable intervention. We are aware that music has soothing properties, and is used successfully as an anxiolytic (Aldridge, 1993c). It can also be inspiring and uplifting (see Table 1). In its sacred use, it can transport the listener to other realms of consciousness, and is used in this way during the final stages of dying (Schroeder-Sheker, 1993). Indeed, the power of music is precisely its ability to calm us or to stir us in so many dimensions (see Table 2).

Music therapy, with the potential for bringing form out of chaos, should offer hope in situations of seeming hopelessness, and therefore a means of transcendence.

Working with therapists in a creative way to enhance the quality of living can help patients make sense out of dying (Aldridge, 1987a). It is important for the dying, or those with terminal illness, that approaches to help them integrate the physical, psychological, social and spiritual dimensions of their being (Feifel, 1990; Gary, 1992; Herth, 1990), for terminally ill patients face many new areas in which they must learn to cope (Table 3).

In music therapy, the patient is required to be an active self-defining agent. Each situation is unique and requires a creative response. In this sense, the creative act is similar to play, which lies between the external world of objects and the sphere of the most personal, intimate and subjective (Winnicott, 1951). For the ill, music bridges the internal world of the individual with the external world of the therapeutic relationship (Robbins, 1992).

In art an intuitive recognition of inner knowledge is projected as outer form: subjective is made objective but in the terms of the subject and thereby unique. In artistic expression, we thus have the possibility of making perceptible an inner experience. Music, drama and visual art are concerned, not with the stimulation of feeling, but with the expression of feeling. It may be more accurate to say here that feelings are not necessarily emotional states, but more an expression of what the person knows as inner life (Aldridge, 1989).

Table 1
Music Therapy and Fostering Different Dimensions of Hope

Dimension of Hope	Role of Music Therapy
Interpersonal-relationship with others	Relationship between therapist & patient
Beliefs and cognitions, identifying attainable aims	Melody brings feeling into form helping the patient find orientation
Spiritual	Uplifting music, the traditional role of sacred music, transcending the moment
Personal attributes	Being creative, being musical
Light-heartedness	Play in therapy
Uplifting memories	Listening to music, playing and singing remembered songs
Affirmation of worth	Activity of actual music-making

This table itemizes many different pathways in which an individual can come to feel hope and how music therapy can elicit this restorative emotion in each of them.

Table 2
Different Aspects of Music and Their Individual Effects

Aspects of Music	Effects
Popular	Inducing motions of the body
Technical	Satisfying the intellect
Artistic	Inducing a sense of beauty and grace
Appealing	Piercing the heart
Uplifting	That is which the soul hears the harmony of the spheres

This table itemizes assorted facets of music and the effects of each on an individual, indicating the richly complex experience of music and its deep value as a therapy.

Table 3
Coping Requirements and Changes Associated With Terminal Illness

Coping Requirements	Changes
Coping with physical change	Anticipation of pain Management of pain Management of the physical consequences of illness (nausea, incontinence) and changes in physical appearance Management of the physical consequences of treatment
Coping with personal attitudinal changes	Loss of hope, fitness and identity Anxiety and depression about the future Loss of role in family and in employment Frustration and helplessness
Coping with relationship changes	Resolution of conflict Change in parental roles Anxiety about future welfare (emotional and financial) Anticipated hospital contacts & treatment Anticipated loss of a family member Planning the future Social isolation Changes in family boundary, and of family and marital distance Negotiation of dependence/independence Saying "good-bye" and talking about dying Handling the above personal and physical changes within the context of an intimate relationship Changes in, and loss of, sexual activity
Coping with spiritual changes	Feelings of loss, alienation, and abandonment Understanding suffering Accepting dependence Handling anger and frustration Forgiving others Discovering peace Discussing death Grieving Planning the funeral Discovering hope and the value of living

It must be emphasized that the changes listed here have ramifications at differing levels. For example, personal changes have implications for an intimate relationship, within the family and throughout the social environment.

Music therapy serves many ends. This listing identifies considerations to guide its use, both initially and over time (Table 4).

Our treatment initiatives should also be made early in the patient's illness career, soon after diagnosis, such that a relationship is made with the patient, and with the patient's carers (Table 4). One value of introducing music therapy early in the illness comes from the field of rehabilitation medicine with coma patients and working with the elderly. Music therapy has proved to be a useful diagnostic tool for ascertaining levels of awareness and intentionality.

Table 4
Guidelines for Introducing and Using Music Therapy Practice

Guidelines
Start early after diagnosis
Consider creative music therapy as a diagnostic tool
Develop a stable team; encourage long-term stability
Include the caregivers or partner in the therapy plan
Establish a support group for the professional caregiving team
Promote teamwork and identify common aims
Be ready for changes in physical status of the patient
Integrate the physical, psychological, social, and spiritual
Be aware of the existential anxiety of working with patients whose lives are challenged—by contagion, disempowerment, death

More broadly, the therapeutic relationship offers intimacy at a time when the individual often is threatened with isolation and rejection. We can help our patients discover their own sense of meaning by enabling them to live out their lives in individual creative acts within the context of the therapeutic relationship. Robbins (1992) refers to such situations as "creative holding environments" (p. 178). What we need is the time, and the opportunity, to maintain long-term stability in the relationship, even as the physical consequences of the disease continually remind us of the precariousness of corporeal existence. It is this very balance between the temporal aspects of the body and the existential act of living in that body which is at the crux of the therapeutic act.

Comments on a Needed Shift in Research and Practice

Music therapy can be used as an adjuvant therapy complementary to medical initiatives in palliative care.

In modern scientific medicine, people are transformed into the subjects of research. They are classified into disease groupings. This subjectification, and the additional requirement that they remain passive to keep the status of "being sick," has been challenged both by AIDS activists and women lobbyists seeking better breast cancer treatment. The creative therapies equally expect the patient to be an active self-defining agent. The patient, that is, is moral, actively partaking, and self-defining, even when he or she is sick and suffering. In this sense, patients are not subject to our morality and definition, passive and judged (Aldridge, 1991a).

At the center of the AIDS debate is a massive existential anxiety that both patients and we as therapists face. This anxiety is based upon the confrontation with death, the fear of contagion, the challenge to our sexual orientation, the exercise of power over another, and the reality of poverty in a material world. Death, the inevitable end process of living that is so often ignored, comes into the foreground; and thereby the normal expectation of the medical endeavor, that the patient will recover to a state of normative health, is challenged. Contagion, the fear of being invaded, is ever present. (Despite our knowledge of the transmission of the virus, our fears of contagion have little to do with such rationality.) For example, in the late 1980s, talks with general practitioners and oncologists about working with cancer patients revealed that the doctors feared of "catching cancer," an irrational fear in a purportedly rational scientific enterprise (Aldridge, 1987c).

In the creative therapies, sexuality, which we learn to express and which we take for granted as part of our identity, is seen as a matter of choice and preference and not as solely dictated by our genetic make-up. The notion of "sex" makes it possible to group together in an artificial unity anatomical elements, biological functions, conduct, sensations and pleasures, all presumably suitable to the scrutiny of modern scientific medicine (Dreyfus, 1987). Foucault (1988, 1989) describes this tendency to normalize all aspects of human behavior and bring them under medical control, as bio-power. The effect of this power on the patient is to categorize and "unify" the patient, the assumption being that the patient can react in only one way to a particular situation, as if the human range of possible responses had become reduced to one form. For Foucault, the therapeutic act is to bring about a change in such structuring, to give the life of the patient the stability and the uniqueness of a work of art.

We know, too, that patients are socially vulnerable, and that their caregivers, particularly in regard to children with AIDS, are economically disadvantaged. Poverty is a challenge to us all, for no matter what therapeutic skills we bring to bear and no matter how we strive for our own empowerment, we are continually faced with the blight of material neglect. How we care for the poor, the sick and the dying, no matter how they contracted their disease, is both a matter of our own personal responsibility and a collective measure of our humanity (Aldridge, 1991b)

LIVING AS JAZZ

> Classical music is the expression of a fully formed culture. Jazz, however, is the creation of people under constant pressure to conform to conditions imposed on them. (Benzon, 1993)

Music therapy, with its emphasis on personal contact and the value of the patient as a creative, productive human being, has a significant role to play in the fostering of hope in the individual. Hope involves feelings and thoughts, and it necessitates action; it is dynamic and susceptible to human influence. Stimulating the awareness of living in the face of dying is a feature of the hospice movement. Being becomes more important than having. In creative arts activities, the opportunity for the patient to be remade anew in the moment, to assert in the context of another person (the therapist) an identity that is aesthetic, to be separate yet not abandoned, is an activity invested with the vital quality of hope. For the therapist, hope is a replacement for therapeutic nihilism, enabling us to offer constructive effort and sound expectations (Menninger, 1959). In this way, our lives will not conform to the beauties of the past, whether immunologically or psychologically, although that past has an informing influence. Our lives must be created new in the moment, improvising upon current themes. Life is jazz. Our immunological status must adapt to the new. Our psychological status too.

Any therapeutic task, then, must concentrate on the restoration of hope. It must help the patient in a variety of critical tasks: accommodating to feelings of loss, isolation and abandonment; understanding suffering; forgiving others; accepting dependency while remaining independent; making sense of dying. Creative arts therapies can be powerful tools in such a process of change.

These changes can be categorized within the overall rubric "quality of life." While quality-of-life scales exist for the general clinical status of cancer patients as a group, they fall short of meeting the requirements for individual patients. Expectations of life quality differ. Furthermore, the elusive life qualities inherent in creative activities—joy, release, satisfaction, simply being—are not readily susceptible to rating scales. We can, however, hear them when they are played, see them when they are painted or danced, and feel them when they are expressed dramaturgically. The therapeutic question becomes not "What am I?" a question that lies in the realm of categorization and cognition, but "How am I?" a question of being.

In our treatment initiatives it is also necessary to care for the caregivers, the family, friends or partner of the patient. We must additionally bear in mind the psychological burden on health workers themselves. Although working with couples and families may be alien to some individual therapeutic directions, we must accept that the overwhelming burden of care and the suffering of daily living lies outside of the clinic. When clinical care is necessary, we are also best guided to attend to ourselves and our colleagues too as we accompany our patients on the long journey which awaits us all. Social disruption, isolation, conflict and neglect are the doors to the house of despair. Creative arts therapies must respond to those who enter that house, but it is at a social level that we must be the architects of change. People will die. It is what we contribute to the quality of their living that is of importance.

Music and the expressive arts represent a spontaneous activity. Improvisation demands the maintenance of a theme that must change to gain liveliness. Our lives are similarly improvised, from the cellular to the cerebral, to maintain our identities intact. In all such processes, listening to each other is a central method for gaining information, negotiating relationship, and maintaining credibility, whether it is the cell communicating with the cell, person with person, or community with community. To the degree that our selves require a spontaneous adaptation to survive and that our existence depends upon expression, then living is jazz.

The body has a central role in post-modern society. The relationship with the self is mediated through the body. It is in the body that we have the interface of internal and external, between the individual and society. How we experience the unfolding of our experience is reflected in our bodies. The reason that the expressive arts as therapies are so powerful is that they emphasize the lived body as being sensed, not only as being said. Expressing ourselves as a musical identity, as a danced piece, even as a dramatic event, may stay closer than a strictly medical assessment to the reality of symptoms as they are expressed in the body. For symptoms too are bodily expressions involving feelings and cognitions, sometimes conforming to a medical interpretation but also demanding an existential interpretation that cannot be spoken. From this perspective, we can perhaps understand that some seemingly chronic diseases, predominantly those seen as psychosomatic, are problems that are being dynamically expressed upon the stage of the body and are being inadequately interpreted in the context of treatment.

While symptoms are the embodiment of distress, we have to understand how people "do" their lives. It is what people do together that binds them with the groups with whom they perform their lives. If we wish to encourage people to do something differently, we have to understand that the process will be intimately connected with their identity as individuals and with the people with whom that identity is validated.

Music therapy offers the patient the chance to do something differently. A new identity can be performed. However, the patient is not left alone to find his or her own way, the music therapist accompanies the patient. Rather than just describing the way forward for someone, we accompany the person along part of the journey, reviving the old notion of therapist as one who attends to the needs of a fellow traveler as well as being the musical accompanist who provides a basis from which the other can perform.

In creative music therapy lies the possibility to hear in a dynamic way the individual as a whole self as well as a person in relationship with another person. We can hear the person coming into being as he or she creates a relationship in time. Music therapy offers individuals a chance to experience concretely the self in time, literally to hear their own selves coming into being. If human survival is concerned with a repertoire of flexible coping responses to both internal and external demands, then in the playing of improvised music may be heard the creative way in which a person meets those demands.

It could be that illness is a state where there is: (a) a restriction in the ability of the person as a whole to improvise creatively (that is, develop new solutions to problems), or (b) a limited repertoire of coping responses. By promoting creative coping responses we may be establishing the possibilities for renewed health. These possibilities are based on the creative qualities of the whole person that promote autonomy. This catalyzation of self-healing properties is a central feature of the art of medicine that can work in concert with the science of medicine.

There is an old notion taken from the Christian Bible and reflected in other doctrines that says that although we are many, we are one body (Aldridge, 1987b). While many of our therapeutic endeavors are designed to encourage others to perform themselves authentically, we can sometimes discern that what is performed by our sisters and brothers, even in sickness, has ramifications for the way in which we ourselves have our own being.

REFERENCES

Aldridge, D. (1987a). Families, cancer and dying. *Family Practice, 4,* 212–218.

Aldridge, D. (1987b). *One body: A guide to healing in the Church.* London: SPCK.

Aldridge, D. (1987c). A team approach to terminal care: Personal implications for patients and practitioners. *Journal of the Royal College of General Practitioners, 37*, 364.

Aldridge, D. (1989). A phenomenological comparison of the organization of music and the self. *The Arts in Psychotherapy, 16,* 91–97.

Aldridge, D. (1991a). Aesthetics and the individual in the practice of medical research: A discussion paper. *Journal of the Royal Society of Medicine, 84,* 147–150.

Aldridge, D. (1991b). Healing and medicine. *Journal of the Royal Society of Medicine, 84,* 516–518.

Aldridge, D. (1991c). Spirituality, healing and medicine. *Journal of British General Practices, 41*, 425–427.

Aldridge, D. (1993a). Hope, meaning and the creative art therapies in the treatment of AIDS. *The Arts in Psychotherapy, 20,* 285–297.

Aldridge, D. (1993b). Music and Alzheimers' disease—assessment and therapy: A discussion paper. *Journal of the Royal Society of Medicine. 86,* 93–95.

Aldridge, D. (1993c). The music of the body. Music therapy in medical settings. *Advances in Mind-Body Medicine, 9,* 17–35.

Aldridge, G. (1996). A walk through Paris: The development of melodic expression in music therapy with a breast-cancer patient. *The Arts in Psychotherapy, 23,* 207–223.

Bailey, L. M. (1983). The effects of live music versus tape-recorded music on hospitalized cancer patients. *Music Therapy, 3,* 17–28.

Benzon, W. L. (1993). Stages in the evolution of music. *Journal of the Society of Evolutionary System, 16,* 273–296.

Carter, B. J. (1994). Surviving breast cancer. A problematic work re-entry. *Cancer Practice, 2,* 135–140.

Carter, R. E., & Carter, C. A. (1993). Individual and marital adjustment in spouse pairs subsequent to mastectomy. *American Journal of Family Therapy, 21,* 291–300.

Dreyfus, H. (1987). Foucault's critique of psychiatric medicine. *The Journal of Medicine and Philosophy, 2,* 311–333.

Feifel, H. (1990). Psychology and death. Meaningful rediscovery. *American Psychologist, 45,* 537–543.

Foucault, M. (1988). *The use of pleasure: The history of sexuality*. London: Peregrine.

Foucault, M. (1989). *The birth of the clinic*. London: Routledge.

Gary, G. A. (1992). Facing terminal illness in children with AIDS. Developing a philosophy of care for patients, families, and caregivers. *Home Health Nurse, 10,* 40–43.

Herth, K. (1990). Fostering hope in terminally-ill people. *Journal of Advanced Nursing, 15,* 1250–1259.

Jacobsen, P. B., Bovbjerg, D. H., & Redd, W. H. (1993). Anticipatory anxiety in women receiving chemotherapy for breast cancer. *Health Psychology, 12,* 469–475.

Khan, I. (1983). *The music of life.* Santa Fe: Omega Press.

Khan, S. I. (1979). *The bowl of saki*. Geneva: Sufi Publishing Co., Ltd.

Menninger, K. (1959). Hope. *The American Journal of Psychiatry, 116,* 481–491.

Nattiez, J. J. (1990). *Music and discourse. Towards a semiology of music.* New Jersey: Princeton University Press.

Rabinow, P. (1986). *The Foucault reader.* London: Penguin.

Robbins, A. (1992). The play of psychotherapeutic artistry and psychoaesthetics. *The Arts in Psychotherapy, 19,* 177–186.

Saudia, T. L., Kinney, M. R., Brown, K. C., & Young, W. L. (1991). Health locus of control and helpfulness of prayer. *Heart Lung, 20,* 60–65.

Schroeder-Sheker, T. (1993). Music for the dying: The new field of music thanatology. *Advances, 9,* 36–48.

Siegel, B. (1995). Exploring what can't be explained [Letter]. *Advances in Mind-Body Medicine, 11,* 4.

Spiegel, D. (1991). A psychosocial intervention and survival time of patients with metastatic breast cancer. *Advances, The Journal of Mind-Body Health, 7,* 10–19.

Tournier, P. (1981). *Creative suffering*. London: SCM Press.

Wear, D. (1993). Your breasts/sliced off: Literary images of breast cancer. *Women and Health, 20,* 81–100.

Wiedermann, C., & Wiedermann, M. (1988). Psychoimmunology: Systems medicine at the molecular level. *Family Systems Medicine, 6,* 94–106.

Wilkinson, S., & Kitzinger, C. (1993). Whose breast is it anyway? A Feminist consideration of advice and treatment for breast cancer. *Women's Studies International Forum, 16*, 229–238.

Winnicott, D. (1951). Transitional objects and transitional phenomena. In D. Winnicott (Ed.), *Collected papers* (pp. 229–242). New York: Basic Books.

Wong, C. A., & Bramwell, L. (1992). Uncertainty and anxiety after mastectomy for breast cancer. *Cancer Nursing, 15,* 363–371.

Yates, P. (1993). Towards a reconceptualization of hope for patients with a diagnosis of cancer. *Journal of Advanced Nursing, 18,* 701–706.

"BETTER TRYING THAN CRYING": ANALYTICAL MUSIC THERAPY IN A MEDICAL SETTING

Benedikte Barth Scheiby, MA, CMT, DpMtp

The title of this article refers to an improvised vocal contribution of a patient of mine, Norbert, who inspired me to write this article, and who constantly reminds me of the fact that music therapy treatment is about the relational aspects of being in music together, finding the inner music, letting it play by itself, and using it in interplay with others. Although he initially described himself as being totally unmusical, he nonetheless came a long way on his journey recovering from a stroke, depression, anxiety, cancer of the eye, and internal bleeding. He changed from being very depressed and regressed physically as well as psychologically, and resistant to the idea that music therapy might be able to help him ("I thought it was a bunch of old ladies hanging around singing songs from the old days"), to participating in a men's music therapy group consistently on a weekly basis. After one year of treatment and many tears later, he created an instrumental and vocal group improvisation, "Better Trying Than Crying." A little later he said, "I wish I could move in here" (meaning in the music therapy studio) making the whole group laugh.

Historically, Analytical Music Therapy (AMT) is a form of supportive/insight music psychotherapy founded by the British music therapist, Mary Priestley in the 1970s. Priestley, who was a performing violinist and pianist, went through her own analysis. She became inspired to transform the philosophy and treatment that she had received into a music therapy treatment form where goals, objectives, and interventions were processed and worked with in the medium of improvised and composed music, with an additional verbal integration if possible. Priestley was inspired by psychoanalysts such as Freud, Jung, Klein, and Adler, and in her later years by transpersonal psychology theorists as well. The theory behind her method in its musical and verbal dimensions is a reflection of these different orientations. The method took form while she was working primarily with an adult psychiatric population and prisoners. Her trainees (including me) have been further developing the approach, and it has been proven to be very effective with a variety of populations, including patients with medical problems in short- and long-term treatment, as is illustrated in the present chapter.

According to Priestley (1994), AMT is "the analytically-informed symbolic use of improvised music by the music therapist and client. It is used as a creative tool with which to explore the client's inner life so as to provide the way forward for growth and greater self-knowledge" (p. 3).

I would like to expand upon the definition: Analytical Music Therapy is the analytically-informed symbolic use of improvised or composed music as intervention in order to effect therapeutic change. Musical experiences and the musical relationship between client and music therapist are the main dynamic factors in the therapeutic process.

Characteristic of the approach is its focus on:

1. Using primarily improvised tonal/atonal music as the primary agent of change and "transportational tool." Composed music may also be used. For example, the music therapist may compose a song or piece of music together with the patient that embodies the here-and-now issues with which the patient is struggling. Another way of using composed music may be to replace a well-known song's text with an improvised text that relates to the patient's situation. In cases where the patient initially is unable or unwilling to play/sing, the music therapist may use pre-recorded music or play/sing precomposed music that the patient likes.

2. Integrating music and words, when words are accessible. If the patient can verbalize about the music, this is encouraged by the music therapist, who asks such questions as: "What was the music about for you?" In many cases, I have realized that the patient's verbalizations about the content, meaning, and associations related to the music can be very different from what the music therapist perceives. Therefore, it is important to have the verbal feedback from the patient, so misinterpretations and misperceptions can be avoided. A specific melody or musical gestalt may carry a significant meaning for the patient that the music therapist may not have realized. If words are not available, the processing of the music may be done through art, such as a drawing of how the music sounded, or a clay sculpture that speaks for the music. This is particularly helpful in work with speech-impaired patients or children, both of whom may be intimidated by verbal communication.

3. Addressing psychodynamic phenomena, such as musical transference, musical countertransference (Scheiby, 1998), musical resistance (Scheiby, in press), somatic and musical empathy, defenses, and regression as dynamic parts of the treatment. An important part of AMT work lies in understanding that one of the healing factors of the music is the relationship between the patient and the music therapist and how this develops and is reflected in the music. It is the job of the music therapist to identify conscious and unconscious (transferential) elements of the patient's music. Musical transference is defined as "sound patterns that reflect the client's re-experiences and re-enactments of unfinished gestalts from previous relationships or distortions of experiences of the present"(Scheiby, 1992, p. 14). The quality of the contact in the musical transference is often characterized by a "child-parent" dynamic, rather than as a relationship between peers. The music therapist can help the patient to gain insight and to begin owning unconscious feelings, such as depression, anger, anxiety, and loneliness, by letting the patient listen to his or her own recorded music in the session, or through the music therapist's mirroring or musical reinforcement of the patient's transferential music. It is also the job of the music therapist to identify his or her own musical countertransferences, which are defined as "sound patterns that reflect the music therapist's own unconscious transference distortions of what is going on in the relationship with the client" (Scheiby, 1998, p. 217). These are activated by the patient's musical and nonmusical presence and can be harmful to the music therapy process if

undiscovered. There are several forms of musical countertransferences (Priestley, 1975, 1994; Scheiby, 1998). Because music is such a subjective medium in which to work, and because the AMT therapist often plays/sings together with the patient, it is important to identify the unconscious parts of the music therapist's music, i.e., those unconscious reactions the patient evokes in the music therapist.

The Analytical Music Therapist must also identify if the patient has musical resistance, and if so, make a qualified decision either to respect it or to help the patient confront and overcome it, if appropriate and if the patient is willing. Musical resistances can take many gestalts, but the first and most common to this particular population is resistance towards singing or vocalizing. Many patients who have suffered a neurological trauma that impairs their speech or voice are embarrassed about using their voice. They may also feel badly about former musical experiences and dare not play instruments for fear of "making mistakes."

The second form of resistance is observed within the musical expression of the patient. This can be manifested in many ways, such as: (a) a quality of repetitiveness in the music, (b) the patient's inactivity in the musical process, (c) a lack of affect in the music, (d) a contradiction between the musical affect and the affect to which the patient is referring, and (e) a repeated refusal by the patient to begin an improvisation or choose certain instruments. Further information on resistance is given by Priestley (1975, 1994) and Scheiby (in press).

The phenomenon of regression plays an important role in work with short- and long-term rehabilitation patients. Many patients are physically and psychologically regressed because of their neurological trauma, and the music therapist must identify this level of regression from a developmental perspective. From this point, the therapist can decide how to help the patient back to an appropriate level through music. This may involve inventing music that helps the patient to find a rhythm that stimulates his or her walking pace or pattern. It may involve helping the patient to speak, beginning with making baby sounds and progressing to forming a word or sentence through the musical communication. The music therapist can also induce a musical regression to reach the "former intact identity" or the "inner child," thereby accessing resources that the patient has but has forgotten. This can be done through using creative titles, such as "When I Was a Teenager,"or "Going to Church With Mommy," as starting points for improvisations. These titles lead the patient back to events that occurred before the trauma.

No prior musical skill, training, or particular level of musicality is required of the patient, and it is the job of the music therapist to find and create ways of improvising and composing that can meet the goals of the treatment and deal with the specific issues of the patient. The improvisations are performed by patient and music therapist vocally and on instruments, which may include a variety of percussion instruments such as cymbal, drums, maracas, tambourines, shakers, bells, rain stick, metallophones, wood blocks, or gongs. Symphonic instruments such as piano, keyboard, guitar, accordion, cello, violin, and recorder are also available. For patients that are very limited physically, adapted instruments and body suits are available. For example, if the patient can move only a foot, an inlay connected electronically to a keyboard or a drum set can be put in the shoe. The musical sounds are triggered by how, where, and when the patient moves. A microphone can reinforce a voice that is weak.

To be able to practice as an AMT music therapist, one needs a master's degree in music therapy and specific postgraduate training in AMT, including individual and group music therapy self-experience, AMT clinical supervision, Intertherapy (IMT) training, and a theoretical understanding of the basis of the method. In this approach, three basic music therapy competencies are trained: (1) a *technical competency*—the ability to *act* therapeutically appropriate, for example, being able to do the interventions in the music; (2) a *theoretical competency*—the ability to *think* therapeutically appropriate, for example, having a theoretical framework behind the musical and verbal actions; and (3) a *personal competency*—the ability to *be there* in a therapeutically appropriate manner, for example, being able to have an authentic presence and being empathic in and outside the music.

For further information on training, see also Pedersen and Scheiby (in press) and Scheiby (1991). The AMT music therapist working clinically is expected to receive weekly AMT supervision where issues are processed musically and verbally.

After gaining 20 years of clinical experience and training music therapy students in the field for 18 years, I have come to the philosophy and understanding that even having the best training and evaluations does not ensure that the therapist will be able to reach a particular patient. But it helps immensely to have had your own self-experiences in individual and group music therapy and an adequate amount of music therapy supervision, where issues are processed primarily in and through music, rather than in a purely verbal and intellectual mode.

An Analytical Music Therapist must reach the core of the person's musical identity and be able to resonate with it, while coordinating this work with focused musical interventions targeted to addressing specific physical and/or psychological problems. One needs to be familiar with various types of culturally related musical expression as well as its context.

Clinical Needs

I presently work as a music therapy supervisor, researcher, and student supervisor at a short- and long-term rehabilitation hospital, where I see patients 18 years and older, both individually and in groups. Typically, the physician, social worker, or psychologist refers these patients, who have a variety of neurological traumas, stroke, traumatic brain injury, multiple sclerosis, Lyme's Disease, cancer, amputations, coma, heart condition, diabetes, cerebral palsy, or Parkinson's Disease. The patients are referred to music therapy for a variety of needs, as shown in Figure 1.

Depending on the specific needs, goals, and objectives of the patient, music therapy is offered either individually or in group, daily or once or twice a week, in a studio, dining room, or at bedside. With permission of the patients, the sessions are audiotaped or videotaped and documented in written form.

Typical themes that emerge in work with this population are as follows: lack of control, isolation, denial, anger, frustration, hopelessness, fear of the future and/or death, alienation, loss, dependency, confusion, and suicide, as well as feelings of being misunderstood, stuck, invaded, lost, and abandoned. Improvisation titles or composed song material reflect these issues directly or indirectly.

Assessment

A music therapeutic assessment is done in the first session. In 1997, I developed an assessment model that can be used specifically for this population, which includes a large number of musical, social, emotional, cognitive, and psychodynamic factors. These include diagnosis;

Physical Needs	Psychosocial Needs
▪ Pain and cramping reduction	▪ Emotional support
▪ Pain tolerance	▪ Stress management
▪ Relief of insomnia	▪ Improved coping skills
▪ Improved speech	▪ Elevation of mood
▪ Improved short/ long term memory	▪ Refocusing of the mind
▪ Improved cognitive skills	▪ Improvement of self-esteem and confidence
▪ Improved attention span	▪ Improvement in patience
▪ Improved capacity to breathe	▪ Promotion of comfort
▪ Improved motivation to eat	▪ Promotion of hope
▪ Improved endurance	▪ Mobilization of energy
▪ Improved relaxation	▪ Marshalling of spirituality
▪ Reduction of fatigue	▪ Improvement of interpersonal communication
▪ Reduction of depression	▪ Improvement of motivation to participate
▪ Improvement of balance	▪ Improvement of expressivity in general
	▪ Improvement of socialization skills

Figure 1. Physical and Psychosocial Needs in Patients Referred to Music Therapy.

history; cultural context; instrument choices; patient's use of voice, instruments, and body; themes or issues processed; patient's verbalization before, during, and after music; affective information such as emotional qualities, musical transference, musical countertransference; interrelational information (style of connecting); cognitive information (level of organization, structural components); developmental information (ego-function, drives, defenses, differentiation between self and others, authenticity, level of integration/chaos/dissociation); released fantasies and symbolic responses (images, dreams, gestalts, associations mirroring significant experience in past and present); transpersonal information (spiritual quality, meditative quality, altered state of consciousness); aesthetic information (quality of beauty); kinesthetic information (body expressions/sensations released by the music); and creativity information (absence/presence of ideas that develop, playfulness).

My assumption is that each patient moves, feels, speaks, sings, and/or plays in a unique way, based upon the illness, the image of him/herself, and the image of the world that he or she has built through experience. Therefore, each person's musical behavior must be analyzed and interpreted according to this person's individual physical and psychological reality and experience. The patient's own verbal or nonverbal comments in relation to the music must take priority in the process of assessing, deriving clinical data, and developing goals and objectives together with him or her. With patients who cannot communicate verbally, the obvious primary goals are to help improve speech, to develop additional communication channels, and to find expression for the emotions with which he or she may be struggling. For short-term rehabilitation patients, a reassessment of goals and objectives is done once a month, and for long-term rehabilitation patients, it is done every 3 months.

Treatment Procedures

The stages in music therapy treatment can, in general, be described as follows: (a) establishing a relationship and discovering the musical identity of the patient, (b) working in a goal-oriented way at the core of the patient's being, and (c) termination process and help with transition.

The content of the session is not predetermined. Everything depends upon the immediate needs of the patient that day and if the work is in the context of short- or long-term therapy. Some sessions might consist primarily of music; other sessions might consist primarily of verbal contact. One can idealistically describe the session in phases:

- establishing contact verbally/musically
- identifying an issue
- helping to translate the issue into a title of an improvisation, an improvised song, or finding the song that relates to the identified issue
- defining the role of the music therapist (in active listening, accompanying or dialoguing)
- helping the patient find the instrument that appeals to him or her in the moment, and facilitating improvising instrumentally and/or vocally using the title as a guide
- composing a song that deals with the issue, singing a precomposed song that relates to the identified issue
- active listening to the music of the patient
- verbal integration
- processing musically what arose from the verbal integration.

With patients who are cognitively and/or speech impaired, the responsibility both to identify the issues and to decide how to process them musically lies heavily on the music therapist. Therefore, it is that much more important for the music therapist to be trained nonverbally with experience in his or her own personal music therapy, to be able to identify what is communicated through sound, and to be aware of his or her own musical blind spots. In other words, the therapist must be able to interpret transference and countertransference in music.

For patients who are severely neurologically damaged and physically and/or psychologically regressed, there is a greater need for structure in the session, particularly in the beginning and at the end. Often I will take the initiative musically, for instance, by singing an improvised "Welcome" or "Greeting" song, where the patient can fill in words or vocal sounds. The quality of the music might reflect the emotional state or the energy level of the patient to allow him or her to feel seen or heard.

It also is important to mention that the music therapist must rely heavily on his or her musical countertransference as an orientation point and guide for interventions and actions when he or she works with severely impaired or regressed patients who are not able to give clear verbal feedback. Scheiby (1998) provides a more complete discussion of the role of musical countertransference in Analytical Music Therapy.

Guidelines for Improvising and Composing

In creating music during the session, the primary guide is the instrumental and vocal language of the patient. The music therapist encourages the patient(s) to pick instruments whose sound, form, and appearance is attractive, and to sing or vocalize in any way he or she feels comfortable. I try to get to know and reflect the musical identity of the patient at the start of treatment. That means that I have to be flexible to improvise tonal or atonal music in any style that the patient offers or wishes to sing or play. The music therapist does not always have to play together with the patient. The patient might need to play or sing alone in order to feel more independent or to gain self-esteem. A common rule is that the music therapist allows the patient to start and finish the music, but there might be patients who are so depressed or physically handicapped that they are not able to reach out or start a musical communication. Here the music therapist will have to take the musical initiative in the beginning of the treatment, perhaps by choosing an instrument that might appeal to the patient or by creating a "contact" song that reaches the patient.

Techniques

A variety of techniques have been developed to explore conscious material, strengthen the ego, access unconscious material, explore relationships, access spirituality, deal with resistance and denial, stimulate fantasy and imagery, manage pain and stress, and relax the body and mind. A few of the AMT techniques that have been helpful in this particular work merit mentioning.

Musical Holding

The music therapist creates music that serves symbolically as a firm, reliable, and loving parent's arms. It can be created in many ways, such as repeating a certain chord progression, an empathic strong humming vocal accompaniment, a repeated rhythmic pattern on a drum, or a blues-round or gospel-round. This technique can be used for many different purposes with this population. I often use it when certain feelings are extremely overwhelming for the patient, such as pain, deep grief, or anger. Also, when a patient is holding back certain feelings and thereby building up stress, it can be helpful to hold to allow the release of blocked energy. If the patient is experiencing contradictory feelings through the therapist's holding, they can co-exist.

Free Association in Music

The music therapist encourages the patient to play or sing any feeling, image, or scene that comes to mind, and musically reinforces the expression of the patient. This technique may open up doors to discover new ways of viewing one's identity and to help find meaning, particularly when a patient is feeling stuck or trapped in his body and illness.

Splitting in Music

This technique can be very helpful when the treatment focuses on resolving different splits and polarities that the patient is experiencing as a result of the physical trauma. The music therapist facilitates improvisations that reinforce "bridges" and integrative possibilities. Resolving the split relies on the ability of music to simultaneously express contrasting or split ideas, and letting the forces of the music as a transformational tool create the connection between the polarities. Patients with paralyzed or dysfunctional body parts often tend to reject or feel negatively toward certain body parts. Through this technique the person can start to accept his/her "new" body identity and start having a relationship again with the legs that no longer walk or the hand that no longer grasps.

Entering into Somatic Communication

When patients are dealing with somatic symptoms, phantom pain, ulcers, back pain, or pain that may be connected with a psychological reality, the music can be helpful in uncovering an underlying emotion or psychological reason for the physical pain. The patient may improvise being the symptom while the music therapist reinforces, mirrors, or expresses the bypassed emotion(s). The patient is encouraged to explore his or her free associations as they come along, and afterwards the taped recording may be a help for clarification.

Clinical Vignettes

A 67-year-old male, T., was diagnosed with stroke and global aphasia and was characterized by limited vocal output, impaired auditory comprehension, impaired cognitive and memory function, and left side paralysis. He has a previous history of depression and is a retired businessman with a law degree. He is divorced, has three children, and was born in Belgium but immigrated to the U.S. in the 1950s. His interests include listening to classical music, gardening, good food, art, and sailing. He has a girlfriend who visits once in a while, but friends and family are seen rarely. The unit has difficulties in motivating the patient for treatment, in getting him out of bed, and also in the areas of communication and behavior (i.e., being out of control).

My assessment was done at bedside, where I found the deeply depressed and very upset T. lying in his bed, alternating between rage and crying, and in obvious physical pain on his left side. When he saw the instruments, his eyes lit up a little, and they became even wider when I sang "Bonjour" to him ("hello" in French, one of the languages spoken in Belgium). When patients have had a stroke and lose their language, they often seem to regress to their primary language, i.e., that which they spoke when they were children. Therefore, in French, I presented myself as a music therapist and told him I was there to help him.

He signaled to me that he understood but could not speak, and showed angrily that some sounds could come out of his mouth, but they were not words. I started playing with the sounds in an atonal/tonal operatic way, and invited him to dialogue with me. He answered in his own "sound" language, and after some time we both smiled when T. added a touch of humor to the sounds. T. interrupted himself often, and I filled in the "empty spaces" to keep the continuity. Deep sighs of frustration from T. intertwined in the dialogue, which reminded me of some Wagner opera sections, where one experiences long passages of tension, then a short release, and then back to the tension again. I let myself become involved in the "opera" for a while in order to assess T. and to communicate to him that he still was able to communicate something without words.

After our musical dialogue found a natural ending, I placed a keyboard on his lap and suggested that he let his fingers on the right hand play whatever they wanted. It looked as if he were searching for certain harmonies, but could not find them. He stopped in frustration, and I encouraged him to keep searching. He found a C-major triad and also a d-minor triad, and moved back and forth between the two chords. I noticed that T. had not addressed the physical pain during the whole musical communication. When the music ended, the pain seemed to return again, and T. started grinding his teeth, growling and crying.

About 20 minutes had passed, and T.'s attention seemed to disappear. I informed T. that I thought music therapy would be able to help him and told him specifically which goals were appropriate at that point. He nodded and shook his shoulders. I gave him a piece of paper containing information concerning the location and schedule for his individual weekly music therapy sessions. He seemed to be able to read it. When I gave him my hand to say "Au Revoir," he pulled me down and gave me a kiss on the cheek. Was this an instance of music eliciting instant positive transference?

Let us now take an analytical look at this assessment session. The technique used is what Priestley calls "subverbal communication." The patient and therapist improvised together without title, focus, or specific roles for a time period. The technique is used when words fail or become meaningless. Discussion afterwards is not necessary.

In assessing T., I noted the qualities of the transference of his music as follows: sadness, frustration, withheld anger, humor, intentionality, control. In his style of connecting, there was room for both separateness and togetherness, but T. had a tendency to let me take the initiative in the sound making, and he often stopped himself. Cognitively, the music reflected an intact organization of structural components. T. was able to vary rhythm, dynamics, melody, and form, and to imitate me. He could also identify a major and minor chord.

Developmentally, two different stages were apparent: (1) the vocal communication in the "opera" had similarities to the way a mother communicates nonverbally with her infant, as there was mirroring, initiating, reinforcement, playfulness, and humor; and (2) the keyboard music reflected an adult level of communication and consciousness, including the ability to identify and move between tonalities.

Aesthetically, there was a certain beauty in the operatic dialogue—his sense of aesthetics might have been intact. (This proved to be true later on in his treatment when he stopped himself singing songs or playing music when it did not sound correct.) T. used very skillfully and creatively the "uhs," "ahs," and "ohs" that he had available as words at that time; he used some of my sounds, changed them a bit, and developed them. T.'s bodily expressions during the music were very appropriate to the musical expressions that we were experiencing together. The physical pain seemed to return when the musical communication stopped. All this information gave me an idea of the goals and objectives for future sessions with T.

The following were designated as short-term goals for T.: pain reduction and pain tolerance, improvement of speech, relief of depression, improvement of long- and short-term memory, improvement of coping skills, improvement of attention span, improvement of nonverbal expressive skills, and improvement of behavior.

The basic tools implemented to reach these goals in the framework of a 50-minute individual session were as follows:

1. Vocal and instrumental improvisations on keyboard and percussion instruments together with T., helping him to give himself permission to give sound to any emotional and physical state that he was in, such as anger, pain, depression, and frustration. Here, the use of techniques such as Holding, Splitting, and Entering into Somatic Communication were helpful.

2. Singing French and English songs that related to T.'s past and present, for example, "La Marseillaise," a French song that reflects war, victory, and marching. T. was in a war with his words and with the left side of his body; he could not walk. We also sang French children's songs that carried positive memories. I left room for T. in the songs to spontaneously fill in words.

3. Finding classical music that T. had listened to before his stroke, and constructing an audio tape with this so he could listen to it in his room.

4. Inventing musical forms that forced T. to be the leader; I therefore would have to follow him to help him to reestablish his superego.

5. Inventing dialogue improvisations that helped T. to feel less isolated.

6. Playing and singing improvisations that were based on guided imagery, with titles such as "Taking a Walk in the Botanical Gardens"or "Sailing on My Boat."

After having worked for a while with T., he did get out of bed, and by the time of his fourth session, he was working in the music therapy studio. He seemed to become less depressed, the physical pain receded somewhat, and he started uttering words in French and English, such as "Oui" or "Yes," but was still not able to form a whole sentence and make himself understood.

In my work, I encountered several men who had had strokes and who were struggling with some of the same issues as T, i.e., depression, anger, frustration, pain, loss of identity, loss of ability to speak and remember, and feeling out of control. I decided to form a "Men's Music Therapy Group" for men who had experienced severe, debilitating strokes; who had various degrees of physical, mental, and verbal problems; and who were compatible intellectually. Here, T. could feel at home, be accepted, and communicate nonverbally with men who experienced some of the same obstacles.

My role would be a musical and verbal facilitator and supporter of the musical processing of issues and themes of the group members. The group started meeting once a week for 1 hour.

Two scenes in particular stand out in my fond memories of working with this group. In the second group session, T. was in particularly severe pain and in a bad mood. He started crying, and the three other men on percussion instruments, and I on keyboard, started playing some improvised music that had the quality of a rocking and consoling lullaby in a slow rhythm. Norbert recited over the music: "You are crying our tears, T. Men are also allowed to cry." This improvisation facilitated the release of the stored up tears in other group members, and a touching talk ensued about issues of feeling isolated, missing wives, missing family, being in physical pain, and feeling frustration over being dismissed from occupational, physical, and speech therapy. The session ended with singing, humming, and playing at Norbert's request, "Somewhere Over the Rainbow." T. looked relieved, and a little smile was growing on his face. The song resonated with the key material of this session.

The second scene was in session 21, where I suggested that one Cuban group member contribute with a vocal solo that we could accompany. This particular group member had difficulties taking initiative and was often stuck emotionally and dynamically in the music's rhythm or melody. He started out singing in Spanish about a beautiful woman, and the rest of the group played a vivid Cuban rhythm, mambo, on percussion instruments. Before we knew it, there was an atmosphere of a Cuban night club with everyone vividly engaged in their musical activities. After the music, all of the group members looked much more alive physically with their eyes shining. They spoke about going dancing in night clubs, their life before the stroke, women, preferred drinks—things that were very far away from the reality of a hospital, but, if imagined, can help to access resources and positive memories. T. took a big step forward in his speech during the group sessions, and he was able to make himself understood with single English or French words. The closeness that these men developed was seen in their connections outside the sessions, for at times, one could find three of the men hanging out together in the hospital cafeteria in the afternoon.*

In conclusion, I would like to mention briefly the countertransference reactions in and outside the music that the music therapist often experiences in work with a neurologically impaired population: (a) a tendency to offer too much structure, holding, and support in the music; (b) taking too much leadership in and outside the music; (c) a tendency to be too fast in tempo in all aspects of the session; (d) issues of control in the music, such as choosing the song, title of the improvisation, what to do next, picking the instruments for the patient, etc.; (e) being overly helpful, extending one's self more than that which is appropriate; (f) feeling isolated, which might then produce the need to want to play/sing with the patient—fuse in the music; (g) feeling helpless, not good enough, depressed, burned out; and (h) problems with memory.

To avoid or deal with these countertransference issues, the Analytical Music Therapist should receive private weekly music therapy supervision, which would provide a relevant, neutral place to bring in issues related to work with patients and to process them verbally and musically. This can be done in many ways, but personally, I have been helped by improvising my countertransference issues and then listening to a recording of my music. I have also role-played the patient and then myself as a music therapist to identify possible solutions to problems. I usually bring in selected audio or video materials to the supervision session, present the problem, and go from there. If there are other music therapy colleagues, it is possible to form a peer supervision group that can meet weekly for mutual support. Peer supervision groups are also possible by inviting music therapists from the area to meet once a month, for example. Models of peer supervision have been described by Montello and Scheiby (1994), and Priestley (1975).

Teamwork, of course, is also recommended, because often a patient may be displaying the same dynamics in work with other staff members. For music therapists who are not able to get together with peers, the method of "self-clearing" before sessions can be very useful and provide a means for focusing before the session. This involves creating an improvisation with the patient in mind, or engaging in a musical meditation or relaxation experience. One may also listen to the taped session or make notes right after the session to analyze what the dynamics were that caused the countertransference. Writing session notes immediately following the session may also help to identify and understand the countertransference dynamics in the music itself. And finally, it is important to make sure that one's musical self is nurtured. Bruscia (1999) provides additional suggestions for counteracting countertransferences.

*For further information about this type of group music psychotherapy work, see also Tomaino, Scheiby, Asmussen, Ramsey, Shah, and Goldstein (1999) and Scheiby (in press).

References

Bruscia, K. E. (1999). Techniques for uncovering and working with countertransference. In K. E. Bruscia (Ed.), *The dynamics of music psychotherapy* (pp. 93–120). Gilsum, NH: Barcelona.

Montello, L., & Scheiby, B. B. (1994). Introduction to psychodynamic peer supervision in music therapy. *Proceedings of the AAMT annual conference* (pp. 217–223). New York: AAMT.

Pedersen, I. N., & Scheiby, B. B. (in press). Intertherapy as part of an integrated MA program in music therapy at Aalborg University, DK. *Nordic Journal of Music Therapy*.

Priestley, M. (1975). *Music therapy in action.* London: Constable.

Priestley, M. (1994). *Essays on analytical music therapy.* Phoenixville, PA: Barcelona.

Scheiby, B. B. (1991). Mia's fourteenth—the symphony of fate: Psychodynamic improvisation therapy with a music therapy student in training. In K. E. Bruscia (Ed.), *Case studies in music therapy* (pp. 275–290). Phoenixville PA: Barcelona.

Scheiby, B. B. (1992). Musical transference and countertransference: Fellow travelers or stowaways on the musical journey. *Proceedings of the AAMT annual conference* (pp. 13–23). New York: AAMT.

Scheiby, B. B. (1998). The role of musical countertransference in analytical music therapy. In K. E. Bruscia (Ed.), *The dynamics of music psychotherapy* (pp. 213-249). Gilsum, NH: Barcelona.

Scheiby, B. B. (in press). Music as symbolic expression: An introduction to analytical music therapy. In D. J. Wiener (Ed.), *Beyond talk therapy: Using movement and expressive techniques in clinical practice.* Washington, DC: American Psychological Association.

Tomaino, C. M., Scheiby, B. B., Asmussen, S. M., Ramsey, D., Shah, V., & Goldstein, A. (1999). *The effects of a music therapy intervention on the levels of depression, anxiety/agitation, and quality of life experienced by individuals diagnosed with early and middle stage dementias: A controlled study.* Final Report, 1996 Dementia Grant Projects, Office of Continuing Care, New York State Department of Health.

Homeodynamic Mechanisms of Improvisational Music Therapy

Mark Rider, PhD, RMT

ONE OF THE DIFFICULTIES that music therapy poses for the scientific community is in first enumerating and then validating the seemingly infinite number of mechanisms presumably operating during this form of therapy. This is in part due to the fact that music, perhaps more than any other alternative therapy, functions with equal power on the four levels of interaction upon the human body: the physical, emotional, mental, and sociospiritual. However, a mechanism has been recently discovered which does account for the medical effects of all alternative therapies, regardless of the interaction level on which they participate. This mechanism is called homeodynamism (Rider, 1997).

Homeodynamism is a complementary mechanism to homeostasis. Whereas homeostasis regulates against macrovariations in internal environments that may become dangerous to health, homeodynamism relies upon dynamic microvariations in systems to confer physiological resilience in preparation for change. In cybernetic language, both homeostasis and homeodynamism employ negative feedback to prevent chaotic instability. In more basic terms, homeodynamic theory states that therapeutic interventions which create both (a) physiological shifts, and (b) physiological resonance are healthy to all systems in the body.

Homeodynamism was originally developed as an underlying mechanism for psychoneuroimmunology (PNI) (Rider, 1992). Neurological shifts were found to be advantageous to the immune system, whereas a lack of neurological shifting was detrimental to immunological health. Neurological shifts are hereby defined as relative power shifts in the electroencephalogram (EEG) among the frequency bands of delta (1–4 Hz), theta (4–8 Hz), alpha (8–12 Hz), and beta (above 12 Hz). These neurological shifts are hypothesized in homeodynamic theory to represent signaling by the immune system to the brain to shift to different EEG frequency bands (brainwaves) when various immune responses are needed. Different brainwaves during sleep and wake have been found to be associated with the various stages of the immune response (Moldofsky, Lue, Eisen, Keystone, & Gorczynski, 1986). Physiological variability has also been found to be beneficial to the cardiovascular (Singer et al., 1988) and musculoskeletal (Rider,

1997) systems. Therefore, homeodynamic mechanisms appear to be universal healing phenomena within the body.

Entrainment Music and Imagery

To shed some history on the discovery of homeodynamic mechanisms, this author became intrigued in the late 1970s with the work of a group of clinician/researchers successfully using mental imagery in improving medical conditions involving cancer, pain, and autoimmune disease (Achterberg, Lawlis, Simonton, & Simonton, 1977). Two features became immediately obvious as I explored this work clinically: (1) music enhanced the relaxation and imagery process (Kibler & Rider, 1983), and (2) physiological changes seemed to manifest themselves at the same time that imagery components (i.e., vividness, content, activity, etc.) shifted (Rider & Achterberg, 1989; Rider, Achterberg, Lawlis, Goven, Toledo, & Butler, 1990).

Further exploratory work demonstrated that a novel type of music dubbed "entrainment" music was the most efficacious in stimulating imagery shifts, particularly in those whose imagery was weak or blocked. Entrainment music is similar to the Nordoff and Robbins' improvisational approach (Nordoff & Robbins, 1977), except applied to cognitive behavior (imagery) instead of the more classic verbal-motor behavior.

Entrainment music was developed because there were patients (especially those with intense chronic pain) for whom sedative music had no demonstrable effect on either imagery or relaxation. The question was raised that if music could be developed which started with a symbolic representation of their pain/disease and then (as in the Nordoff and Robbins' approach), gradually transitioned into music designed to produce images of healing and/or pain relief, would the effects on the body and mind be greater?

The entrainment improvisation process is described as follows: With the patient lying down in the center of a small group of people with Orff and odd-percussion musical instruments, the conductor leads the improvisation of music designed to match the patient's disease/pain imagery. After several minutes, or when the leader determines from the patient's body language that he or she is resonating with the disease/pain music, the music is transitioned gradually into that designed to produce images of the alleviation/management of the disease/pain. The musicians can be untrained as musicians or therapists, but the conductor must have music therapy training.

Entrainment music was found to be more effective than traditional anxiolytic or preferred music in producing the desired physiological changes (Rider, 1985). Furthermore, the process was significantly more powerful when improvised live than when utilizing a tape of entrainment music previously recorded (Rider & Weldin, 1990). As I continued to work with the entrainment process, I became more convinced that the shift in consciousness that was produced by the music was related to the physiological shifts observed. Was it simply the empowered imagery that was effecting the healing response, or did the shift itself have something to do with wellness? This sojourn was to lead to homeodynamic theory.

Rhythms and Health

The idea of rhythmic shifting's relevance to health first became apparent when I was studying PNI phenomena in patients with multiple personality disorder (MPD). Researchers in the field of

MPD had documented extremely rapid healing and/or physiological changes in all systems of the body of these patients when they shifted among different personalities or "alters" (Braun, 1983; Hurley, 1985). These clients' EEG power amplitudes were especially more variable in the beta frequency band than controls acting out different personalities (Putnam, 1984). In this same study, visual evoked potentials also differed significantly more among MPD alters than among actors portraying different roles.

Wondering if the high neurological variance had anything to do with PNI activity, I began hunting for other disorders characterized by EEG shifts. Schizophrenia seemed a conceivable choice, and, as it turned out, large theta power increases had been documented just prior to hallucinations (Whitton, Moldofsky, & Lue, 1978). Although hallucinations are problematic to normal psychosocial communication, they do appear to yield health benefits to schizophrenics. Several authors have noted that schizophrenics are less prone to certain diseases, particularly cancer (Achterberg, 1985; Whitmont, 1993). The inductive logic for a homeodynamic theory of psychoneuroimmunology was expanding.

In one of the epidemiological studies cited above, another population—the developmentally disabled—was also noted for its startling immunity to cancer (Achterberg, 1985). While neurological deficits have been documented in this population (Psatta, Goldstein, & Matei, 1991), another EEG anomaly characterized by large electrical shifts is quite prevalent with this group, i.e., seizures. The notion that epilepsy could confer some immunological protection to its victims has been supported by clinical demonstrations. Specific immune cells called eosinophils provoke seizures when their numbers become too low, thus restoring the eosinophilic balance (Halberg, Engel, Halberg, & Passouant, 1952). The homeodynamic evidence continued to rise.

The next goal of associating neurological shifting with immunocompetence was to ascertain if a lack of EEG deficits, either in reduced band power or in reduced variability, accounted for immunosuppression. The first evidence emerged from the EEG literature on depression. Research has indicated that depressed individuals display reduced alpha power (Maurer & Dierks, 1991). Furthermore, depression has been linked with a suppressed immune system (Kronfol, Silva, & Greden, 1983) and increased risk of cancer (Shekelle et al., 1981).

Another population was found to exhibit EEG reductions—attention deficit disorder (ADD). In terms of EEG spectral power, individuals with ADD have been found to yield too little beta (Lubar, 1989). Conforming to homeodynamic theory, children with ADD have also demonstrated an increased occurrence of immunological problems consisting of upper respiratory infections and otitis media (Barkley, 1990). Therefore, it did not seem to matter whether it was depressed individuals' inability to increase alpha power or ADD clients' inability to increase beta power; the lack of shifting was apparently correlated with the suppression of the immune response.

In the only studies discovered in the literature on EEG and immunity, Moldofsky and his colleagues correlated a lack of delta-wave (deep) sleep with rheumatoid arthritis (Moldofsky & Scarisbrick, 1976; Moldofsky, Scarisbrick, England, & Smythe, 1975). These researchers also concluded that interleukin-1 was produced during delta-wave sleep, affirming that at least one of the EEG bands is necessary to optimum immunological functioning (Moldofsky et al., 1986). Since other immune cells are generated at other phases of sleep-wake cycles, it is hypothetical that each of the EEG bands is important to one or more phases of the immune response.

Due to the unavailability of any such research, I decided to conduct the first study of patients with various immune disorders using standard waking EEG protocols. With the help of Texas

Woman's University psychologist Dan Miller, I conducted Fast Fourier and evoked potential comparisons between a patient population and a healthy control group (Rider, 1997). Patients (all women) were solicited for participation based upon their active disease status involving immunological mechanisms which did not affect brain functioning. Four patients had autoimmune disease (lupus, uveitis, and two with rheumatoid arthritis); three had cancer (breast, lung, and ovarian); and four had fibromyalgia/chronic fatigue syndrome. This group was contrasted with a control group of four healthy women.

The general pattern exhibited by the immune patients' EEGs consisted of (a) significantly reduced relative power in the alpha and delta bands, and (b) significantly increased relative power in the theta and beta bands (significant at the .05 level). The visual evoked potential was also significantly higher for the healthy population. Thus, this pilot sample adds validity to the homeodynamic theory that each of the EEG brainwaves is perhaps essential for optimal functioning of the immune system. Through various activities or therapies, EEG power apparently needs to be focused at different times through the various EEG bands. Each EEG band may have an electrical threshold that needs to be obtained in order to activate events in the immune and/or endocrine system.

HARMONICS AND HEALTH

The more I searched and researched into the mind, brain, and immune system, I became increasingly convinced that they are essentially the same thing. Furthermore, the more I studied the term *homeodynamic,* the more I realized the following: (a) part of the word refers to the dynamic neurological nature of a healthy body; and (b) the other part, *homeo,* may have more referential meaning than was originally intended, i.e., an oppositional principle to that of homeostasis. It could also refer to the identical nature of mind and body (*homeo* means like or similar). Elsewhere I cover in greater detail both structural and functional similarities of the mind and body that demonstrate that their most salient representatives, the nervous and immune systems, are in many ways identical (Rider, 1997).

One of the most interesting resonant features of the mind, nervous system, and immune systems that demonstrates their capability for intercommunication involves a rhythmic principle called harmonic organization. This principle is borrowed from physics and is most easily demonstrated as the phenomenon that makes musical instruments sound different from one another. Assuming they all play the same fundamental frequency or pitch, harmonics are derived by multiplying the fundamental pitch (in cycles-per-second or Hz) by consecutive integers (e.g., 2, 3, 4, etc.). The note we hear is actually a combination of the fundamental and harmonics. Musical instruments sound differently due to the varying amplitudes associated with each of the harmonics—a concept referred to as timbre. A flute is close to a sine wave with very little energy found in the harmonics, whereas the clarinet's spectral energy includes significant amplitudes in the odd numbered harmonics.

I discovered the harmonic organization of the mind while doing research on synesthesia, in this case, the rare ability of some to see colors when hearing specific musical tones. After first determining that there was little consistency in the tone-color associations, I began to glean that there were individual patterns that yielded fascinating information about the language of the mind. For example, while the musical note C might evoke different colors to different people, it always evoked a more similar color to a harmonic relative to C, instead of a nonharmonic, but nearby neighbor (alphabetically) to C. In music, "harmonic relatives" are those tones that are a "perfect fifth" in musical distance (five white notes on the piano including starting and ending note). These harmonic relatives of C are G and F (going forwards and backwards, respectively), and share 4 of the first 12 harmonics of C. These harmonic relatives also contain 6 of the 7 scale notes of C. Notes close in physical distance to C (B and C#, for example) share only 1 harmonic in the first 12 and only 2 scale notes, and are therefore labeled "nonharmonic."

In other words, a synesthetic might see blue to C and the similar color purple to F or G, but the nonharmonic tones of B or C# might elicit the color of yellow. Therefore, the language of the mind appears to have harmonic organization.

This is not totally surprising due to the fact that the EEG has also been found to demonstrate a harmonic organization (Bickford et al., 1973; Brown, 1974). With delta considered as the fundamental frequency, sometimes theta is double and sometimes triple delta's frequency. Alpha is double theta and beta is double alpha. As a musical instrument, the brain would have a spectral analysis with predominant energies at the 2nd, 4th, and 8th harmonics when theta is delta doubled, or at the 3rd, 6th, and 12th harmonics when theta is delta tripled.

However, another way of looking at these rhythms is that they evolved historically in a bottom-to-top manner with delta being the oldest and beta being the newest (in terms of both phylogeny and ontogeny). Furthermore, to reiterate the musical analogy, activating the higher brainwaves may be similar to blowing on a trumpet at different intensities to obtain higher notes in the harmonic series. The higher the harmonic that is produced in the brain, the more alert the individual. It has been speculated that the physiological purpose for harmonic organization is to (a) enable fine-tuning of transmitted information, (b) reduce the background noise much the same way that frequency modulation (FM) accomplishes this in radio transmission, and (c) more efficiently remove metabolites from tissues (Carnes, Goodman, & Lent, 1991).

The implications of the harmonic organization of the brain toward health did not fully impact us until we completed our EEG study of people with immune disorders. What no one had before discovered was that unhealthy people seem to produce a nonharmonic EEG! Every single one of our immune patients, regardless of diagnosis, had spectral EEGs containing extra harmonics that were nonmultiples of fundamental frequencies. For example, in one cancer patient, the spectral analysis showed approximate harmonic multiples of 5, 10, and 20 Hz for theta, alpha, and beta, respectively. However, also present were peaks at 8 and 15 Hz. Interestingly, although this second competing set of alpha and beta frequencies is nonharmonic with the first set, it too exhibits perhaps a second harmonic pattern with 15 being nearly double 8. Theoretically, this phenomenon would be like a radio receiver trying to pick up two radio stations at frequencies too close to each other, thus causing interference.

Improvisational Music Therapy: The Quintessential Homeodynamic Therapy

With mounting validity of a homeodynamic theory of psychoneuroimmunology, I began to ask the question of whether this mechanism was involved in alternative therapies. In looking at the alternative healing techniques of sleep, deep breathing, exercise, therapeutic touch, acupuncture, bioelectric therapies, nutrition, psychotherapy, music therapy, biofeedback, cognitive therapy, hypnosis, imagery, social support, and healing-at-a-distance, I discovered that all therapuetic modalities effected positive changes in health and the immune system. Furthermore, each alternative therapy induced a dynamic, resonant shift in brainwave activity, therefore establishing each as homeodynamic (Rider, 1997).

Because improvisational music therapy utilizing entrainment imagery operates on more levels than perhaps any other alternative therapy, it likely involves the widest possible variety of homeodynamic shifts and thus healing potentials. (The research associated with these levels is covered in more detail in Rider, 1997). On the physical, or first interactional level, music entrains the breathing and thalamic motor response, each of which have been found to produce synchronized alpha brainwaves. Sometimes, the patient being improvised for has been found to be humming or toning along with the final soothing portion of the entrainment procedure. Toning not only employs breathing mechanisms but has also been found to stimulate theta and delta brainwaves.

The second interactional level, the emotional, has been demonstrated to be the most physiologically enhanced with music over any other behavior, including sex. The entrainment process often produces emotional catharsis in patients. Cathartic psychotherapy has been documented to produce both synchronized alpha as well as better delta-wave sleep.

The third and fourth levels, the cognitive and sociospiritual, are the hallmark of the entrainment process. Cognitive mechanisms are quite complex, but mostly involve imagery, which has been found to increase synchronized beta brainwaves. Relaxational meditation, on the other hand, has predominantly yielded increased synchronized alpha, whereas hypnotic trance has tended to increase theta activity. The transpersonal healing intentions directed by the improvisers toward the patient cannot be overlooked. Research has demonstrated that guided intention from a healer to a patient produced increased synchronized alpha and beta. Thus, improvisational music therapy utilizing entrainment imagery offers potential synchronized EEG increases among all of the brainwave bands, enabling the greatest possible activation of the different components of the immune response and healing.

A fascinating observation of our patients' EEGs was that as imagery became more effective, the competing nonharmonic frequencies subsided and healing and/or disease management increased (Rider, 1997). The overall spectral power of the EEG also increased, suggesting that more electrical energy was available to enable a healthy immune response.

The power of improvisational music therapy using entrainment imagery has been demonstrated to be so powerful that single session partial remissions of disease states have been reported by patients. These patients have all commented that they can easily remember one or two specific instruments (e.g., someone toning a lullaby or the simple melody of a xylophone) in their improvisation, the imagery of which was still vivid and able to produce considerably lengthy disease/pain management.

REFERENCES

Achterberg, J. (1985). *Imagery in healing.* Boston: New Science Library.

Achterberg, J., Lawlis, G. F., Simonton, O. C., & Simonton, S. (1977). Psychological factors and blood chemistries as disease outcome predictors for cancer patients. *Multivariate Experimental Clinical Research, 3,* 107–122.

Barkley, R. A. (1990). *Attention deficit hyperactivity disorder*. New York: Guilford Press.

Bickford, R. G., Brimm, J., Berger, L., et al. (1973). Application of compressed spectral array in clinical EEG. In P. Kellaway & I. Petersen (Eds.), *Automation in clinical electroencephalography*. New York: Raven Press.

Braun, B. G. (1983). Psychophysiologic phenomena in multiple personality and hypnosis. *American Journal of Clinical Hypnosis, 26,* 124–137.

Brown, B. (1974). *New mind, new body*. New York: Harper & Row.

Carnes, M., Goodman, B. M., & Lent, S. J. (1991). High resolution spectral analysis of plasma adrenocorticotropin reveals a multi-factorial frequency structure. *Endocrinology, 128,* 902–910.

Halberg, F., Engel, R., Halberg, E., & Passouant, P. (1952). Diurnal variations in amount of electroencephalographic paroxysmal discharge and diurnal eosinophil rhythm of epileptics on days with clinical seizures. *Federal Proceedings, 11,* 62.

Hurley, T. J. (1985). Multiple personality—Mirrors of a new model of mind? *Investigations, 1,* 1–23.

Kibler, V. E., & Rider, M. (1983). Effects of progressive muscle relaxation and music on stress as measured by finger temperature response. *Journal of Clinical Psychology, 39*(2), 213–215.

Kronfol, Z., Silva, J., & Greden, J. (1983). Impaired lymphocyte function in depressive illness. *Life Sciences, 33*, 241–247.

Lubar, J. F. (1989). Electroencephalographic biofeedback and neurological applications. In J. V. Basmajian (Ed.), *Biofeedback* (pp. 67–90). Baltimore: Williams & Wilkins.

Maurer, K., & Dierks, T. (1991). *Atlas of brain mapping*. New York: Springer-Verlag.

Moldofsky, H., Lue, F. A., Eisen, J., Keystone, E., & Gorczynski, R. M. (1986). The relationship interleukin-1 and immune functions to sleep in humans. *Psychosomatic Medicine, 48,* 309–318.

Moldofsky, H., & Scarisbrick, P. (1976). Induction of neurasthenic musculoskeletal pain syndrome by selective sleep stage deprivation. *Psychosomatic Medicine, 38*, 35–44.

Moldofsky, H., Scarisbrick, P., England, R., & Smythe, H. (1975). Musculoskeletal symptoms and non-REM sleep disturbance in patients with "fibrositis syndrome" and healthy subjects. *Psychosomatic Medicine, 37*, 341–351.

Nordoff, P., & Robbins, C. (1977). *Creative music therapy*. New York: John Day.

Psatta, D. M., Goldstein, R., & Matei, M. (1991). EEG mapping in mentally retarded children by synthetic arginine vasotocin administration. *Romanian Journal of Neurological Psychiatry, 29,* 9–16.

Putnam, F. W. (1984). The psychophysiologic investigation of multiple personality disorder. *Psychiatric Clinics of North America, 7,* 31–39.

Rider, M. (1985). Entrainment mechanisms are involved in pain reduction, muscle relaxation, and music-mediated imagery. *Journal of Music Therapy, 22*(1), 46–58.

Rider, M. (1992). Mental shifts and resonance: Necessities for healing? Foundations for a homeodynamic theory of psychoneuroimmunology. *Revision, 14(*3), 149–157.

Rider, M. (1997). *The rhythmic language of health and disease*. St. Louis: MMB.

Rider, M., & Achterberg, J. (1989). Effect of music-assisted imagery on neutrophils and lymphocytes. *Biofeedback and Self-Regulation, 14*, 247–257.

Rider, M., Achterberg, J., Lawlis, G. F., Goven, A., Toledo, R., & Butler, J. R. (1990). Effect of immune system imagery on secretory IgA. *Biofeedback and Self-Regulation, 15,* 317–333.

Rider, M., & Weldin, C. (1990). Imagery, improvisation, and immunity. *The Arts in Psychotherapy, 17,* 211–216.

Shekelle, R. B., Raynor, W. J., Ostfeld, A. M., Garron, D. C., Bieliauskas, L., Liu, S. C., Maliza, C., & Paul, O. (1981). Psychological depression and 17-year risk of death from cancer. *Psychosomatic Medicine, 43,* 117–125.

Singer, D. H., Martin, G. J., Magid, N., Weiss, J. S., Schaad, J. W., Kehoe, R., Zheutlin, T., Fintel, D. J., Hsieh, A. M., & Lesch, M. (1988). Low heart rate variability and sudden cardiac death. *Journal of Electrocardiology,* Supplement, S46–S55.

Whitmont, E. C. (1993). *The alchemy of healing.* Berkeley, CA: North Atlantic Books.

Whitton, J. L., Moldofsky, H., & Lue, F. (1978). EEG frequency patterns associated with hallucinations in schizophrenic and "creativity" in normals. *Biological Psychology, 13,* 123–133.

11

ACTIVE MUSIC THERAPY APPROACHES FOR NEUROLOGICALLY IMPAIRED PATIENTS

Concetta M. Tomaino, DA, MT-BC

THE TERM *NEUROLOGICALLY IMPAIRED* includes all syndromes and injuries related to damage of the brain and nervous system. This encompasses a wide range of abilities and disabilities. In this chapter, however, I will focus on the types of neurologic disorders typically encountered by therapists working in subacute care, short-term rehabilitation, and long-term care. Neurologic patients in these settings may have an admitting diagnosis of cerebral vascular accident (CVA) or stroke, traumatic brain injury (TBI), multiple sclerosis, Parkinson's disease, or Alzheimer's disease. Each diagnosis may include additional medical problems as well as mood-related disorders, secondary to loss of function, resulting in the need for extended treatment. Even with a specific diagnosis, the range of abilities and disabilities related to a neurological disease can vary greatly with each individual. The music therapist must have an understanding of the various disease and neurological processes to adequately assess functional ability and plan appropriate use of music for the course of treatment.

The medical needs of neurologic patients appropriate for referral to music therapy include: memory deficits, depression, balance/gait problems, fine motor problems, agitation/aggressive behaviors, acute or chronic pain, poor attention, decreased vocal projection, expressive aphasia, poor motivation, reduced muscle strength, Alzheimer's disease (nonspecific), multiple sclerosis (nonspecific), Parkinson's disease (nonspecific), and stroke, which may also include problems related to comprehension, concentration, attention span, memory, problem-solving, communication, and physical function (Davis, Gfeller, & Thaut, 1992, p. 254).

The theoretical approaches of music therapists working with this population vary, depending on training and orientation of the therapist as well as the presenting needs of the client. Over the past 20 years I have developed my own approach for this population by gleaning from principles of humanistic psychology, neuroscience, and neuropsychology. I believe that regardless of medical diagnosis or presenting medical need, each patient enters into the therapeutic process differently.

Patients' perspectives on their rehabilitation goals and coping strategies can greatly affect the outcome of therapy. For example, I recently worked with two medically similar yet contrasting patients. Two male patients were admitted to the short-term rehabilitation program following a stroke. Both were the same age and had a right side hemiparesis with weakness in both the arm and leg. The first man was retired and spent most of his time at home. His primary goal was to be able to care for himself and achieve enough functional ability to be able to dress himself and walk to the local store. The second was a professional musician, who was primarily concerned with regaining full use of his right arm and hand. Both men were highly motivated in their therapy, and both regained some function on the affected side. However, the musician was not motivated to relearn activities of daily living (ADL) skills, e.g., dressing and bathing. Rather, he wanted to work on his fine motor skills and coordination. The attending physiatrist stated that full recovery of finger dexterity following stroke was very difficult and highly unlikely according to the literature. However, this man, as a life long musician, may have a better chance of recovering these skills, because his brain representation of this function would theoretically be different than that of the average person. He did indeed recover more function than was expected. Despite his partial recovery, he needed to deal with the potential loss of one aspect of his career and explore options and strategies for maintaining an active role in his musical community. The needs of the individual and the potential he or she brings to the therapy situation must always be taken into account.

Many persons with neurological disorders have problems in cognition and in receptive and expressive speech. The therapist must be able to detect subtle cues from the patient, translate them, and interpret their meaning. The therapist is a message-sender as well as an observer, the dynamics of the therapeutic relationship always being a factor in the outcome of the intervention (Shapiro, 1967). Equally important to understanding therapeutic process is a knowledge of the underlying neural mechanisms and how various neurologic diseases affect human function. Patients' ability to benefit from music therapy is dependent on their ability to perceive and process musical stimuli.

Working alongside Dr. Oliver Sacks for the past 19 years has greatly influenced my understanding of neurologic function. His case studies (Sacks, 1973, 1995), as well as those of A. R. Luria (1972), have provided much insight into the minds of those living with neurologic problems and have been a great source of inspiration and learning.

The use of music as a therapeutic tool for persons with neurologic disease has tremendous potential because of the many ways the individual properties of music, i.e., rhythm, melody, and harmony, induce sometimes predictable neurologic responses. Some examples of this are auditory cuing for gait (Thaut & McIntosh, 1992), and the use of music as a retrieval mechanism for those with memory impairment (Tomaino, 1998). People's experience with music throughout their lives can influence how they will respond to rhythm and sounds presented during therapy sessions. Research in neuroscience indicates there is a strong connection between the auditory system and the limbic system. This biological link makes it possible for sound to be processed almost immediately by the areas of the brain that are associated with long-term memory and the emotions (Tomaino, 1993). This link is also mediated at a subcortical level, making it possible for the processing of information despite higher cortical damage. This is evidenced clinically by the strong emotional responses to familiar music we observe in persons with memory deficits, such as multi-infarct dementia or Alzheimer's disease. Familiar songs become a tool for connecting to seemingly lost parts of the personality by providing a necessary link to the "self." We have memories for not only the particulars of a song, such as the melody or lyrics, but also the rich associations that keep the melodies alive for us throughout our life. Memories are not actually lost with dementia or with other brain injuries; rather, the ability to retrieve and gain access to these is damaged. Music, then, can provide access not only to specific moods and memories, but also to the entire thought-structure and personality of the past.

As we possess memories for factual information, we also possess memories or "motor templates" for physical movements. Many adults are institutionalized following a stroke that leaves them with a weakness or paralysis on one side of the body. Even persons with dementia may lose the ability to initiate movements. Music, and in particular rhythm, can play a essential role in treatment by providing the necessary cues to reintegrate the sense of movement. The loss of neurologic function can trigger the activation of compensatory mechanisms, which have been lying dormant within the brain, to partially or completely "take over" the absent function. This phenomenon is known as "neural plasticity." There are many alternate nerve pathways and connections that can be used to re-establish behaviors. Damasio (1994) indicated that neurologic function includes the recruitment of certain neural pathways, depending on the type of stimulus or the subsequent response. In persons with hemiparesis, it may be possible to stimulate alternate motor pathways with the "right" music/rhythm. For example, walking and dancing, though both physical movements, use different postural schema. By stimulating a similar but neurologically different physical activity through music therapy, we have the ability to help patients reintegrate the sense of movement that they have lost. For example, a stroke patient who had played the piano as a child and has now lost the ability to move his fingers in a sequential pattern, may spontaneously do so if encouraged to play "für Elise." Although the patient may remark that he cannot play it, he may find his fingers moving automatically. Likewise, there is clinical evidence of preserved musical abilities in musicians with early to mid-stage advanced Alzheimer's disease. Crystal, Grober, and Mazur (1989) state that the skill of playing previously learned piano compositions from memory represents a special kind of procedural memory and is stored al least in part in the neostriatum, an area of the brain spared until the latest stages of Alzheimer's. The anatomical structure of procedural memory is presumed to involve striato-prefrontal circuits, whereas the substrate of declarative memory, i.e., memory for specific facts and information, is presumed to involve circuits connecting the hippocampus, subiculum, and association cortex. Much of the pathology of Alzheimer's disease is found in these latter regions.

Because neurologic damage resulting from head trauma, early to mid-stage Alzheimer's disease, and some strokes occurs in higher cortical areas, finding responses that are mediated at a sub-cortical level can greatly enhance the recovery of function. In persons with severe dementia, music, with a strong rhythmic base, can allow for spontaneous movement, thus keeping limbs and joints free from possible atrophy and contractures. For persons with language disorders secondary to stroke, we have also seen improvements through music therapy. Those with expressive aphasia (difficulty in word retrieval but with good comprehension) can often sing familiar musical phrases without a problem. Using singing to stimulate language centers of the brain can aid in nonmusical word retrieval, making it eventually possible for purposeful speech (Berlin et al., 1996). Likewise, persons with dysarthria, a motor speech problem that makes verbal communication difficult, can also be helped through music therapy. Many dysarthric patients, though able to learn speech techniques intelligibly, have problems in carry over and thus are not able to employ them consistently. By engaging such patients in vocal expression that utilizes specific tempi, melodies, and enhancement of phrasing inherent in the music, the therapist can provide the patient with a real sense of what correct breathing and phrasing feels like.

The type of sound, rhythm, or melody that is chosen by the music therapist in conjunction with the patient during the therapy session should then depend on the target outcomes and goals of the therapeutic process. Davis et al. (1992) provide a good overview of goal planning for specific populations. Some of the common areas addressed with neurologic patients in therapy and the related uses of music are:

Physical functioning—The rhythmic character of music serves as an auditory cue to influence timing and readiness (potentiation) of the nervous system, and consequently supports more precise and sustained physical movements. Nonrhythmic, slow tempos, and/or low frequencies can entrain brain frequencies to levels that reduce relaxation and facilitate the alleviation of pain. The use of MIDI equipment, such as digital drum pads and specially designed MIDI triggers (see chapter by David Ramsey), makes music-making accessible to those with limited movement. Such activity can reinforce occupational therapy goals for range of motion because the instruments can be situated in a variety of positions around the patient. With special software and computer equipment, the numbers that comprise the digital signal in the MIDI drum pads can be downloaded and evaluated to measure changes in force.

Cognitive functioning—The structural characteristics of music can stimulate attention and memory and facilitate learning. For example, music that is repetitive, predictable, and symmetrical can be used as a mnemonic device to assist with recall. Interesting rhythmic patterns and novel or familiar music may increase both attention and motivation. By using contrasting qualities of sounds, e.g., pitch and timbre, and/or varying the location of the sound in the environment, the therapist can enhance the patient's spatial orientation. Instruments placed outside of the visual field of someone with an hemianopia or visual neglect can encourage improvement in visual perception.

Emotional and social needs—Melodic and rhythmic improvisations and musical dialogues between client and therapist or among group members can promote expression of deep emotions and facilitate more adaptive emotional and social functioning.

Communication—Structural features of music, such as melodic inflection and rhythm, can facilitate word retrieval and vocal production with some types of speech disorders. The content of the lyrics, expressive qualities of the melodic line, or qualities of musical sounds can represent ideas and also have symbolic meaning (Gfeller, Tomaino, & Wheeler, 1998).

Patients are referred to music therapy by the attending physician and/or by the admitting social worker. To ensure that patients who can benefit from music therapy are referred, regular inservices are provided by music therapy staff to medical and social service departments. Once a patient is referred, a full assessment is made. During the assessment process, the following information is collected:

Full history—Including musical preferences, musical background, formal training, level of involvement in music (professional, amateur, occasional, listener, dancer). Levels of physical functioning, including vision and hearing. Psychological state and ability to be engaged in the therapeutic process.

Medical needs—Taken from medical referral to music therapy. Prior medical history, other medical problems (arteriosclerotic heart disease, diabetes, substance abuse, vascular, hypertension).

Assessment of musical function—Identify the type of music used during assessment. Describe patient's:

- sensorioperceptual ability (state of consciousness, e.g., alert, drowsy, lethargic)
- verbal ability (*verbal character*: mute, single words, short sentences, conversation; *verbal quality*: unintelligible, perseveration, inarticulate speech, articulate speech)
- nonverbal communication (expressions: smiles, gestures, inexpressive, sad)
- affect (flat, elated, appropriate, anxious)
- attention level (attends to music, nonreactive)
- behavioral (patient to patient and patient to therapist: verbal, nonverbal, animation)
- rhythmic expression (follows rhythm, clapping hands, tapping feet, nodding head, moving body, integration, complexity)
- musical expression (congruence with verbal, ability to choose instrument, willingness to share instruments, improvises)
- music memory (recalls lyrics, recalls song titles, recalls melody)
- relatedness in music (self, therapist)
- motor functioning (fine/gross motor, gait: pace, balance, symmetry/asymmetry)
- memory (immediate, recent, long-term)
- reminiscence (spontaneous, prompted)
- physical and emotional responses to familiar music
- ability to sing song lyrics
- pitch/melodic discrimination
- pattern of melodic and rhythmic responses.

(Some of the items above adapted from *Music Therapy Assessment Tool*, Glynn, 1992, adapted and revised in Tomaino, Scheiby, Asmussen, Ramsey, Shah, & Goldstein, 1999.)

All assessments are documented in the patient's chart within 48 hours of the referral. Upon evaluation, the music therapist states whether the patient is an appropriate candidate for music therapy. All goals need to be measurable and time-specific. This is especially important if music therapy services are reimbursable through outside insurance providers. Documentation may include video- and audiotapes of sessions. Progress notes are completed every 14 or 30 days, depending on whether the patient is in short-term rehabilitation or long-term care. Besides written documentation, regular meetings with the interdisciplinary team take place to coordinate care plan strategies.

How music is used during the session and how the therapeutic process unfolds is difficult to describe in a set formula. For example, in using music therapy with a person who has Parkinson's disease and who needs assistance in initiating movement, the session may be used to explore various rhythmic patterns to assist in normalizing and synchronizing gait. Once coordination and ease of walking are established within the music therapy session, time is spent to help the patient internalize this rhythmic beat, either through singing or recalling a song in the same tempo. Sacks (1973) has illustrated that the irregular EEGs of post-encephalitic Parkinson's patients became normalized when thinking about certain musical works.

For a person with expressive aphasia, singing familiar lyrics or phrases may be employed to increase stimulation of preserved language areas and to teach strategies that the individual can use after discharge. However, for the patient who is in denial, has depression, and possesses limited cognitive ability, the initial therapy sessions may include a variety of techniques. These may include improvisation and music listening to explore the scope of skills available to this individual and provide a safe environment for self expression. In such a case, establishing a trusting relationship is essential for therapy to take place. Music can serve as a bridge between therapist and patient to facilitate self-expression and communication as the following case illustrates.

Ms. B., a 70-year-old German immigrant who came to the U.S. to escape religious persecution, was admitted with a severe neuromuscular disease. She could not use her hands, nor could she walk, and she was admitted for long-term nursing care. Ms. B. was from a wealthy family, was very proud, and had always been independent. She was well-educated and part of a musical family; she herself had aspired to be a classical vocalist. She brought a private attendant to care for her when she arrived at this facility. Ms. B. was referred to music therapy because she refused to leave her room (she did not want anyone to see her in her limited condition). Refusing to discuss her anger and depression with the psychiatrist, she also would not accept any medications other than analgesics for pain. She remarked that she had no interest in music or in therapy. She had been a friend to a leading psychoanalyst in Germany and remarked that she knew all the "tricks."

I knew that I could not get her to leave her room and that she had already refused to listen to taped music at bedside (which the recreation worker and the physiatrist had suggested). When I introduced myself, I mentioned my collection of German lieder and asked if she had ever heard Anderson or Dietrich Fischer-Dieskau sing. Our first conversation consisted of her reminiscing and criticizing both singers and others. From this exchange, I was able get a better glimpse into her personality. I spoke of the music studio at the facility with its excellent sound system and remarked that it was a shame that she could not leave her room. The next afternoon she was at the studio and asked if I still had the Anderson recordings of Schumann. Our session consisted of listening to music, followed by her analysis of its quality. The songs were in German, and I often asked her to translate the lyrics for me and describe what the song was trying to convey. I *did* know the translations, but wanted to hear how she would translate them. Up until this point, I had met her on an intellectual level; she had not been able to achieve even this with any other staff.

With each session she started to personalize the music and her own experiences. As she disclosed more and more about herself, I changed the music to Schubert's "Die Schoene Mullerin." This contains a passage where one of the characters finds that his love is not reciprocated and asks the river to let him rest. As Ms. B. translated this to me, she broke into tears. Although she had shown no emotion until this moment, she did remark this was what she too was feeling. The notion of "love being lost, life being over, and suicide the only choice left" became the link to the deeper therapy that followed. The words and the music had brought her to the level of realization that she had been repressing the anger she was feeling toward others. The next week she remarked how lucky she was to still have her mind, as other patients on her unit could not speak or move. She asked if she could invite some of the others to listen to the music with her.

Although this case material is not typical of how I use music in my sessions, it clearly illustrates the need to connect with the individual in a way that he or she can be met. The music provided a path to communication, yet I needed to know how and when to introduce different music, which I thought might reflect her own feelings. The music I chose could have been interpreted in several ways, so I did leave an opening for her. I needed to be a quiet listener and observer for several sessions, introducing new music only when I thought that she was ready to hear it. Another therapist may have challenged her earlier, but my judgment was that I would have alienated her had I pushed an issue on her. She needed to come to this herself.

The role of the music therapist in all the above situations is multifaceted. Shapiro (1967), a humanistic psychologist, compares himself to an instrument in his role as a therapist. This reflects my own philosophy both literally and figuratively:

> What I really mean by an "instrument" is the capability of my guts, my body, and my computer-brain to pick up subtle cues given by other people, the environment, and myself as I encounter people and move through the world. . . . Not only do I pick up cues, but I also decode them, translate them, and I express myself. I am message sender as well as recorder. . . . I suppose I am just as much computer, too, as a recorder, and I am also a musical instrument. Not only do I try to listen to the music as well as the words that people say, but I also sometimes play a tune myself on the instrument. My tune could be my pattern of feelings expressed, my voice, my facial expression, a sigh or frown, or it could be something less tangible for which others might have to listen. . . . I often tell people, "Listen for the music, not the words." (p. 235)

And yet, I believe that the music therapist still does more. The music therapist needs to have a wide repertoire which may serve to draw in the patient and engage that person in a meaningful exchange. The music may be of any genre as well as including principles of psychoacoustics and vibration. Even when the music is prescriptive, such as using a melodic phrase to aid communication, the therapist needs to assess what melodic phrase, including range and interval will work for the patient. Additionally, the music therapist needs to know how neurologic disease affects perception and capacity for cognitive, emotional, and physical response. The benefits of this knowledge and understanding are immeasurable, as the music therapist will have the ability to effectively treat those with neurologic impairments on a level that cannot be met by other therapeutic modalities.

References

Berlin, P., Eeckhout, P. V., Zilbovicius, M., Remy, P., François, C., Guillaume, S., Chain, F., Rancurel, G., & Samson, Y. (1996). Recovery from nonfluent aphasia after M.I.T.: A PET study. *Neurology, 47,* 1504–1511.

Crystal, H. A., Grober, E., & Mazur, D. (1989). Preservation of musical memory in Alzheimer's disease. *Journal of Neurology, Neurosurgery, and Psychiatry, 52,* 1414–1416.

Damasio, A. R. (1994). *Descartes' error: Emotion, reason and the human brain.* New York: Grosset/Putnam Books.

Davis, W. B., Gfeller, K. E., & Thaut, M. H. (1992). *An introduction to music therapy.* Iowa: Wm. C. Brown.

Gfeller, K., Tomaino, C., & Wheeler, B. (1998, November 20). Unpublished white paper on scope of music therapy practice. AMTA Board of Directors Meeting.

Glynn, N. J. (1992). The music therapy assessment tool in Alzheimer's patients. *Journal of Gerontological Nursing, 18*(1), 3–10.

Luria, A. R. (1972/1987). *The man with a shattered world* [Reprint]. Cambridge, MA: Harvard University Press.

Sacks, O. W. (1973). *Awakenings*. New York: E. P. Dutton.

Sacks, O. W. (1995). *An anthropologist on Mars*. New York: Alfred A. Knopf.

Shapiro, S. B. (1967). Myself as an instrument. In J. F. Bugental (Ed.), *Challenges of humanistic psychology* (pp. 235–239). New York: McGraw-Hill.

Thaut, M. H., & McIntosh, G. C.(1992). Effects of rhythmic auditory cueing on stride and EMG patterns in normal gait. *Journal of Neurologic Rehabilitation, 6,* 185–190.

Tomaino, C. M. (1993). Music and the limbic system. In F. J. Bejjani (Ed.), *Current research in arts medicine.* Chicago: A Cappella Books.

Tomaino, C. M. (1998). *Music on their minds: A qualitative study of the effects of using familiar music to stimulate preserved memory function in persons with dementia.* Unpublished doctoral dissertation, New York University, New York.

Tomaino, C., Scheiby, B., Asmussen, S., Ramsey, D., Shah, V., & Goldstein, A. (1999). *The effects of a music therapy intervention on the levels of depression, anxiety/agitation, and quality of life experienced by individuals diagnosed with early and middle stage dementias: A controlled study.* Final Report to 1996 Dementia Grants Projects, Office of Continuing Care, New York State Department of Health.

12

Restoration of Essential Human Experiences Through the Implementation of Adaptive MIDI Technology

David W. Ramsey, MA, ACMT

> Neurology's favourite word is "deficit," denoting an impairment or incapacity of neurological function: loss of speech, loss of language, loss of memory, loss of vision, loss of dexterity, loss of identity and myriad other lacks and losses of specific functions (or faculties).
>
> —Oliver Sacks, 1989, p. 3

WEBSTER DEFINES the word *rehabilitate* as "to restore to former capacity; to reinstate." In a rehabilitation hospital, the parameters of this restoration are defined and processed through the lens of those health care providers who see illness as a conglomerate of deficits. These deficits are usually related to global functions that enable the person to perform the activities of daily living in a manner independent of care providers. Once persons are able to carry out functions of daily living that allow them to communicate needs and to feed, clean, and mobilize themselves, they are discontinued from rehabilitation treatment. Those who cannot make progress according to managed care calculations and prescribed timelines are terminated.

This chapter concerns itself with the latter—patients who are unable to make progress according to managed care guidelines, but who are nonetheless assigned the role of patient in a long term rehabilitation/health care facility. *Maintenance* is the overriding term in describing the approach to their treatment. Music and music-based relationships can play a unique role in restoring "deficits" not recognized within the medical model, specifically those that involve certain functions of basic humanity and social networking. Music therapists, while still adhering to the goals determined by managed care and insurance reimbursing agencies, can assure themselves as to the other "real" work being provided through music therapy and adapted MIDI technology.

My patients are typically classified as neurologically impaired, a term that encompasses a wide range of injuries and syndromes related to compromised parts of the nervous system. Patients who have experienced cerebrovascular accidents/strokes, traumatic brain injuries, multiple sclerosis, Parkinson's disease, or coma seem to benefit from a music therapy group designed (a) to meet them at their level of physical functioning, and (b) to provide a means for restoring social contact. I tend to select patients who have expressed an inclination towards music, as this existing motivation helps sustain them throughout the initial excitement of being able to play a MIDI musical instrument. I also like to choose patients with limited speech, who cannot enter into everyday conversations, and who are thereby excluded from spontaneous social interactions. Finally, I typically select patients with limited physical capabilities. It is a challenge to modify, adapt, and arrange the MIDI triggers to meet the available movements of these severely impaired patients, and this, in a fundamental way, provides for opportunities not possible with any other mode of intervention.

BILLA'S STORY

Last year I decided to start a music therapy group comprised of the hospital's most physically impaired patients. I planned to incorporate sophisticated MIDI technology in my group to convert the patients' limited movements into lush, synthesized sounds that were programmed into "mistake free" scales and sound patterns. I selected those patients who could not speak and who had severe physical handicaps, but who were still cognitively intact and interested in music. Most of these patients had already been discontinued from speech, physical, or occupational therapy because they had been determined to have reached their maximum level of functioning, and thus had been placed at the long-term health care section of the facility.

On the first day of the scheduled group, one patient showed up uninvited. Billa was a 38-year-old quadriplegic male who was admitted to the hospital 8 years previously with traumatic brain injury resulting from an automobile accident. He could move only his head and was unable to speak. However, he could communicate through an electronic speaking device that was manipulated by an infrared light strapped to his forehead. Billa loved to "talk" and joke around, but never expressed much interest in actually playing music. We had worked together for almost 2 years in individual music therapy, during which time we had listened to music and engaged in remembrances of his teenage days. We had also done song-lyric writing and discussed the significance of the lyrics with regard to his life situation. My therapeutic goals had been to provide an outlet for self-expression as well as a means for him to come to terms with his extremely difficult circumstances. However, he appeared to be more interested in joking around and social contact than in analysis, cognitive reconstruction, or emotional catharsis. Because of this, I had not considered him for my new group, even though he met all of the requirements.

I had set the room up for three other patients with stations equipped with very sophisticated MIDI-triggered instruments capable of capturing and calibrating any movements of the patient and converting them into programmed, pentatonic synthesized music. Although I had not planned on Billa's visit, I invited him in nevertheless.

Billa watched and smiled at the other patients as they manipulated the triggers to produce music that was full, rhythmic, and expressive. One patient was playing a beautiful flute sound by moving his right arm back and forth about 6 inches—the extent of his stretching capacity. Another patient was tapping on an electronic drum trigger that produced deep, resonant drum sounds. At one point, I started playing country music in a waltz tempo as it seemed conducive to a call and response format. I stopped to ask Billa if he would join us by spelling out "Yee Haw" on his talking machine and by activating it during the end of particular phrases. When it came time for Billa to say, "Yee Haw," he began to laugh uncontrollably; I had seen him laugh before, but never like this. This particular laugh was akin to an infant's first laugh when playing with an overhead mobile, and his whole body shook with excitement. I asked myself later why this laugh seemed different than his previous responses to hearing a joke or to seeing a clumsy music therapist drop a very expensive, irreplaceable MIDI music instrument.

Suddenly, I realized something that I had never considered before: Billa was being confronted with "time" in a way that he had not experienced since his accident. At this instant, the other members were watching and waiting for him to say "Yee Haw." His response was necessary for the continuation of the music, and it was a moment alive with possibilities and power. He held in his control the destinies of four other persons who needed his contribution to continue with their music. It was a situation characterized by fun, support, power, and control. After this incident, I began to compare this fully alive moment to his typical way of being in the world. Usually Billa is forced to spell out each letter, each word, each sentence by using the infrared light; it is a time-consuming communication process, characterized by long periods of waiting to convey basic chunks of condensed information. What was lacking from these communication exchanges was the element of "real time," and thus I began to realize that certain forms of expression are dependent upon the manipulation of time. Yes, we could say we are angry, but through the timing of the delivery of this message, we could convey this anger in a completely unique way, as certain dimensions of this expression exist only within the context of spontaneity. It seemed to me also that certain forms of humor, aggression, affirmation, and affection were indeed dependent upon the manipulation of time, and Billa had not had the opportunity to experience these expressions while living in "step time," which is limited by calculated, type-written communication.

After working as a music therapist for over 17 years, I began to challenge the concepts and goals that defined my work. I began to question terms so often used to describe music therapy, such as *nonverbal communication* and *nonverbal expressions of the self in music*. I had always been concerned and interested in subtle forms of nonverbal communication and had even completed a postgraduate certification program at the New York Institute for Neurolinguistic Programming, an approach dedicated to the most subtle of cues to determine meaning in communication. This work in a rehabilitation hospital, however, increased and renewed my interest in investigating these dimensions of music therapy. Could there be an entire world of "time dependent" behaviors and experiences that exist and contribute to our experience of being fully human? Could these nonverbal expressions and time-dependent experiences be observed, described, and labeled? If these sorts of things do exist, where would they fit into the world of rehabilitation medicine, or even music therapy?

NONVERBAL COMMUNICATION

In his book, *Essentials of Nonverbal Communications*, Mark Knapp (1980) has cited over 300 studies relating to how information is conveyed through nonverbal means. Body movements, facial expression, vocal tones, use of space, use of time, physical appearance, and many other nonverbal cues are seen as significant components of human interaction. Birdwhistel (1970) has concluded that the strategic interactions conveyed through the sometimes unconscious movement of our bodies comprise the majority of all communications. Hall (1966) considers the use of space and time as the most important elements in communication within a culture. Studies that looked at communications that transcend the verbal content exchanged reminds the music therapist that beyond the music played exist experiences dependent upon communications allowed for in the music. If the music therapist looks solely at the structure, dynamic, or mode of a musical piece to determine the meaning of the patient's expressions and experiences, he or she may miss exchanges that reveal significant social dynamics. Synchronicity, for instance, may reflect an experience of acceptance and community. The intentional hesitation from a patient who commands the dominant drum in an established groove-oriented improvisation may reflect hostility. Strong syncopated beats against an established straight pulse may reflect an assertion of command and power in a socially acceptable format. For patients who have lost their ability to join in on community or social interactions because of speech or physical disabilities, these interactions are significant and warrant acknowledgment and affirmation. Although it would be difficult to attribute a specific meaning to a particular extra-musical behavior, as each person may demonstrate unique nonverbal communications in music-making, it would be correct to say that the re-establishment of communication experiences through music-making is essentially restorative.

Adaptive MIDI Instruments in Neurological Rehabilitation

I have been implementing MIDI technology for over 10 years now in my music therapy practice. By adapting this technology to drums, shirt sleeves, and table tops, lush sounds can be produced by the most physically challenged patient with the simplest of movements. For several years I brought in my own "homemade" MIDI equipment to use in music therapy groups. Then the music therapy department acquired several high-tech manufactured MIDI instruments that accommodated a variety of physical movements in sound production. The following sections provide a more detailed account of the equipment suitable for adaptation to this population's needs (Ramsey, 1998).

Soundbeam

Soundbeam is a device that produces a sound wave across a predetermined linear space. The invisible beam of sound can be interrupted by waving a foot, an arm, or any other object through the beam. This interruption is converted into MIDI information and passed onto a sound source, i.e., a synthesizer sound module. The soundbeam can be programmed to play individual notes for each interruption, thus producing one note at each time of manipulation. Another option involves moving through the beam to manipulate a scale, one that is preprogrammed (major, minor, and pentatonic scales) or original as created by the programmer. Soundbeam, in this way, allows for real time movements to be converted into harmonic sounds to fit particular modal improvisations. The range of the beam can be programmed so that movements as grand as 6 feet in extension can produce one octave of a scale, or so an entire scale can be produced by moving within a 6-inch range of motion. For patients with limited motion, this latter option is very useful.

Electronic Pizzo Triggers

Electronic pizzo triggers can be purchased at most music stores that sell electronic drum equipment. They are essentially electronic pick-ups that produce a simple electronic on/off signal when activated by pressure. These triggers are usually small round metal dots with an attached wired input jack to which a quarter inch patch chord can attach. The guitar chord (quarter-inch patch) can be plugged into a drum sound source to act as an additional drum pad, or it can be plugged into a MIDI converter that enables the music therapist to access any MIDI sound source. For a music therapist on a limited budget, this is the most economical way of accessing the limited movement of physically challenged patients.

Electronic Drum Pads

Electronic drums are readily available at most music stores. In essence, these are electronic versions of the traditional trap drum set, including a foot pedal trigger for the bass drum, and drum pads arranged on a rack to provide snare and tom tom drums, as well as a variety of cymbal and Latin percussion sounds. These pads can be placed on individual stands and adjusted to meet the angle of movement available to the patient. Since the sound source for these drum sets is usually MIDI capable, the triggers can be linked to other sound sources to produce not only percussion sounds but also harmonic synthesized sounds. With this capability, the pads can be programmed so that, for example, a flute sound is played in a blues scale when tapped in succession.

Miburi

The Miburi MIDI suit is produced by a major company but is not yet available for purchase. Our music therapy program was fortunate enough to be the first to use this instrument to determine its effectiveness in music therapy with neurologically impaired patients. The Miburi is essentially a body suit with MIDI triggers implanted at various joints. Unlike pizzo triggers that need pressure to be activated, the Miburi triggers are activated by movement, e.g., by the bending of the 3-inch flexible electrode. Each trigger can be programmed to produce individual sounds or scales with organized movements.

Because neurologically impaired patients may be unable to fit easily into the spandex body suit, I adapted the system by removing the triggers and placing them in positions accessible to the patient's movements. For patients who are unable to apply sufficient pressure to their movements, the Miburi can be very effective. The triggers can be attached to flexible stands and manipulated to a wide variety of body parts and angles according to patients' capabilities.

There are many other MIDI instruments available on the market today that are able to convert almost any physical signal into MIDI information and subsequently synthesized musical sounds. Some of these instruments can convert even EEG signals into MIDI information; some convert video signals into MIDI information as well. These instruments are truly awe inspiring, but for the music therapist interested in facilitating personal musical expressions, i.e., expressions that are easily identified by the patients as being the result of their own efforts, simple triggers are better than those that measure subtle responses, such as EEG.

Organization of Equipment

The electronic MIDI music therapy group is set up with four music stations. Each station is equipped with different MIDI instruments, which are specifically chosen to match the physical capabilities of the patient. All instruments are programmed to a particular mode, and improvisations are employed using these modes. The music is usually rhythmic in nature, at least initially, to provide a foundation for the improvisation and enhance the patient's success. Although the rhythmic aspect of the music is important for this reason, it is also important to allow for space and dynamics in the music improvisations. Once a rhythmic improvisation has been established, the music therapist's music can drop back to allow for the group to live in the dynamics of the music. If the patients are unable to carry the music without a strong rhythmic structure from the music therapist, he or she can manipulate the timing and dynamics of the music to encourage personal input from the patients. These musical dynamics often provide the only real source of control for the patient in a world where control is provided by caregivers. But much more than this, the music allows patients to experience camaraderie and affection for one another. I have often noticed one patient drop out of the improvisation just to watch the musical interactions between the other two patients. These observations are often accompanied by a fully alive smile and an expression of joy at being socially active once again, an experience that involves the manipulation and sharing of time.

Conclusion

When persons suffer a cerebrovascular accident, traumatic brain injury, or any physical disability that takes away their ability to move fully or speak fluently, the mechanisms that allow for social connections and individual expression are compromised. Although music does not restore a person's ability to exchange specific ideas, thoughts, and feelings, it does, however, provide a context for nonverbal communications to exist and, thus, essential human experiences of community, power, and shared emotions. Sometimes it is best to utilize modern technology to provide for this musical means to reconnect. Sensitive MIDI triggers are useful in adapting the existing movements of the disabled into fully expressive sounds and allow for musical exchanges and personal dynamics to flourish.

References

Birdwhistel, R. L. (1970). *Kinesics and context: Essays on body motion communication.* Pennsylvania: University of Pennsylvania Press.

Hall, E. T. (1966). *The hidden dimension.* New York: Doubleday.

Knapp, M. L. (1980). *Essentials of nonverbal communication.* New York: Holt, Rinehart and Winston.

Ramsey, D. W. (1998, November). *Implications of MIDI in rehabilitative music therapy.* Paper presented at the Music Therapy in Rehabilitation Symposium of the annual conference of the American Music Therapy Association, Cleveland, Ohio.

Sacks, O. W. (1989). *Seeing voices: A journey into the world of the deaf.* Berkeley: University of California Press.

13

THE USE OF MUSICAL WIND INSTRUMENTS IN THE TREATMENT OF CHRONIC PULMONARY DISEASES

Ellen Griggs-Drane, MM, MT-BC

ASTHMA, CYSTIC FIBROSIS (CF), and Chronic Obstructive Pulmonary Disease (COPD) are three pulmonary diseases that differ in etiology, yet are quite similar in treatment protocol. The use of musical wind instruments in music therapy treatment is basically the same among all three diagnoses. Specific characteristics of each of these diseases, as well as a definition of terms, are included in the Appendix at the end of this chapter.

The goals in treating these illnesses are (a) to slow down the rate of decline in lung function, (b) to control symptoms, and (c) to restore normalcy to the life of patients. Traditionally, physicians, pulmonologists, and respiratory therapists have employed different devices to enhance the overall pulmonary fitness of the patient as well as enhance the ability for airway clearance. Music therapy interventions using wind instruments incorporate the same focus areas that are addressed using other pulmonary devices. These include: (a) diaphragmatic breathing with increased resistance levels as an elementary technique in instrumental training, which may assist with pulmonary fitness; (b) exhalation resistances provided by playing a musical instrument, which later may be increased by changing the instrument and by improved musical skill; and (c) respiratory endurance, which may be enhanced by one's ability to sustain a note for longer periods of time.

In addition, the use of musical wind instruments with these populations may also address (a) treatment compliance, which may improve the amount of time an individual spends using a treatment technique; (b) school and work attendance and integration, by allowing for involvement with an instrumental music program, which may enhance socialization, self-esteem, and improve overall absenteeism; and (c) enhanced pursed lip breathing, expectoration, self-esteem, and overall respiratory fitness. Due to the motivating, social, and creative qualities of music therapy, using a musical wind instrument may be as effective as traditional interventions for pulmonary fitness and may prove to be more reinforcing in the areas of treatment compliance, cost effectiveness, and quality of life.

The use of music to enhance correct breathing techniques with pulmonary patients has been found to be an effective, nontraditional intervention that has resulted in emotional, physiological, and physical benefits. Several studies have pointed to the respiratory benefits of playing musical wind instruments.

Bouhuys (1964) studied 452 male professional wind instrument players and compared data concerning their pulmonary function with results obtained from nonwind players. It was found that vital capacity, total lung capacity, and forced expiration were greater in the wind instrumentalists than in the control group. Bouhuys (1964) concluded that wind instruments and singing require a regulation of exhaled air flow that develops as the performer is taught to use lung volume or vital capacity to the fullest possible extent and exhaling to the maximum degree.

The use of instrumental music has been shown to be an effective rehabilitation technique in the treatment of children with asthma (Marks, 1974). As breathing exercises are a necessary part of the respiratory process for asthmatic children, these can be implemented through wind instrumental performance. Constant practice on a wind instrument often improves pulmonary function, thus reducing progression of the disease. "It is believed that training the abdominal muscles to assist the diaphragm in some of the work of breathing helps many children to moderate and even control attacks of bronchospasm" (Marks, 1974, p. 314).

Griggs-Drane (1989) found that the use of musical wind instruments as an expiratory treatment technique with Chronic Obstructive Pulmonary Disease (chronic bronchitis, emphysema, asthma) patients was as effective as the traditional treatment of using an Inspiratory Muscle Trainer. The subjects who received treatment using a musical wind instrument demonstrated improvements in endurance for walking and treatment compliance. Enjoyment, self-motivation, concentration, awareness of correct posture and breathing techniques, maximum effort used, flexibility of treatment into one's daily life, and personal achievements were all higher for subjects receiving music therapy. These results suggest the motivating and rehabilitating qualities of music.

In a safety study with Cystic Fibrosis subjects, Griggs-Drane (1998) found that playing a musical wind instrument of choice was beneficial for subjects in increasing the amount of expiratory pressure produced by playing wind instruments as compared to the use of a Positive Expiratory Pressure (PEP) Mask and Flutter Device. There was also an increase in the subjects' ability to sustain a single pitch, suggesting that playing a wind instrument may positively influence respiratory endurance. It was also found that subjects playing wind instruments spent a greater amount of time practicing instruments than in using their traditional methods of treatment. Perceptions of enjoyment of treatment, awareness of correct posture, breathing, and the desire to continue playing a musical wind instrument were greater among the music-treatment subjects when using the wind instrument of choice over their prescribed PEP Mask or Flutter Device.

Musicians use diaphragmatic/costal (DC) breathing as a technique while playing an instrument or singing. The incorporation of DC breathing provides exercise of the respiratory muscles and coordinates the movement between the rib cage and the abdomen. Skilled musicians were found to have smooth and coordinated movements between the rib cage and abdominal muscles, thus allowing expiratory airflow to be maintained at a constant value (Cugell, 1986). This consistent expiratory airflow is the desired response for pulmonary patients, providing for a thorough and complete exhalation with a level of positive expiratory pressure for increased clearing of the airways. DC breathing is an important technique in the application of expiratory treatment techniques for patients with pulmonary diseases.

Playing a woodwind instrument involves blowing against a resistive force as demonstrated when blowing into the mouthpiece. Both musical wind instruments and traditional equipment, such as the PEP Mask, Flutter Device, and Inspiratory Muscle Trainer (IMT), use contrasting bore sizes, thus allowing for various levels of resistance. The larger bore-sized instruments (e.g., tuba, euphonium, baritone horn, trombone, baritone saxophone, tenor saxophone, and bass clarinet) may provide less expiratory resistance. Instruments with narrowing bore sizes (e.g., cornet, trumpet, French horn, alto saxophone, alto clarinet, B♭ clarinet, E♭ clarinet, bassoon, English horn, and oboe) may provide a greater resistance.

Expiratory and inspiratory treatments (PEP Mask, Flutter, IMT) are designed to stimulate the expectoration of mucus and excess air in the lungs, possibly increasing Pulmonary Function Tests and achieving a longer period of open airways. Playing a wind instrument also provides an increased air resistance comparable to the PEP Mask, Flutter, and IMT, which aids in the expectoration of mucus. Further, through the use of music vibrato techniques, an oscillating effect is achieved similar to that found in the Flutter Device.

Successful respiratory therapy is related to the amount of time involved in patient intervention and the amount of time the patient takes in following through with the prescribed exercises (Nickerson & Keens, 1982). Music helps to increase the amount of time spent on the treatment, because it provides an interesting form of therapy that will stimulate motivation and thus provide for further health benefits.

Based on the previously cited research, it is possible to infer that some of the problems associated with the identified pulmonary diseases (e.g., increased levels of mucus in the airways, constriction of the airways, and decreased respiration benefits) may improve with the use of an instrumental music intervention. This technique seems to be effective because it allows the patient to take a part in active therapy and to exercise some control over a disabling condition. Like the traditional pulmonary rehabilitation devices, the use of musical wind instruments presents an expiratory treatment technique that demands increased levels of expiratory pressure; this may be used independently and with lesser amount of daily practice.

Clinical Approach

In preparing for working with individuals with a pulmonary disease, music therapists need to understand the underlying symptoms and traditional treatments of each disease and also have an understanding of instrumental pedagogy. Before beginning this type of treatment, clients must be referred by their pulmonologist and be assessed for a previous history of atelectasis (partial collapse of an expanded lung). The music therapist should also establish a relationship with the respiratory therapist and clinical nurse. The patient's prior history should be obtained, and a plan developed for assessing pulmonary function.

Instrument Selection

Appropriate physical characteristics of the subjects must be considered during the instrument selection process based on hand size, lips, presence of teeth, and current pulmonary function. Of primary concern is the instrument of choice. The author advises limiting the initial instrument choices to one of four instruments: clarinet, saxophone, trumpet, and trombone. Flute is not a good initial choice because it mimics pursed lip breathing without the benefit of additional expiratory pressure. All instruments should be new; this is of particular significance for patients who have Cystic Fibrosis because of infection control issues. These patients are especially susceptible to Burkholderia Cepasia and MUST not share instruments or perform on a used instrument.

The reed strength should be at a beginner's level. As the individual progresses, the thickness of the reed should likewise increase. This is one way of adding expiratory pressure without increasing musical expectation.

Breathing and Posture

Both posture and diaphragmatic/costal (DC) breathing must be stressed. The therapist should keep in mind the exact focus of this type of treatment and pay careful attention to back, neck, and head posture, as tension and poor posture may negatively influence airflow. It is helpful to begin with training in DC breathing. The emphasis should be placed on a thorough exhalation followed by a deep and thorough inhalation. By teaching this in a reverse format, the pulmonary impaired individual can begin the inhalation process with a more normalized lung capacity. A helpful way to accomplish this quickly is to have the client lie down on the floor with a telephone book on his or her stomach and practice DC. This limits the amount of upper body movement that can occur while learning this often unfamiliar process. When DC breathing has become somewhat comfortable, long tones exercises may then be practiced. These will allow the client to begin making music and will also provide the therapist with a baseline of the duration of a sustained long tone. In addition to documenting this, the therapist may record the metronome marking used, as well as the note played. The ability to sustain pitches varies from note to note. This information should be shared with clients, so that they may begin self-monitoring their pulmonary progress.

More oxygen and breath support are required when tonguing begins. The music therapist should inform the client of this so he or she can be prepared for the greater breath support and endurance that this musical technique requires. Educating the client about the demands of each new technique will help ameliorate feelings of inadequacy should the new skill take a while to accomplish. Each session should be designed to include warm-ups using long tones and arpeggios; performance of musical selections; and, should the individual become fatigued, relaxation and listening activities to facilitate imitation of a well produced tone.

Intonation is important for clinical purposes and musicality. When the client has an understanding of how to play a pitch correctly, playing flat (not supporting the note with enough breath) and playing sharp (over blowing) can be monitored by the client to determine if maximum effort is being used. Playing a musical wind instrument offers the individual the ability to focus on the task at hand and receive immediate feedback from the music if the technique is being performed correctly. Traditional pulmonary rehabilitation devices do not provide this feedback.

As soon as sufficient musicianship is acquired, the individual may be transitioned into an ensemble (e.g., in the community or school). This provides an opportunity to socialize with people who have similar interests and to increase self-esteem, while also working on pulmonary fitness goals. Children with asthma and Cystic Fibrosis are often excluded from physically demanding activities, and the school wind instrument program is a wonderful alternative for them.

Assessment and Measurement

When developing treatment protocols for these populations, the music therapist needs to consider a variety of monitoring techniques to assess pulmonary function, treatment compliance, quality of life issues, and musical skill development. To this end, the following assessment/evaluation procedures may be useful, and baseline information may often be obtained from the clinical nurse or medical records in most of the nonmusical areas.

Pulmonary Function

- Changes in spirometry measurements from a Pulmonary Function Test (PFT)
- Changes in lung volumes
- The overall progression of the disease as indicated by the PFT, monitoring based on deterioration of lung function from baseline (the goal is to decrease the rate of lung decline)
- The ability of the client to sustain a pitch on an individual instrument (the pitch should be predetermined and based on its ease of execution on each of the instruments; this must remain consistent when measuring progress) with metronome markings kept consistent. This should be assessed monthly.
- The ability/length of time the subject can exhale using pursed lip breathing while the duration is measured (MM = 60). This should be assessed every 3 months.
- Positive expiratory measurement through a manometer reading.

Treatment Compliance Measurements

- The amount of time clients spend using the traditional techniques versus the time spent using the selected musical wind instrument.
- The client's involvement in any performing ensembles.

Quality of Life Measurements

- The number of required hospitalizations.
- The number of infections acquired.
- The amount and type of medications used.
- The length of time that the prescribed treatment needed to be altered due to an acute exacerbation of the disease.
- The number of days missed from either work or school due to illness.

Musical Skill Level Measurements

- The musical maturity of the client monthly based on progress in the method books demonstrating the correct use of DC breathing, posture, thorough exhalation, and musical techniques (phrasing, articulation, dynamics).
- The client's involvement with school or community ensembles and the difficulty of the music being performed.
- The amount of practice time on the instruments.

SUMMARY

The use of instrumental music provides the client with an active role of therapy that allows for increased self-disclosure and an avenue for further discussion between the therapist and the client. Musical instrument intervention stimulates the patient's desire to follow the prescribed course of treatment because of potentially improved respiration as well as success in a performance medium. The music provides a secondary benefit to the primary goal of improved respiratory health.

A unique advantage of this form of music therapy is that both the instrument and the music can be adapted to meet the needs of the patient. Patients who have pulmonary diseases need to learn complete exhalation and successful diaphragmatic breathing. The use of musical wind instruments as an expiratory therapy mimics traditional treatment techniques by providing an increased expiratory resistance. Musical phrasing encourages this and may be altered for gradual extension of exhalation exercises. The goal is to encourage the patient to reach an extended exhalation period, thus permitting thorough emptying of the lungs against an increased expiratory resistance. Long tones and slurred arpeggios are taught initially; expectations are increased to include articulated rhythmic patterns. The use of tonguing on a wind instrument, in addition to providing the client with additional musical selections, also requires more breath support and more thorough exhalation and may increase levels of secretion removal. Tempos of musical selections are flexible and decided by the performer, and this encourages creativity and independence.

In addition to improving respiratory health, the beneficial qualities that music therapy may bring to the pulmonary impaired patient are independence for musical interpretation and self-monitoring behaviors, which encourage improved self esteem; leisure time activities; respiratory fitness; and socialization. The continuity of wind instrument instruction facilitates rehabilitation and provides motivation. Diaphragmatic breathing and proper posture may become habitual as the patient is able to hear a breath-supported sound versus a nonsupported sound. When appropriate posture and breathing are occurring, a fuller and richer musical sound ensues. Thus, the patient receives immediate auditory reinforcement.

Traditional pulmonary treatments may enhance health, but the use of music therapy also influences one's quality of life. A clinical setting is typically one where individuals are reminded of their physical problems. With the implementation of a successful instrumental music program, the environment becomes a more aesthetically attractive setting and a venue for the development of an individual's strengths and creative expression. This indeed can contribute to the patient's overall quality of life.

REFERENCES

Adams, P., & Marano, M. (1995). Current estimates from the National Health Interview Survey. *Vital Health Stat, 10,* 94.

Altose, M. E. (1985). Assessment and management of breathlessness. *Chest, 88*(2), 77s–83s.

Bouhuys, A. (1964). Lung volumes and breathing patterns in wind instrument players. *Journal of Applied Physiology, 19*(6), 967–975.

Cugell, D. (1986). Interaction of chest wall and abdominal muscles in wind instrument players. *Cleveland Clinic Quarterly, 53,* 15–20.

Cunningham, J., & Taussig, L. (1989). *A guide to cystic fibrosis for parents and children.* Tuscon, AZ: Tucson Cystic Fibrosis Center, Pediatric Pulmonary Section, The University of Arizona Health Sciences Center.

Griggs-Drane, E. (1989). *The use of musical wind instruments as an expiratory therapy with chronic obstructive pulmonary disease patients.* Unpublished master's thesis, Western Michigan University, Kalamazoo.

Griggs-Drane, E. R. (1998). *The use of musical wind instruments as an expiratory therapy with cystic fibrosis: A safety study.* Unpublished manuscript.

Konstan, M., Stern, R., & Doershuk, C. (1994). Efficacy of the flutter device for airway mucus clearance in patients with cystic fibrosis. *The Journal of Pediatrics, 124*(5), Pt. I, 689–693.

Lertzman, M., & Cherniack, R. (1976). Rehabilitation in patients with chronic obstructive pulmonary disease. *American Review of Respiratory Disease, 114,* 1145–1165.

Mahlmeister, M., Fink, J., Hoffman, G., & Fifer, L. (1991). Positive-expiratory-pressure mask therapy: Theoretical and practical considerations and a review of the literature. *Respiratory Care, 3,* 1218–1229.

Marks, M. (1974). Musical wind instruments in rehabilitation of asthmatic children. *Annals of Allergy, 33*(6), 313–319.

National Institutes of Health National Heart, Lung, and Blood Institute. (1995). *Pocket Guide for Asthma Management and Prevention* (NIH Publication No. 96-3659B). Rockville, MD.

National Institutes of Health National Heart, Lung, and Blood Institute. (1997). *Guidelines for the Diagnosis and Management of Asthma* (NIH Publication No. 97-4051). Rockville, MD: Expert Panel 2.

Nickerson, B., & Keens, T. (1982). Measuring ventilatory muscle endurance in humans as sustainable inspiratory pressure. *Journal of Applied Physiology, 52,* 768–772.

Pryor, J., Webber, G., Hodson, M., & Batten, J. (1979). Evaluation of the forced expiration technique as an adjunct to postural drainage in treatment of cystic fibrosis. *British Medical Journal, 2,* 417–418.

Rosenburg, S. (1999). Asthma—a very treatable disease. *Pediatric Pulmonary & Asthma Center* [On-line]. Available: www.erols.com/ppac/asthma.htm.

Rossman, C., Waldes, R., Sampson, D., & Newhouse, M. (1982). Effect of chest physiotherapy on the removal of mucus in patients with cystic fibrosis. *American Review of Respiratory Disease, 126,* 131–135.

Sutton, P., Parker, R., Webber, B., Newman, S., Garland, N., Lopez-Vidriero, M., Pavia, D., & Clarke, S. (1983). Assessment of the forced expiration technique, postural drainage and directed coughing in chest physiotherapy. *European Journal of Respiratory Disease, 64,* 62–68.

APPENDIX

Definition of Terms

In order for music therapists to provide treatment for individuals suffering from these pulmonary diseases, it is critical that the following terms be correctly understood.

Asthma: Asthma is defined as "a chronic inflammatory disease of the airways" (Adams & Marano, 1995, p. 1) and affects 14 million individuals and specifically 4.8 million children in the United States alone (Adams & Marano, 1995). The symptoms of asthma are variable. Wheezing is the most commonly discussed symptom; other symptoms include coughing, chest tightness, difficulty breathing, and excessive fatigue (National Institutes of Health National Heart, Lung, and Blood Institute, 1995; Rosenberg, 1999). Symptomatic triggers may include viral infections; environmental, animal or food allergens; exercise; smoke inhalation; and chemical irritants such as cleaning products or perfumes. Usually an asthmatic patient will take maintenance medications to try to keep the symptoms under control. There are a variety of medications used in treating asthmatic patients, most of which are maintenance or immediate bronchodilaters and anti-inflammatory agents. Some individuals will also monitor their progress using a Peak Expiratory Flow Meter, which can be used to assess basic breathing capabilities throughout the day. Physical exercise is encouraged, as well as a normal routine. The goal is to maintain normal activities without asthmatic episodes. The National Institutes of Health National Heart, Lung and Blood Institute (1997) has identified the four categories of asthma for the purpose of diagnosis and treatment. The first level is *Intermittent Asthma,* which is defined as symptoms occurring less than one time a week. *Mild Persistent Asthma* is defined as symptoms occurring one or less times a week but less than one time a day. Moderate Persistent Asthma is identified as daily episodes, which may also impact the patient's affect. The most chronic condition is *Severe Persistent Asthma,* which is defined as continuous symptoms with limited physical activity.

Chronic Obstructive Pulmonary Disease: Chronic Obstructive Pulmonary Disease (COPD) is a major health problem ranking second only to coronary disease as a cause of permanent disability for individuals above 40 years of age (Lertzman & Cherniack, 1976). COPD refers to a condition where the patient has difficulty expelling air from the lungs. There are three diseases that cause COPD: chronic bronchitis, emphysema, and asthma. The most common symptom of COPD patients is dyspnea or breathlessness. Altose (1985) states there are presently no effective methods of treating dyspnea; however, overall conditioning and respiratory muscle performance may be helpful.

When the diaphragmatic muscles fatigue and are no longer able to aid in respiration, a laborious breathing pattern begins. To compensate for the lack of strong diaphragm muscles, many COPD patients rely on accessory and rib cage muscles. Pursed lips breathing is a technique taught to patients with COPD in an attempt to provide the patients with the knowledge to form a continuous resistance level during exhalation through pursed lips. Often individuals will whistle as a result of using the pursed lip breathing technique.

Cystic Fibrosis: CF is a hereditary disorder affecting the exocrine or outward secreting glands. Secretions may plug up ducts and other passageways in the lungs and pancreas and can interfere with vital body functions, such as breathing and digestion (Cunningham & Taussig, 1989). Characteristics of this disease include "recurrent wheezing, persistent cough and excessive mucus, recurrent pneumonia, failure to gain weight, abnormal bowel movements, nasal polyps, and clubbing of the fingers" (Cunningham & Taussig, 1989, p. 14). Interventions that are used in the treatment of CF include medications, airway clearance techniques, and self-care management. Medications for CF include antibiotics to treat the recurring pulmonary infections that are the result of impaired clearance of thick secretions. Bronchodilators are usually administered through nebulizer treatments and mucolytic agents to increase the airway opening, thus assisting with airway clearance. Airway clearance techniques for CF are identified as Chest Physiotherapy or Chest Physical Therapy (Rossman, Waldes, Sampson, & Newhouse, 1982). These methods include Forced Expiration Technique (FET), Postural Drainage (PD), Huff coughing, and chest percussion (Sutton et al., 1983). FET is described as a "technique of forced expirations interspersed with carefully controlled diaphragmatic breathing" (Pryor, Webber, Hodson, & Batten, 1979, p. 417). The key to the effectiveness of this procedure is the patient's ability to use diaphragmatic breathing while performing the FET. PD is defined as a technique that is used to assist with draining the thick mucus out of the small and large airways. Huff coughing is preceded by a period of forced deep breaths with an open mouth to ensure an open glottis followed by coughing. Chest percussion is also typically done during PD. Chest percussion requires either a trained professional or a trained parent who cups his or her hands and repeatedly claps the lung area to dislodge any additional mucus that is not removed through PD. Pursed-lips breathing is also used with individuals with CF. This technique relieves air trapping caused by collapse of unstable airways during expiration (Mahlmeister, Fink, Hoffman, & Fifer, 1991).

The Positive Expiratory Pressure (PEP) Mask and the Flutter device apply an increased level of resistance during expiration, which distends airways and increases the amount of mucus removal from the lungs.

> The Flutter is a hand-held device designed to facilitate clearance of mucus in hyper secretory lung disorders. Exhalation through the Flutter results in oscillations of expiratory pressure and airflow, which vibrate the airway walls (loosening mucus), decrease the collapsibility of the airways, and accelerate airflow, facilitating movement of mucus up the airways. (Konstan, Stern, & Doershuk, 1994, p. 689)

The Flutter differs from the PEP Mask in that it is the oscillations of the ball in the device which loosen mucus, whereas in the PEP Mask, the increased levels of positive expiratory pressure provide the treatment. Both the PEP Mask and Flutter device have been found to require much less time than other treatments.

Forced Expiratory Volume (FEV1): The amount of expired forced air in 1 second.

Functional Residual Capacity (FRC): Volume of gas in lungs at resting expiratory volume.

Hyperinflation: Increased functional residual capacity during quiet breathing. This results in expanded lungs, which requires the COPD patient to force air out during expiration.

Maximal Sustained Ventilatory Capacity (MSVC): Objective measures of respiratory muscle work capacity.

Residual Volume: Volume of gas in lungs at end of maximum expiration.

Total Lung Capacity: Volume of gas in lungs at end of maximal inspiration.

14

A Music Therapy Wellness Model for Illness Prevention

Kay Roskam, PhD, MT-BC
Barbara Reuer, PhD, MT-BC

We live in a world that is beginning to acknowledge the connection between the body and the mind, and research is supporting this connection. Being well is no longer just the opposite of being sick. All people experience a continuum between disease and health throughout life. When this continuum leads away from disease and toward health, often and at least partially, it is a personal choice, made in order to improve the individual's potential. Learning to be healthy is a process—an awareness that, even in the disorientation and dismay of illness, a person can maintain attention to those things, people, sensory stimuli, and moment-to-moment experiences that remember and reinforce wellness.

"Health and disease are not fixed entities; they are concepts used to characterize a process of adapting to the changing demands of life and the changing meanings given to living" (Aldridge, 1996, p. 54). "Remembered wellness" describes the interconnections between mind and body in the process of any recovery. Benson (1996) identified three components of this phenomenon: "(1) Belief and expectancy on the part of the patient, (2) Belief and expectancy on the part of the caregiver, and (3) Belief and expectancies generated by the relationship between the patient and the caregiver" (p. 32).

This conceptual map leads to a holistic event that includes the experiential history of the patient, the experiential history of the caregiver, and the dynamic interaction between the two—a formula that underscores a cooperative belief system in the process of healing.

In addition to the personal striving for health, the so-called "wellness movement" is a powerful societal phenomenon which seems to be embracing beliefs, attitudes, behaviors, and positive interactive experiences that can impact the quality of health. It is not just a clever marketing strategy to increase the profits of a particular product (Belli, 1994). Rather, music-making itself is emerging as a new way of "applying music beyond (passive) entertainment. Instead, active music-making is viewed as an integral component within education, social activities and ultimately wellness. *Put quite simply, music making is inherently good for people*" (Belli, 1996, preface).

The medical model has transitioned into the bio-psycho-social-spiritual model, giving credence to all aspects of a person's needs and systems, i.e., physical, affective, cognitive, and social. The ancient roots and practical implementation of these ideas coexist even today in many non-Western cultures. Now, Americans also seem ready to assume responsibility, both individually and collectively, for wellness as a way of life.

In the world of music therapy, an unprecedented study is currently being completed, exploring the effects of music making on healthy, active older adults. The Music Making and Wellness Project (1999) is a three-phase, multi-year study that grew out of a decade of research conducted at the University of Miami. Under investigation are the effects of music therapy on health and wellness, including a federally funded study demonstrating how active music making positively affected the biology and behavior of Alzheimer's patients. The current project defines wellness as being free of disease, successfully coping with stress, feeling competent, and being in control of one's life—all of this encompassed in a matrix of social support, and available and adequate healthcare. The multidisciplinary team conducting the current project, headed by Dr. Fredrick Tims, measured the effects of music making (specifically group keyboard lessons) on the immune systems of healthy older adults. Their findings show significant increases in the human growth hormone, which is an important factor in maintaining immunity from disease. In addition, there were significant decreases in anxiety, depression, and loneliness for the well elderly people in the experimental group.

During the past 15 years, many large corporations and organizations have developed wellness programs. As an example, Motorola designed and implemented a plan for employees, focusing on providing information and care in seven areas: life and health attitudes, social connectedness, emotional well-being, rest, pleasure and play, purpose and meaning, and self-care. The United States Coast Guard has also introduced a program supporting health and fitness. Dr. Terry Golden, Chief of Clinical Medicine and Wellness for the Coast Guard, has stated that the "bio-psycho-social model represents a paradigm shift from the mechanical/industrial model of reality to the quantum model. . . . If you want to effect health, you have to affect social health. We need to think of the Coast Guard as a family, or a living organism, not just 40,000 individuals working together" (Muir, 1997, p. 7). These are just two examples of large group models incorporating the concept of wellness. The results for these organizations and many others like them are improved employee job satisfaction, reduced absenteeism, and direct dollar savings.

The common thread between individuals and large groups, through all the wellness literature, books, articles, holistic journals, public presentations, and media attention, is quite simple. How can optimal health be promoted, improved, established, and maintained in a world so complex and frenetic as ours? For music therapists, one of the answers is through the use of music.

> Music can and does influence an individual's behavior. The extent of this influence, or the form it may take, remains somewhat enigmatic. We do know that the influence involves a combination of musical and experiential factors. Rhythm—or pulse that is regular or irregular, fast, or slow, changing gradually or changing abruptly—can affect behavior. Increase in dynamic levels, instrumentation, the quality of sound, tonal aspects of music, as well as a myriad of other musical entities can all be responsible for subtle and not so subtle actions and reactions. Over all lie the experiences of a lifetime that make every musical response unique and private. (Roskam, 1993, p. 8)

The profession of music therapy is the conscious application of this knowledge, specifically "a systematic process of intervention wherein the therapist helps the client to promote health, using music experiences and the relationship that develops through them as dynamic forces of change" (Bruscia, 1998, p. 20). The beauty of this definition is that it embraces the complete continuum of wellness and illness, allowing a more inclusive and dynamic meaning of music as therapy.

As music therapists, we are trained to look for and document the nonmusical outcomes, the "dynamic change." Acknowledging nonmusical outcomes is recognizing that the result of a musical experience has gone beyond the aesthetic pleasure involved in the hearing of or the making of music. This subtle awareness of music as pleasure is placed in storage in the limbic system for future reference and is used again and again when the circumstances or mood calls for positive change in feeling or functioning. In other words, the recipient of the therapeutic experience can be any person who has a need that is nonmusical that is fulfilled by music. So the therapeutic benefits of music occur, in a broad sense, anytime someone has a musical experience resulting in their "feeling better" or in functioning in a way that is more satisfying. This seems to be one of the commonalities of being human, that our thoughts and feelings respond in ways that allow us to be comforted, nurtured, stimulated, motivated, saddened, and sometimes even angered by the sounds of music. Often, when a person is initially told of a professional field called music therapy, there is an immediate recognition of the "sense" of it all, for, after all, he or she has been having just this kind of musical involvement for many years.

Farbman (1994) has clearly outlined what music offers for getting well and staying well, even for nonmusicians:

- anxiety and stress reduction
- an outlet for expression of feeling
- nonpharmacological management of pain and discomfort
- structure which promotes physical rehabilitation
- sense of control over life through experiencing success and mastery
- positive changes in mood and emotional states
- memory recall which contributes to reminiscence and life satisfaction
- opportunities to interact socially
- emotional intimacy when spouses and families share creative music experiences.

Schmid (1994), past-president of the Music Educators National Conference (MENC), also reports a growing interest from music educators in music and wellness. This area of clinical practice for music therapists thus is a shared concept, as music educators are also committed to using music to develop well-functioning individuals, creativity, higher levels of self awareness, and growth of self.

As music therapy struggles for recognition as a legitimate and valuable part of the health-care system, it is always invigorating to experience the commitment to music of other professionals, especially members of the medical establishment. Deepak Chopra (1991) chronicles the influence of music in India in his book, *Perfect Health: The Complete Mind/Body Guide.* He addressed a conference for doctors on the clinical uses of Gandharva music. Chopra demonstrated music's effects by asking participants to take the pulse of the person on their right, and then on their left. A woman singer then sang a melody that specifically balanced "Vata - dosha, a stimulating, exhilarating, alert, cheerful, optimistic, and flexible function of the body." The pulses all dropped below normal. After a second quicker melody, the pulses increased again, by a clearly noticeable amount.

Chopra (1991) discusses the interconnectedness of mind and body, through three operating principles called "doshas." He describes these as the basic functions of controlling movement, metabolism, and structure. The body needs all three to be healthy. The Gandharva melody that the woman had sung seemed to manipulate the bodies' responses through sound. Chopra contends that a dosha is balanced by certain tones and disturbed by others. When properly played, Gandharva melodies are said to have universal effects. This kind of therapy forms a standard part of the in-patient programs at Chopra's clinics. He states that there is benefit in playing Gandharva music continuously, even when a person is not in the room. Gandharva "charges the atmosphere with happy vibration" (p. 158), and he believes this effect is possible even when a person lacks the cultural familiarity with the ragas and musical schemas of India.

For music therapists, this kind of information is both reassuring and frustrating. Nowhere in Dr. Chopra's description of music's effects is there any mention of quantitative data. Instead, he talks of the benefit of 10 minutes of Gandharva music "as a gentle wakeup in the morning; after a meal to settle digestion; just before bedtime as an aid to sleep; and during the recovery period when you are sick" (Chopra, 1991, p. 157). Chopra instructs the reader to simply listen, while sitting still with closed eyes, letting his or her attention stay easily on the melody. In other words, try it, and if the participant feels pleasantly refreshed, or able to sleep better, or seems to have fewer digestive problems, the music is working. This is an example of a therapeutic experience that would surely be subject to the belief system mentioned earlier.

On the other hand, data do suggest that music influences endocrine reactions by lowering stress hormone levels. A recent study (Berk, 1997) utilized music combined with beautiful nature scenes and affirmations of wellness with cancer patients. The researchers measured three neuroendocrine stress hormones that interfere with natural healing. All three dropped between 16–20% after the patients viewed the videotape. Several other studies have also concluded that music boosts immune responses (Rider, 1997). If music can produce these results in subjects who are on the disease end of the continuum, it is quite credible that people who are moving toward health can reinforce and increase this movement in a positive manner with music. In one such study with normal adults, it was suggested that sedative music is an effective method for enhancing the immune system (Tsao, Gordon, Dileo-Maranto, Lerman, & Murasko, 1991).

One of the most intriguing theories concerning music and wellness is presented in *The Rhythmic Language of Health and Disease*. Rider (1997), a clinical psychologist and music therapist, postulates physical health benefits from brain wave shifting. This mental shifting is characterized by frequency shifts in electroencephalogram tracings (EEG) and frequent changes in the level of brain functioning. These shifts include thoughts, feelings, perceptions of connectedness, and electrochemical changes measured on the skin surface. Rider (1997) explains that

> The brain likes to shift cerebral hemispheres back and forth about every 90 minutes. If continuous activity is engaged in with only one hemisphere, then health problems usually ensue. For example, if you spend an entire workday in primarily one type of activity (whether it is making calculations, painting, or making managerial decisions) you will

> probably have a headache by the end of the day. In other words, stress can be caused by too much homeostasis. (p. 2)

Rider (1997) asserts three conclusions from his work:

1. People who demonstrate frequent shifts of brain wave patterns seem to also exhibit strengthened immunity.
2. People who tend to be low in shifting, meaning exhibit stasis in mood such as depression, also have compromised immune systems.
3. It seems that brain wave shifts are responsible for accelerating ions in the human system, one aspect of functioning which allows us to think more clearly and defend ourselves through a heightened immune system.

Rider contends that music, as no other human behavior, can totally engage the brain in eliciting these homeodynamic shifts. In one study, live music elicited as high of an immunological boost in one session as recorded music accomplished in 6 weeks (Rider & Weldin, 1990).

The fact that music has the power to create such changes is due in great part to the importance of the auditory system in survival of the species. There is no way to close the ear or to mitigate sound. The human ear can hear 1,378 different tones within the vibratory range of 16–25,000 Hz. Of all the senses, hearing is the response provider for newborn and unborn babies. Hearing is also the one sense that seems most resistant to habituation, so repetition has less effect on shifting brain waves. Music has retained its evolutionary capability for profoundly affecting an individual physically and emotionally.

Rider (1997) categorizes music as the most important aspect of emotion shifting. He identifies five mechanisms involved in the promotion of physical healing:

> The first, and perhaps most prolifically studied level is the limbic, or emotional, response to music. Second, music elicits fantasy, thought, and imagery, and consequently, this level is the cortical, or cognitive response to music. Next, there is the thalamic response in which musical rhythms entrain rhythmic movements within the body. A newer area of research pertains to the direct stimulation by sound of peripheral and cutaneous nerves. Finally, group music-making involves spiritual, or psychosocial mechanism, which play a major role in health maintenance. Entrainment is undoubtedly involved in the first three levels, but research on the latter two has only scratched the surface. (p. 96)

Rider also reinforces what music therapists know and use—that familiarity and preference also allow the shifting of brain wave patterns more readily than music that does not fall into these categories.

Sacks (1995), lending support from the medical community, eloquently described the power of music in an interview with Clayton Collins (1994). Sacks stated that "the key is for patients to learn to be well again. Music can restore to them the identity that predates the illness. There's a health to music, a life to music" (p. 41). Sacks gave an example of a young amnesiac patient experiencing "remembered wellness" through music:

> I had heard, from the hospital social worker, that he had a passion for music, especially for rock-and-roll bands of the sixties; I saw piles of records as soon as I entered his room and a guitar lying against his bed. So now I asked him about this, and with this there came

> a complete transformation—he lost his disconnectedness, his indifference, and spoke with great animation about his favorite rock bands and pieces—above all, of the Grateful Dead. "I went to see them at the Fillmore East, and in Central Park," he said. He remembered the entire program in detail, but "my favorite," he added, "is 'Tobacco Road.'" The title evoked the tune, and Greg sang the whole song with great feeling and conviction—a depth of feeling of which, hitherto, he had not shown the least sign. He seemed transformed, a different person, a whole person, as he sang. (p. 47)

The wellness movement is a shift in paradigms, moving control from health professionals to individuals themselves. People want to be well and to stay well. It is becoming increasingly clear that active music making and well chosen music for listening can be strong components for health and wellness. Early detection of potential health problems can mean living life so you don't get the problem. Society is doing more and more self-care/guided care. We have known for some time that good nutrition, appropriate physical exercise, attitude, and stress management are components of wellness. In addition, research indicates that people perceive themselves as healthier when they "belong" and continue to engage socially, especially as they age. Active music making programs for older adults have shown that music facilitates and helps to maintain feelings of relaxation. Music promotes and directs cognitive activity, emotional expression and communication, and management of moods. Music is, and has always been, a natural and spontaneous way to provide community, uniting people of all ages and ethnic groups, and making significant contributions to rendering life worth living.

Music therapists in the American Music Therapy Association have begun the process of including wellness as a category in their *Standards of Clinical Practice*. At this date, the standard is identified as:

> the specialized use of music to enhance the quality of life, maximize well-being and potential, and increase self-awareness in individuals seeking music therapy services. Assessment in this practice area may be informal in nature as agreed upon by the music therapist and the client, and programming will be based on a mutual agreement for services. (AMTA, 1999)

Though music therapists are well aware of the benefits of music therapy interventions with a broad range of clients, little formal use of specific music therapy techniques and strategies has taken place with well populations (Reuer & Crowe, 1995). The potential for expanding music therapy strategies for people who are coming into the therapy process to improve quality of life is great. The Rhythm for Life (RFL) model, developed out of an Administration on Aging funded-grant at the San Diego State University Center on Aging, is a model that implements the aforementioned standard.

The percussion and rhythm sessions were divided into four components to offer all participants a wide variety of experiences. These components were:

1. WARM-UP (Sharing)

   The first component served as a means to bring the group together. It is very important to offer these types of "ice-breaker" activities to encourage and build a feeling of trust within the group. The goals were to:

   - encourage social interaction in a structured environment.

- provide an alternative means of social interaction.
- provide opportunity for individual choice within the group.
- improve concentration.
- offer opportunity for reinforcing short-term memory.

2. GROUP FOCUS (Community and/or Team Building)
   The second component consisted of activities designed to help participants become focused, while at the same time developing a greater awareness of the group. Many of these activities were basic rhythm warm-up exercises or simple relaxation techniques, which encouraged participants to feel a basic pulse with their whole body. The goals were to:
   - provide participants with alternative strategies for dealing with stress.
   - improve attention span.
   - provide opportunity for increased body awareness.
3. RHYTHM/DRUMMING ACTIVITIES (Working on Skill Development)
   These activities involved basic team-building exercises combined with percussive skill development and basic ethnomusicological information. The goals were to:
   - encourage feelings of self-worth through the process of creating something meaningful.
   - encourage feelings of self-worth via the process of learning a new skill.
   - encourage participants to spontaneously interact with others.
   - encourage self-expression.
   - maintain visual/motor skills and prevent deterioration of muscle tone.
   - provide opportunities for individual choice within the group.
   - provide opportunities for participants to work cooperatively with others.
   - improve concentration and increase attention span.
   - offer opportunity for reinforcing short/long-term memory.
   - develop interest in music as a redirection of leisure time.
   - learn (relearn) to enjoy music and movement simply for its own inherent qualities.
   - have fun.
4. CLOSURE
   The final section served as a means for the group leader to say good-bye to the participants and helped to frame the group experience by ending with a structured activity. (Reuer & Crowe, 1995, pp. 20–21)

The RFL model, developed for group work, can be adapted to meet individual needs throughout the lifespan on the continuum between disease and health. For music to be used for wellness, it must be purposefully chosen and applied. Krout (1996) reports using these Rhythm for Life wellness techniques with his college students, as well as his subsequent excitement when he observed the students adapting these musical experiences to a variety of child, adolescent, adult, and senior populations, all of whom were clinical challenges.

The theory of music as a tool for therapeutic change begins with an innate response to rhythm. This theory is well demonstrated in the model cited. Every person's response to rhythm is expanded through life experience and by the relationships one builds throughout life.

This model can be utilized and expanded to include various music therapy clinical approaches, e.g., song writing, improvisation, GIM, lyric analysis, etc. Potential populations are many. Music wellness programs can be used for staff support and/or team building at hospitals, schools, and corporations; one can find music wellness programs in senior centers, retirement communities, churches, early childhood programs, assisted childbirth classes, integrated health care offices and programs, stress management programs, and the list goes on. These programs may need to be adapted to the ages, cultural backgrounds, and preferences of clients. However, music therapists have been "adapting" since the inception of the profession. That—if we are successful—is what we do best.

When the seeds of positive behavior patterns can be established through musical experiences such as these, the ultimate goal of therapy has been achieved. When intellect, interest, skill, and feeling become positively channeled into pleasurable sound, the intervention is considered successful. When the love of sound connects positively with the love for oneself, with one's family and friends, and with the larger community, then music has functioned as a therapeutic process (Roskam, 1993, p. 65).

The real change comes in including the new clinical population—the well—into our practices. Wellness is the integration of body, mind, and spirit, with an understanding and acknowledgment of this interconnectedness. It is writing a song about "being me" with "things that I would change and things that I hold dear." It is working with an intergenerational bell choir. It is leading a drum circle of employees for a large corporation. It is about changing behavior. It is about having no identified problem, but still getting better. It is about expressing oneself with a joyful noise. It is about music.

References

Aldridge, D. (1996). Notes on the phenomenon of "becoming healthy": Body, identity, and lifestyle. *Advances in Mind-Body Medicine, 12*(1) 51–58.

American Music Therapy Association (AMTA). (1999, January 24). AMTA Standards of Clinical Practice [Draft].

Belli, R. (1994). A view from the music industry: Music therapists as partners. *Music Therapy Perspectives, 14*(1), 5–6.

Belli, R. (1996). *Think drums* [Guest Editorial]. North Hollywood, CA: Remo, Inc.

Benson, H. (1996). *Timeless healing: The power and biology of belief.* New York: Fireside.

Berk, L. (1997, April 14). Research uses of music to ease cancer pain. *The San Bernardino County Sun.*

Bruscia, K. (1998). *Defining music therapy* (2nd ed). Spring City, PA: Barcelona.

Chopra, D. (1991). *Perfect health: The complete mind/body guide.* New York: Harmony Books.

Collins, C. (1994, February). Doctor of the soul. *Profiles.*

Farbman, A. (1994, September). Music therapy and the music products industry: An alliance whose time has come. *Think Drums.* North Hollywood, CA: Remo, Inc.

Krout, R. (1996, March). Enhancing the beat: Creative percussion-based application in music education university curriculum. *Think Drums.* North Hollywood, CA: Remo, Inc.

Muir, M. (1997, February). Enlightened self-interest: Corporate wellness programs find a new paradigm. *Alternative & Complementary Therapies, 3*(1), 6–12.

Music Making & Wellness Project (in progress). University of Miami.

Reuer, B., & Crowe, B. (1995). *Best practices in music therapy: Utilizing group percussion strategies for promoting volunteerism in the well older adult.* San Diego, CA: San Diego State University Center on Aging.

Rider, M. (1997). *The rhythmic language of health and disease*. St. Louis: MMB.

Rider, M., & Weldin, C. (1990). Imagery, improvisation and immunity. *The Arts in Psychotherapy, 17*, 211–216.

Roskam, K. (1993). *Feeling the sound: The influence of music on behavior*. San Francisco: San Francisco Press.

Sacks, O. (1995). *An anthropologist on Mars*. New York: Vintage Books.

Schmid, W. (1994, October). New drumming markets in music education. *Think Drums.* North Hollywood, CA: Remo, Inc.

Tsao, C. C., Gordon, T. F., Dileo-Maranto, C., Lerman, C., & Murasko, D. (1991). The effects of music and biological imagery on immune response (S-IgA). In C. Dileo-Maranto (Ed.), *Applications of music in medicine* (pp. 85–121). Washington, DC: National Association for Music Therapy, Inc.

Part III:
Song Approaches

15

SONGS FOR LIVING: THE USE OF SONGS IN THE TREATMENT OF ONCOLOGY PATIENTS

Cheryl Dileo, PhD, MT-BC

> The dark labyrinth of life does not have a simple escape route. Each juncture of the journey presents a choice, a turning point; whether to split ourselves off from our own experience, or make what is happening, horrific though it may be, part of our larger process of Becoming. For if we fully inhabit our life when it is both most painfully constricted and paradoxically frought with potential—if, even as our feet carry us into the maze, we can proceed with our eyes open rather than squeezed shut—we will inevitably discern a path of creative response. (Barasch, 1993, p. 16)

THE PURPOSE OF THIS CHAPTER is to describe stages of a potential music therapy process, from a mind-body-spirit perspective, with patients who have cancer. The rationale for the specific stages described is drawn from the current literature in behavioral medicine that emphasizes this model of illness and healing. Also, examples of music therapy interventions relying primarily on the use of songs are provided. In addition, some critical components of the therapeutic relationship and therapist are mentioned.

CLINICAL NEEDS AND THEORETICAL APPROACH

Anyone who has been fortunate enough never to have heard a physician say "You have cancer" cannot fathom the terror, isolation, shock, and anxiety that these words summon. Lerner likens it to "being pushed out of a helicopter into a jungle war without any training, any familiarity with the terrain, or any sense of how to survive" (Dienstfrey, 1994, p. 28). Further, Spiegel (1991) states: "Cancer seems to evoke a unique fear in patients. It frightens patients in a way that goes beyond the fear of mortality, and patients who suffer from cancer and its attendant dread need a special degree of understanding to help them cope with it" (p. 12).

Cancer affects all aspects of the individual. Physically, the individual is weakened, may be in pain, and is at the mercy of an unpredictable and savage internal invader that threatens his or her survival. Emotionally, the individual has become a "victim" of this invader, is often depressed, and may be struggling desperately to identify the emotional resources to cope or, perhaps, may use all these resources to deny the disease. Cognitively, the individual is trying to take in all the medical information, understand and process it, and make life-hinging decisions about treatment. Socially, all of the individual's relationship are called into question and tested; the person experiences extreme isolation Spiritually, the person may interpret the meaning of cancer in many ways, for example, as a punishment from God, as a lesson one must learn, as a retribution for "unacceptable" behavior, etc. The meaning of life, in the face of death, beckons contemplation. Cancer affects and may fragment the individual's identity on all of these levels.

It can be theorized as well that cancer occurs as a result of a combination of many factors: *physical*—genetic predisposition, lifestyle, environmental toxins; *emotional*—suppressed emotions, hopelessness, early traumas; *cognitive*—explanatory style; *social*—isolation, lack of close relationships; and *spiritual*—lack of purpose in life. Several of these areas will be discussed in more detail later in the chapter. Obviously, it is important to identify the role these factors play in increasing susceptibility to cancer insofar as prevention is concerned.

Embracing a bio-psycho-social-spiritual etiological model of cancer implies several issues for treatment/healing for the individual:

1. A fragmented identity on any of these levels may contribute to, as well as result from, cancer.
2. These factors are interrelated in the individual in terms of etiology and treatment.
3. An overriding goal of treatment is to help the individual "re-member" the dismembered/fragmented parts to achieve wholeness, and this whole identity will allow the individual to live fully "through" the illness.
4. Healing and the achievement of wholeness come from within the individual.
5. As no person experiences cancer in the same way, all treatment must be patient-centered.
6. Healing cannot be equated with curing the illness, as healing may or may not imply a cure for the disease.

It is also extremely important to stress that this etiological view of cancer should not be used to blame or hold responsible the cancer patient for his illness, as has been the unfortunate case in some recent writings. Rather, cancer can be viewed as an opening for needed "re-membering" an identity to occur on any or all of these levels.

Clinical Approach

Songs represents one method, but certainly not the only one, in working with cancer patients. However, various uses of songs are particularly appropriate within a bio-psycho-social-spiritual model for the following reasons:

1. Songs accompany us through our lives and often become associated with various difficult life events. Songs then become tools for recall and re-experiencing those events that may be relevant to a therapeutic process and, at the same time, provide resources for resolving conflicts.
2. Because of their emotional and social contexts, songs deliver important messages and meanings for life with which individuals readily identify. Because of these contexts, these messages and meanings are often considered "truths."

3. Songs are capable of influencing all aspects of the individual simultaneously, i.e., physical, emotional, cognitive, social, and spiritual.

4. Songs are capable of being experienced in both active and receptive ways, thereby overcoming various resistances to either approach, and also accommodating a range of physically-limiting medical conditions.

5. Song experiences provide opportunities for creativity and self-expression within forms that are accessible and familiar; the traditional song forms (e.g., strophic, verse and refrain, through-composed, call and response, blues, etc.) can be used according to the needs of the client.

6. Sharing songs facilitates intimacy, interpersonal connections, and reductions in perceived isolation.

7. Song lyrics allow individuals to safely project their own feelings onto the music and the composer's words, particularly in those individuals who have difficulty with emotional expression. Songs, therefore, provide opportunities for meaningful assessment and subsequent treatment.

8. Songs stimulate intrapersonal communication by bringing awareness of and insight into one's own feelings and thoughts.

9. Songs are capable of integrating apparent polarities, such as thinking and feeling, being and doing, giving and receiving, etc.

10. Songs can provide a means of communicating information, new ideas, and new ways of thinking, thereby enhancing decision-making.

11. Words and meanings, important for change in the individual, take on more significance because of the emotional intensity of the music.

12. Songs provide a mechanism for examining and reinforcing an individual's spiritual life.

13. Songs provide a means for individuals to tell the stories of their lives and illness.

14. Songs allow opportunities for individuals to listen to the message/wisdom of the illness.

15. Songs can enhance feelings of hope, joy, satisfaction, and triumph.

Bruscia (1989), in summarizing the role of songs, states:

> Songs are our connections to life. They connect us to our inner world; they bring us closer to others; they keep us company when we are alone. They articulate our beliefs and reaffirm our values. They arouse, they accompany, and they release. And as the years pass, our songs bear witness to our lives and give voice to our experiences. They rekindle the past, reflect the present, and project the future. Songs weave tales of our joys and sorrows; they express our dreams and disappointments, our fears and triumphs. They are our musical diaries, our life stories. They are the sounds of our development. (p. 1)

Because each patient experiences cancer in a unique way (thereby necessitating a patient-centered approach), it seems contradictory to describe a "typical" music therapy process! Indeed, the music therapy process that unfolds with each patient will be truly unique. This reality notwithstanding, generalities of this process are described in the following sections of this chapter in a somewhat generic fashion. Implicit in this is the realization that some stages of this process may be relevant to individuals with certain types of needs, and not others; the order of these stages, depending on their relevance, will indeed vary for each patient. Also, working through each of the various stages may constitute a process in and of itself. These stages then represent a broad range of some of the clinical possibilities. The goals for and issues addressed in each stage are based on the bio-psycho-social-spiritual variables associated with healing as identified in the clinical and research literature.

ASSESSMENT: CONCEPTUALIZING HEALTH

> Only metaphor can express the bafflement, the panic, combined with the beatitude of the threatened person. (Broyard, 1992)

Assessment is an extremely important part of the therapeutic process, as the patient's view or conceptualization of his or her health is a significant factor in both predisposition to illness as well as the course of illness. Research has indicated that the concept of our own health has more accurate predictive value than other more objective measures, such as physical symptoms, laboratory tests, or health-related behaviors (Idler & Kasl, 1991).

In addition, personality factors and coping styles are significant factors in health, and those found to be related to health, specific illnesses, and survival/recovery from cancer should be assessed at the beginning of treatment. Recent research has suggested a personality profile, the "Type C" personality, that has been correlated with cancer (Temoshok & Dreher, 1992). A person fitting this profile (a) is overwhelmed by emotions that are unexpressed, unresolved, and repressed; (b) has high social desirability and a strong desire to please others; (c) is self-sacrificing; (d) experiences loneliness, hopelessness, and the ability to cope; and (e) has less than satisfactory interpersonal relationships, including a lack of closeness with his or her parents (Hafen, Karren, Frandsen, & Smith, 1996).

Other important personality factors and coping styles related to health and illness in general include (a) explanatory style, (b) locus of control, and (c) self-esteem. *Optimistic and pessimistic explanatory styles* are potent predictors of health and influence immunity, the time it takes for healing, survival time, as well as the course of the illness. Explanatory style refers to the ways that individuals explain the negative events in their lives.

> Optimists see the causes of such events as temporary, limited to the present case, and the result of circumstances, bad luck, or other people's actions. A pessimist sees success at work, in love, or in friendship as due to luck; an optimist as due to his or her own efforts and skill. (Hafen et al., 1996, pp. 463–464)

Locus of control refers to the beliefs of the patient regarding his or her ability to master the environment. Individuals with an external locus of control believe that the things that happen in their lives are externally imposed and unrelated to what they do. Patients with an internal locus of control attribute life events to their own actions. Locus of control is associated with the biochemical balance in the body, influencing the release or nonrelease of serotonin (regulating moods and pain); dopamine (associated with feelings of pleasure); and norepinephrine (when depleted, associated with depression); as well as immune response. Some researchers believe that locus of control has a stronger influence on health than stress (Hafen et al., 1996).

Self-esteem refers to the positive regard the individual has for him or herself. Individuals with high levels of self-esteem are compassionate and have the confidence to exert control over their life's circumstances. On the other hand, individuals with low self-esteem are more apt to view themselves as passive victims and are more susceptible to stress and illness. (Hafen et al., 1996).

Similarly, researchers have identified personality variables that are associated with general health and well-being (Hafen et al., 1996), including (a) empowerment and control, (b) connectedness and acceptance, (c) meaning and purpose in life, and (d) hope. A sense of *empowerment and personal control* implies "control over one's responses, not necessarily over the environment, the ability to live by one's deepest values (integrity), and feeling heard and valued" (Hafen et al., 1996, p. 588). Healthy individuals experience "a sense of *connectedness and acceptance* to one's deepest self, to other people, to the earth and the cosmos, and to all regarded as good, and to the source of one's spiritual strength" (Hafen et al., 1996, p. 588). The sense of *meaning and purpose* implies "giving of self for a purpose of value; a caring sense of mission, finding meaning and wisdom in here-and-now difficulties, enjoying the process of growth, and having a vision of one's potential" (Hafen et al., 1996, p. 588). *Hope* implies "positive expectation and the ability to envision what one wants before it happens" (Hafen et al., 1996, p. 588). With this information in mind, music therapy assessment attempts to identify how the patient views his or her own health, what is "well" with the patient, what is in need of healing, and the patient's coping style and personality variables (mentioned above) that have contributed to the illness and which may optimize recovery.

Diagnostic song choice is an assessment tool in which the patient identifies those songs or particular lyrics from songs that best represent his feelings, attitudes, and coping style with regard to his or her illness. This can be accomplished in several ways: (a) by asking the patient to spontaneously sing songs and/or particular lyrics in response to directed "identity"questions from the therapist, such as "What song best describes your health?" "What song describes how you are dealing with your illness?"; (b) by providing a list of songs and/or lyrics that may suggest different representations of feelings, attitudes, etc., and by asking the patient to select from among them in response to designated questions; or (c) by having the patient listen to various songs and/or lyrics performed by the therapist and beginning a discussion of how closely the patient identifies with any of the lyrics. In implementing one or more of these options, certain themes often emerge that are useful in assessing the status of the patient with regard to any of the aforementioned factors.

The therapist may also use song discussion in a metaphoric way, focusing on the elements of music in the songs as the basis for discussion, such as rhythm (a metaphor for structure and hope), dynamics (a metaphor for control and power), melody (a metaphor for meaning and feeling), and harmony (a metaphor for social relationships) (Decker-Voigt, 1997). After listening to carefully chosen songs in which one or more of these elements is portrayed in a salient way, the therapist may pose such questions as:

- How are you experiencing the rhythm of your life, and does the illness influence this rhythm? What causes joy, sadness, longing in your life's structure? (Rhythm)
- How do you experience your own control and power with regard to your illness? Is your power internal or external to you? What causes joy, sadness, and longing with regard to your perceived control/power in your illness? (Dynamics)
- How do you experience meaning and feeling in your life with regard to your illness? What is causing sadness, joy, and longing with regard to the meaning of your life? (Melody)
- How do you experience being with others when you are ill? What causes joy, sadness, and longing when you are with others? (Harmony)

Another use of songs in assessment is the identification of a patient's "theme song" with regard to the illness, that is, a song that summarizes the patient's identity on one or more levels—physical, cognitive, emotional, etc.

Of course, other methods of music therapy assessment, such as free or structured improvisations (e.g., to identify those parts of the body's music that are well or are in need of healing) are also invaluable sources of information about the patient and may be used in addition to other nonmusical sources of information.

Coping With Anxiety and Pain

> . . . entering the person's illness (for) looking around inside his pathology for suggestions about how the sick man can cope, how he can live parallel to, or even through, his disability. (Broyard, 1992, in describing the genius of Oliver Sacks)

Cancer patients inevitably need strategies (besides those that are pharmacological) to deal with the pain and anxiety of their illness and the medical procedures they must undergo. At this stage of the treatment process, a variety of music-based anxiety- and pain-reducing strategies are used to provide the patient with coping mechanisms. These strategies are seen as palliative and do not involve in-depth work with the patient. (At a later stage in treatment, the patient and therapist may implement a music entrainment process.) It is clear that more comprehensive work cannot be undertaken when pain and anxiety problems interfere with the ability to participate in a process. Therefore, these goals are usually addressed at the beginning of treatment.

A number of music-therapy-based interventions are relevant to treating the symptoms of anxiety and pain and have been demonstrated through research to be effective (Dileo, 1997a; Dileo-Maranto 1993a, 1993b, 1995, 1996b). These include the following receptive strategies: music-based biofeedback, vibroacoustic therapy, and other techniques combining music with progressive muscle relaxation, autogenic training, integrative breathing, meditation, self-hypnosis, systematic desensitization, and imagery. In addition, active strategies such as toning, chanting, and singing pre-composed songs may be also be used according to the needs and preferences of the patient. These receptive and active techniques serve to regulate breathing, provide a distraction, improve mood, enhance immunity, facilitate time-compression, etc. At this stage, music serves as a source of nourishment for the difficulties of the illness and assists in providing a more cohesive physical identity. It also helps in strengthening an internal locus of control, thereby enhancing feelings of empowerment.

Detoxifying Illness and Death

> Just as a novelist turns his anxiety into a story in order to be able to control it to a degree, so a sick person can make a story, a narrative out of his illness as a way of trying to detoxify it. (Broyard, 1992)

Spiegel, Bloom, Kraemer, and Gottheil (1989) and Spiegel (1991) describe the biopsychosocial benefits of group work in patients with metastatic breast cancer. The interventions used in the study were shown to double the survival time for this disease. The notion of detoxifying death, one strategy used, involved directly addressing fears related to dying by breaking them down into smaller issues that could be addressed more readily, such as pain, chemotherapy and radiation, loss of physical abilities and functions, etc.

At this stage in the process, song discussion may be used with the goal of identifying, confronting, discussing, and providing resolution to some of these "smaller" issues. This stage is a continuation of the previous one, in that all of the palliative techniques mastered can be drawn upon as resources in facing these issues.

In addition, other types of psychological and cognitive coping strategies can be acquired through song lyric analysis and song regression strategies. Songs and lyrics selected for discussion may include various models of coping or noncoping that can used to stimulate the patient's awareness of him or herself. Of relevance to the cancer patient are those models that reinforce empowerment, optimism, and self-esteem. Using song regression, the therapist can ask the client to return imaginally to a period of his or her life before the illness and to listen to a song that represents his or her identity at that time (Bruscia, 1989). Previous personal characteristics (sometimes aspects of the fragmented parts of the self) are distinguished and discussed as possible means for coping in the present.

ACTIVATING BELIEF: INSPIRING HOPE

> If I can believe that this might work or that what I am doing matters, I can endure it. If I can believe that this might work, it may in fact make it so. (Bolen, 1996)

What we know from the literature is that coping style, particularly with regard to life-threatening illnesses, can be significantly related to survival. The coping styles most often associated with long-term survival of cancer are fighting spirit and positive avoidance (denial). Dysphoric states, such as stoic acceptance and hopelessness/helplessness, most often limit survival (Hafen et al., 1996) (Figure 1).

An important aspect of the treatment process concerns the activation of the patient's belief system with regard to his or life and treatment. As coping strategies are again emphasized in this stage, music therapy is used to engage and support hope as part of the patient's belief system. Also, at this stage, there is an emphasis on creating the space for positive things to happen or transform, i.e., integration of the various fragmentations of the self.

Song-writing experiences based on individual self-affirmations created by each patient are often used at this stage. Affirmations are used to counteract critical and judgmental thoughts concerning the individual's identity and attitudes that often involve self-blame for illness (Bolen, 1996). These self-affirmations are then set to music that the patient creates. Alternately, lyrics are created and set to pre-existing songs that are meaningful for the individual. The music provides the emotional component needed to engage the person in his or her affirmations. The emotion-colored message is passed to all parts of the self. The process of creating musical self-affirmation is affirming in itself.

FACTORS PROMOTING SURVIVAL FROM CANCER

Social support
Personal attitude
Spirituality
Individual/Group therapy

Specific coping styles
- Determined fighters
- Attitudinally/Behaviorally focused
- Spiritually/Existentially oriented

Existential reorganization
New values and behaviors
Joy
Emotional hardiness
Quality of life
Lack of cooperation/pleasantness

FACTORS IMPAIRING SURVIVAL FROM CANCER

Helplessness/Hopelessness
Lack of fighting spirit
Fatigue/Passivity
Nonexpression of emotion
Negative states
Anger, anxiety, distress, depression

Figure 1. Factors Promoting and Impairing Survival From Cancer.

CREATING HEALTH USING THE IMAGINATION

I have to take my imagery along with my medicine. (Broyard, 1992)

This stage of the process may come at any time during the treatment process, depending on the needs and readiness of the patient. In this stage, the imagination is accessed to allow the patient to create a new vision of his or her own health, acknowledging and balancing his healthy parts with his ill parts. Some examples of how this may occur using a variety of music therapy experiences follow.

Receptive music and imagery experiences may be used to support dialogues between the healthy and ill parts of the individual, thereby gaining insight into why the disease is there and its function in the person's life. Receptive music and imagery experiences, as well as Guided Imagery and Music may be used to facilitate the patient's contact with his or her own "inner healing resources." Receptive music experience may also support "directed visualizations" (Dileo-Maranto, 1993a), in which the music facilitates imagery directed at specific bodily changes, e.g., enhancing the immune system's fight against the disease.

Musical improvisations may be used for a similar purpose, giving a voice to the music of the body, including the parts that are ill and healthy, and to the messages for the patient that these parts and the body as an entity may hold. Musical improvisations may further serve the purpose of integrating the well and sick parts of the body and finding a balance between these parts.

Song-writing may give voice to the musical sounds of the illness, with musical messages from and to the patient.

Doing Versus Being

> God grant me the serenity to accept the things I cannot change,
> The courage to change the things I can,
> And the wisdom to know the difference. (Serenity Prayer)

In light of the information given in previous sections concerning the influence of various factors on coping and survival from illness (hope, fighting spirit, etc.), patients with cancer face an important paradox: in order to learn to take charge and control, they must also learn how to surrender and let go, which is in essence the conflict between doing and being. Doing implies changing what needs to be changed, that is, making the present and self better, striving for what can be. Being, on the other hand, implies accepting, trusting, and embracing the present, allowing what is. Identifying the right balance, "between doing and being, controlling and allowing, resisting and opening, fighting and surrendering, willing and accepting . . . and between the will to live and the acceptance of death" (Wilber, 1993, p. 62) is a major task of the patient.

The contrasting experiences of active versus passive song participation (listening versus singing/composing) can provide opportunities for patients to discover their typical and/or current "doing" versus "being" patterns of life, particularly with regard to their illness and relationships. Feelings and needs are associated with such polarizations, for example, patterns of taking charge of changing all aspects of their illness versus selectively focusing on changes that are within their power to change, or patterns of taking care of others versus taking care of themselves, etc. The metaphors of how they allow themselves to either control or "be" with the music, the therapist and the group often provide important starting points for conscious decision-making, self-awareness, and distinguishing of parts of their identities that can be either accepted and embraced or changed.

Songs, Stories and Feelings of Life

> People who are ill can make an art form of their illness. . . . I would advise every sick person to evolve a style or develop a voice for his or her illness. When you're ill, you instinctively fear a diminishment and disfigurement of yourself. It's that, more than dying, that frightens you. I think you have to develop a style when you're ill to keep from falling out of love with yourself. . . . That's known as the will to live. . . . I'd like to suggest, to invent or imagine or recall, ways of keeping one's desire alive as a way of keeping one's self alive. . . . Always in emergencies we invent stories. We describe what is happening as if to confine the catastrophe. The patient's narrative keeps him from

> falling out of his life and into his illness. Like a great novelist, he gives his anxiety a shape. (Broyard, 1992, pp. 27, 63)

The inability to express or resolve feelings is reported to be associated with the susceptibility to as well as survival from cancer. Thus, the facilitation and support of emotional expression is a critical component of the music therapy process.

> Emotions are neither positive nor negative, but rather innate psychobiological signals that serve as sources of information for the (psychologically aware) individual. . . . In response to illness, each emotion provides specific psychobiological information as part of a process of core psychological growth with parallel physiologic changes. (Dafter, 1996, p. 6)

In this model, each emotion reflects specific "states of autonomic activity and physiological functioning" (Dafter, 1996, p. 6). The expression of a gamut of emotions is thus supported in the music therapy experiences at this stage of the process. The musical structures provided assist the patient in nonverbal expression, which then may lead to catharsis, insight, and integration.

Metaphoric and theme-based referential musical improvisations often create the starting structure for identification and nonverbal expression of emotions. For example, metaphors and themes that involve expressing musically those parts of the patient that are hidden or unavailable may lead to awareness and expression.

Following this exploration, the patient is encouraged to create his or her own life's narrative through song, i.e., a musical song-biography (Bruscia, 1998). With specific structure provided by the therapist or group, the patient selects songs that represent significant times, events, and relationships of the past, including the onset of the illness, as well as specific themes that are essential to the process of integrating or "re-membering" identity. Besides songs that represent biographical milestones and relationships, such as infancy, childhood, mother, father, significant love relationships, dreams for the future, etc., examples of songs that may also be included in this narrative, are those that represent a deep loss, secret longings, experiences of intimacy, health, and being fully alive. These songs are taped and presented to the therapist and/or group. The patient weaves these songs into his or her own personal narrative and is encouraged to re-experience the feelings associated with these events and relationships. Inevitably, very deep, personal emotions are evoked. To assist the patient in going more deeply into these feelings, free and theme-based musical improvisations may be created spontaneously. Themes of these improvisations often involve how the patient is experiencing living with, living against, or living through the illness. The patient is supported in both confronting and embracing these feelings as part of his or her identity.

Finding Love, Intimacy and Resonance

> The patient needs empathic witnessing. The patient is always on the brink of revelation. . . . What a critically ill person needs most is to be understood. Dying is a misunderstanding; you have to get it straightened out before you go. And you can't be understood until (people) know with an intimate knowledge what your illness is like. (Broyard, 1992)

Spiegel (1993) explains his life-extending, group support strategies (upon which these stages are based in part) as follows. By encouraging patients to confront death and the realities of their illness, their lives were not shortened but lengthened. When people address their mortality and make thoughtful decisions about how they want to live, it can perhaps affect them on a biological level. He also attributes the influence of social support as significant. Being together is a response to the threat of not being. Social support appears to buffer adverse effects to physiology. It is possible to understand what life means when we contemplate death or nonexistence.

The biopsychosocial mechanisms involving how social support protects and enhances health have not yet been fully discovered. However, an abundance of research has confirmed that social support may be the most significant biopsychosocial factor in illness, including cancer. Studies confirm that the magnitude of the relationship between isolation, lack of social support, and health is the same as the relationship between smoking and death from various diseases, such as cancer and heart disease (House, Strecher, Metzner, & Robbins, 1986). People who are isolated may have three to five times the mortality rate from all causes. Simply put, people with social ties live longer than people who are isolated. People with connections to others stay well better and longer. Social support protects health in times of crisis (Hafen et al., 1996; Spiegel, 1991).

One interesting finding of these studies is that there are survival benefits for men who are married and for women who have female friends, so being associated with a woman can help people live longer. However, the opposite is also true: social integration with men does not improve health, for either men or women (Spiegel, 1991).

The most important component of this stage, particularly with regard to the patient-therapist or client-group relationship, is "resonance," the ability to of the therapist or another to enter into the client's world on one or more levels, deeply sharing (empathically attuning to) the experience with him or her. Resonance allows people to access and utilize their full spectrum of emotions to enhance their health. Being heard and valued by others allows clients to establish intimate connections with them. "Compassionate empathy may well be the key ingredient that facilitates healing by activating multiple levels of biopsychosocial adjustment intrinsic to emotions" (Dafter, 1996, p. 47).

> The healer's ability to identify and acknowledge a patient's emotional and psychological experiences enables the patient to become more aware of his or her own inner states and their implicit messages for action and change—perhaps in turn activating the multiple pathways for self recognition. Healers selectively acknowledge a patient's inner experience by observing many levels of emotional and biobehavioral responses and then giving back core information to the patient in both verbal and nonverbal ways. In essence, healers act as naturalistic biofeedback systems, selectively amplifying emotional awareness in a person who is repressed, or containing it in the case of a person flooded with affective overload. (Dafter, 1996, p. 47)

In addition to the traditional verbal, cognitive, physical and emotional strategies of achieving resonance, music therapists may further attune to their clients empathically on musical and imaginal levels. Because music therapy offers additional opportunities for resonance through its primary media of music and imagination, it can be assumed that resonance with the client may be more immediate, powerful, and significant, thus validating and offering the client more intense and direct feedback on his own subjective experience (Dileo, 1997c). Resonance thus leads to a re-membering of feelings of connectedness, closeness, intimacy, and love.

Prerequisites to intimacy and social connectedness, however, involve providing safety for patients. That is, individuals must feel that they can feel safe to express vulnerability, have their feelings validated by the therapist or others, have these feelings resonated by others, and are not at risk of being judged for these feelings.

Music therapy approaches that involve shared experiences, physical and emotional proximity in the music, and creative expression are relevant for use. These approaches can be realized in several ways using songs: through "song-dedications" from one member of the group to another/others; through shared listening to or singing of each group member's special song; through paired song listening (back-to-back, holding hands, or in close proximity); through paired toning experiences (taking turns toning back-to-back to experience physical resonance); through group song-writing according to a selected theme; etc.

Existential Reorganization: Meaning and Spirituality

> Any meaning of illness is better than none. . . . Without the recognition of my spirit as well as my illness, I am nothing but my illness. . . . To get to my body, the doctor has to go through my soul. He would see the genius of my illness. (Broyard, 1992)

The basic questions of life's meaning are simple and few (Bolen, 1996):

- What did you come here to do?
- What did you come here to learn?
- What did you come here to heal?
- What and whom did you come here to love?
- What are you here for?

Ascertaining the meaning of their individual lives (one aspect of spirituality) gives people a broader perspective of the illness. Meaning changes people's perceptions of external events and their ability to survive extremely difficult circumstances (Frankl, 1979). "Perhaps there is a greater reality of which we are all part and that our suffering has meaning in these broader terms" (Remen, 1996, p. 28).

People who are spiritual are not defeated by crises, but are able to interpret the crisis in a growth-producing way, and illness frequently presents an opportunity for this growth. The biopsychosocial implications for having a purpose in life are manifold. The research indicates that survival from illness is often associated with existential reorganization (Hafen et al., 1996).

Work at this stage involves a discovery of "each person's special song to sing, music to beat out in relating and creating" (Bolletino & LeShan, 1995, p. 25), or, simply put, "finding the person's bliss." Helping the individual find his or her deepest sense of harmony in life is indeed spiritual/soul work. This is no easy task, as often patients have deeply ingrained habits of putting others' needs first, values of self that are dependent on doing for others, and making decisions based on shame or guilt. However, the turning point in the crisis of illness happens at this spiritual level, in discovering what really matters, that is, re-membering a spiritual and existential identity (Bolen, 1996).

Uses of music therapy therefore center around helping the individual find the music of his life's meaning. Spontaneous song improvisations around specific themes or questions can provide starting points for this spiritual journey. The music therapist will often support the patient musically on instruments or voice during these improvisations. If indicated, the music therapist can provide opportunities for dialogue, feedback, and reflection musically and through lyrics.

Metaphoric approaches to musical improvisation may also be particularly useful to this end. A musical "Orpheus" experience (Spiegel, 1993) may be used for this exploration. A patient is asked to select a group of his favorite instruments and to begin a free improvisation. Periodically during the improvisation, the patient is asked to surrender one of the instruments, constantly reducing the number of instruments he or she can play and thereby diminishing the sounds that can be produced. This continues until there is only one instrument left. The discussion that follows provides the connection between this musical metaphor and life. If only one instrument remains, what will it be? How did it feel to lose all the instruments? Why did the patient surrender the instruments in this particular order? What is the connection between this process and his or her life? Is there an "instrument that the patient cannot surrender in life? What is the meaning of that "instrument"?

FORGIVENESS: LETTING GO

Forgiveness means letting go of the desire for a better yesterday

Forgiveness is an essential part of spirituality, "the ability to release from the mind all the past hurts and failures, all sense of guilt and loss" (Hafen et al., 1996, p. 389). Forgiveness involves "accepting the core of every human being as the same as yourself and giving them the gift of not judging them" (Borysenko, 1987, p. 176). Forgiveness also implies

> a decision to see beyond the limits of another's personality; to be willing to accept responsibility for your own perceptions; to shift your perceptions repeatedly; and to gradually transform yourself from being a helpless victim of your circumstances to being a powerful and loving co-creator of your reality. (Casarjian, 1992, cited in Hafen et al., 1996, pp. 390–391)

For the person with cancer, forgiveness may involve forgiving the self for any unhealthful practices that may have contributed to having cancer, forgiving the illness itself, forgiving others for their personal failings, forgiving doctors, forgiving treatments, forgiving God, etc. Forgiveness allows "re-membering" those parts of the individual that have been frozen in anger and unacknowledged or suppressed because of guilt and shame.

Wolter (1994) describes the components of forgiveness as follows: (a) letting go of the unforgiving position that may be held; (b) realizing that the events and emotions experienced are indeed real; (c) acknowledging that what happened cannot be changed; (d) admitting that there is no longer a need to rely on others for validation, thereby empowering the self for approval; (e) releasing the unrealistic needs for others or the self to atone; and (f) accepting the self and others for who they are rather than who the individual would have them be.

In this stage, several song approaches may provide the opportunity for working through this difficult and painful process. Song reminiscence and song regression can be used as means of stimulating memories of painful events or relationships and allowing an experience and validation of the individual's feelings. Similarly, the creation of song biographies may be instrumental in facilitating an examination of the impact of these painful events/persons on other aspects of the individual's life, and may permit persons to trace and evaluate their development or review their life from this perspective.

Song improvisations can be used as vehicles for the expression and validation of the hurts that have occurred, as well as for exploration of new and creative ways of responding to these painful feelings. Lastly, the process of forgiveness may be finalized with a song written to the person/thing forgiven or as an affirmation to the self as a way of acknowledging in a formal and meaningful way that forgiveness has indeed occurred.

RITUAL : ACKNOWLEDGING CHANGE

Tell me, what you plan to do with your one wild and precious life. (Oliver, 1990)

Perhaps the final stage of the music therapy process involves the realization and acknowledgement of the willingness to change by altering old ways of thinking, feeling, and existence (Barasch, 1993). Implicit in this decision is the movement toward healing. This final step is often honored, acknowledged, and witnessed through the use of musical rituals that both celebrate the transition to healing and change as well as provide closure for the therapy process.

Rituals are outwards signs of interior experiences, and the group provides the love and support to the person during this transition. Rituals symbolize the letting go of the past and moving on (Bolen, 1996). Rituals are highly personal and are always individually designed, carrying the meaning and implications of this rite of passage for the patient. Music is used in a symbolic way to acknowledge that the person has changed.

Rituals may often involve musical gifts from each of the group to the patient, or among all the group members. A shared song, a group toning experience, individual performances of new "theme songs," or spontaneous chanting of messages (which may come from the new theme song or the individual's song of affirmation, for example) all may be meaningful components of the ritual, summarizing and validating what has transpired in the process. Rituals are as varied as the experiences of each individual patient (Bolen, 1996).

CONCLUSIONS AND IMPLICATIONS

The bio-psycho-social-spiritual approach is one that has potential for music therapy practitioners in all clinical specializations, perhaps integrating the diverse practices of music therapy, conceptually, theoretically, and practically. From a biopsychosocial perspective, all music therapy interventions affect the entire person via the mind-body-social-spiritual complex. Even treatment intended for the resolution of psychiatric problems has medical implications (for example, the influence of depression on the immune system is well-documented). Similarly, music therapy interventions aimed at social or spiritual integration in the patient may help prevent illness. Neither the scope of music therapy nor its potential effects can be underestimated or unexamined (Dileo, 1997b, 1997c; Dileo-Maranto, 1996a).

Music therapists who work in this area need to have their own personal work in music therapy. If we are working with ill people, facilitating the acquisition of life's meaning, accompanying our patients into their illness and pain, we need to be adequately evolved as individuals and therapists. A therapist needs to be a model of harmony. When, for example, a cancer patient's life depends upon meaning, creativity, and joy in life, the guide to this process has to have found his or her own way there (Bolen, 1996).

References

Barasch, M. I. (1993). *The healing path: A soul approach to illness.* New York: Arkana.

Bolen, J. S. (1996). *Close to the bone: Life-threatening illness and the search for meaning.* New York: Scribner.

Bolletino, R. C., & LeShan, L. (1995). Cancer patients and "marathon" psychotherapy: A new model. *Advances, 11*(4), 19–35.

Borysenko, J. (1987). *Minding the body, mending the mind.* Reading, MA: Addison-Wesley.

Broyard, A. (1992). *Intoxicated by my illness.* New York: Clarkson-Potter.

Bruscia, K. E. (1989). Songs in psychotherapy. In *Proceedings of the Fourteenth National Conference of the Australian Music Therapy Association.* Melbourne, Australia, August, 1987.

Bruscia, K. E. (1998). Techniques for uncovering and working with countertransference. In K. E. Bruscia (Ed.), *The dynamics of music psychotherapy* (pp. 93–120). Gilsum, NH: Barcelona.

Casarjian, R. (1992). *Forgiveness: A bold choice for a peaceful heart.* New York: Bantam Books.

Dafter, R. E. (1996). Why "negative" emotions can sometimes be positive: The spectrum model of emotions and their role in mind-body health. *Advances, 12*(2), 6–19, 42–51.

Decker-Voigt, H. H. (1997). *Music with cardiac patients.* Paper presented at the Polymedia Music as a Tool for Well-being and Preventive Health Care Mini-Symposium, Hamburg, Germany.

Dienstfrey, H. (1994). Training for cancer: An interview with Michael Lerner. *Advances, 10*(2), 27–37.

Dileo, C. (1997a). The context of music and medicine. In T. Wigram and C. Dileo (Eds.), *Music vibration and health.* Cherry Hill, NJ: Jeffrey Books.

Dileo, C. (1997b). *The process of medical music therapy.* Paper presented at the annual conference of the National Association for Music Therapy, Los Angeles.

Dileo, C. (1997c). Reflections on medical music therapy: Biopsychosocial perspectives of the treatment process. In J. Loewy (Ed.), *Music therapy and pediatric pain.* Cherry Hill, NJ: Jeffrey Books.

Dileo-Maranto, C. (1993a). Applications of music in medicine. In M. Heal and T. Wigram (Eds.), *Music therapy in health and education.* London: Jessica Kingsley.

Dileo-Maranto, C. (1993b). Music therapy and stress management. In P. Lehrer and R. Woolfolk (Eds.), *Principles and practice of stress management.* New York: Guilford Press.

Dileo-Maranto, C. (1995). *Music and the mind-body connection.* Paper presented at the Centennial Conference of the University of Melbourne, Melbourne, Australia.

Dileo-Maranto, C. (1996a). *New directions and research in music therapy and medicine.* Paper presented at the World Congress of Music Therapy, Hamburg, Germany.

Dileo-Maranto, C. (1996b). Research in music and medicine: The state of the art. In M. A. Froehlich (Ed.), *Music therapy for hospitalized children: A creative arts child-life approach.* Cherry Hill, NJ: Jeffrey Books.

Frankl, V. E. (1979). *Logotherapy in action.* Berkeley, CA: Institute of Logotherapy Press.

Hafen, B. Q., Karren, K. J., Frandsen, K. J., & Smith, N. L. (1996). *Mind body health: The effects of attitudes, emotions and relationships.* Boston: Allyn and Bacon.

House, J. S., Strecher, V., Metzner, H. L., & Robbins, C. A. (1986). Occupational stress and health among men and women in the Tecumseh Community Health Study. *Journal of Health and Social Behavior, 27,* 62–77.

Idler, E. I., & Kasl, S. (1991). Health perceptions and survival: Do global evaluations of health status really predict mortality? *Journal of Gerontology, 46,* S55–S65.

Oliver, M. (1990). The summer day. In *House of light.* Boston: Beacon.

Remen, R. N. (1996). All emotions are potentially life affirming. *Advances, 12*(2), 23–28.

Spiegel, D. (1991). A psychosocial intervention and survival time of patients with metastatic breast cancer. *Advances, 7*(3), 10–19.

Spiegel, D. (1993). *Living beyond limits: New hope for facing life-threatening illness.* New York: Random House.

Spiegel, D., Bloom, J., Kraemer, H. C., & Gottheil, E. (1989). Effects of psychosocial treatment on survival of patients with metastatic breast cancer. *The Lancet, 2,* 888–891.

Temoshok, L., & Dreher, H. (1992). *The Type C connection: The behavioral links to cancer and your health.* New York: Random House.

Wilber, K. (1993). *Grace and grit: Spirituality and healing in the life and death of Treya Killam Wilber.* Boston: Shambhala Press.

Wolter, D. L. (1994, Spring). *Lotus,* 53.

16

Creative Song Improvisations With Children and Adults With Cancer

Alan Turry, MA, MT-BC
Ann E. Turry, MA, CMT

> The magic in song only happens when words give destination and meaning to the music and the music gives wings to the words. Together as a song they go places you've never been before. The reason is obvious: Words make you think thoughts. Music makes you feel a feeling. But a song makes you feel a thought. (Meyerson & Harburg, 1993, as cited in Nordoff & Robbins, in press)

> People who are ill can make an art form of their illness. I would advise every sick person to develop a voice for his or her illness. (Broyard, 1992)

Children and adults with cancer can create improvised songs to become aware of, explore, and express thoughts and feelings. Through songs, individuals can tell their stories and embrace painful issues that may otherwise feel overwhelming or threatening. Dileo (1997) describes the importance of emotional expression to the medical patient's overall physical and emotional functioning: "The inability to express emotion is perhaps seen as a . . . significant correlate to illness, in particular, in cancer patients" (p. 133). Improvisation—the unplanned, spontaneous expression of music—allows for the opportunity to be creative and productive and to gain a sense of enhancement, even in the face of physical deterioration. It can be utilized either in the moment to address an acute crisis or over time within the context of an ongoing process. Music is a powerful medium that has the capacity to simultaneously contain and express the ambiguities and subtleties of the human experience as the musical elements are combined to create different textures and colors. The infinite potential of these combinations can reflect the unique quality of each individual. By living in the immediacy of the musical improvisation, defenses can be bypassed, developmental potentials tapped, and repressed feelings acknowledged. Improvisation can accelerate the development of trust, strengthen the therapeutic relationship, and provide opportunities for exploration and integration of complex thoughts and feelings.

In the Nordoff-Robbins Creative Music Therapy approach, the music is considered the primary healing or transformative agent. Music offers "an enormous and potentially unlimited range of *active*, self-integrative experience [that] is available for therapeutic use" (Nordoff &

Robbins, 1977, p. 2). Creative Music Therapy is "based on the belief that everyone has inherent, inborn musicality, regardless of pathology. The therapy process entails engaging the client by creating aesthetic musical forms meant to access these musical sensitivities" (A. Turry, 1998, p. 161). Clinical goals are contained within musical goals, and gains made within the music often can generalize into everyday functioning and interactions.

The approach was named "Creative Music Therapy" because of its emphasis on *creating*. The therapist creates "the musical resources to be used within each therapeutic experience, the therapeutic experiences and techniques to be used in each clinical circumstance, and the process whereby these experiences are sequenced" (Bruscia, 1987, p. 24). The therapist's improvised music is inspired by his or her impressions of the client; the music "creates the emotional substances of the contact and sets the ground for interactivity" (Nordoff & Robbins, 1971, p. 144). To balance the emphasis on spontaneous creativity, each session is recorded and meticulously studied and documented.

Paul Nordoff and Clive Robbins were deeply influenced by the teachings of Rudolf Steiner, the founder of anthroposophy. Aldridge (1996) describes the basic tenets of anthroposophical medicine in this way:

- Each person is a unique individual and treatment decisions must recognize this individuality.
- Scientific, artistic and spiritual insights, which recognize the whole person, need to be applied together in our therapeutic endeavors.
- Life has meaning and purpose. If these qualities are lost then there is a deterioration of health.
- Illness may provide opportunities for positive change and new balance in a person's life. (p. 8)

Clive and Carol Robbins (1991) write that Creative Music Therapy "is directly involved in self-actualization" (p. 70), a concept drawn from the humanistic psychology movement pioneered by Abraham Maslow. A basic tenet of humanistic psychology is that human beings naturally strive to reach their highest potential. Bruscia (1987) states that Nordoff-Robbins music therapy can

> facilitate what Maslow described as peak experiences, those sublime moments wherein one is able to transcend and integrate splits within the person, between persons, within the world, and between the person and the world. Since the arts facilitate the occurrence of peak experiences, aesthetic endeavors are seen to be a central aspect of life and therefore of therapy. (p. 33)

These ideas are consonant with the concept of the "condition child" and the "music child" (Nordoff & Robbins, 1977; Robbins & Robbins, 1991). Improvisational music therapy can access a client's "inherent, inborn musicality, which is so fundamental to human nature" (Robbins & Robbins, 1991, p. 58). As a result, there exists the possibility to develop

> a new nucleus of selfhood which is formed in (or by) musical experience, through musical communication, through the beginnings of musical activity. This musical-personal nucleus then is nurtured, encouraged, challenged, supported, answered by the therapist and begins to take the individuality beyond the previous limits of its functions, beyond the barrier of the condition child. (Robbins & Robbins, 1991, pp. 58–59)

This process of "releasing developmental potentials to give the unfolding personality . . . a positive sense of identity" (Robbins & Robbins, 1991, p. 69) is enabled by the "being child" that exists within the "music child."

Since Creative Music Therapy is closely aligned with the metaphysical teachings of Steiner as well as Maslow's concepts describing human potential and self-actualization, it could be argued that it also corresponds to transpersonal psychology. "Transpersonal psychology seeks to resolve what it considers the disproportionate attention given to man's psychological afflictions at the expense of his greatest potentialities" (Needleman & Eisenberg, 1987, cited in Rugenstein, 1996). Rugenstein, a music therapist who describes her own music therapy work as transpersonal in nature, explains that music "has been used as a model for describing the very essence of life" (p. 20). It can evoke deeply spiritual states and "function as a vehicle to connect us with that which is greater than ourselves, and that which is the essence of the transpersonal approach to psychology" (p. 20). Nordoff-Robbins music therapy, with its emphasis on the intrinsic capacities and dynamic forces embodied in music, can function within the transpersonal realm to transcend patterns that constrict our emotional, psychological, and physical lives.

Case Material

Troy

Troy, a 4-year-old boy with Acute Lymphocytic Leukemia, walked into the playroom with his bandaged finger in the air and tears rolling down his face. "Did you have a fingerstick?" the therapist gently asked. Troy nodded slightly and looked down. "Would you like to make up a song and see if we can make your tears feel better?" He nodded again, continuing to gaze downward. Troy appeared so little, fragile, and helpless at this moment. Based on previous experience with children and procedures and her own emotional response in the moment, the therapist intuitively suspected that underneath the manifest feelings of fear and helplessness were feelings of anger at being stuck and hurt.[1] During the procedure, Troy had experienced a relentless onslaught of sensations and emotions (including fear, pain, anger, and confusion) which made little sense to him, yet overwhelmed his system so that he responded on a purely visceral level. Due to his developmental age and his current emotional state, he was unable to differentiate or process these feelings. When he arrived at the session, he was shaking and couldn't organize his thoughts well enough to speak. He simply nodded in response to the therapist's question and invitation to play music.

The therapist handed him a drumstick, positioned the drum and cymbal nearby, and began to improvise music on her guitar. She made a clinical decision to try to mobilize this anger and began to sing and strum the guitar firmly, attempting to motivate him to action. She sang, "I got a fingerstick; it really hurt, and I feel really mad." At the end of the phrase, Troy struck the cymbal powerfully. He looked up, as if surprised by his own strength, and gave a hesitant smile. Though

[1]Intuition in this context can be defined as an immediate, accurate, and ineffable perception of some aspect of the client or situation. It is a vital faculty for creative music therapists to employ, and it is actively cultivated in the Nordoff-Robbins training. Intuition, though, is balanced with careful scrutiny of all session recordings and the examination of the therapist's personal and creative processes through supervision.

Troy's playing was initially erratic—reflecting his overwhelmed emotional state—he eventually became more focused. His rhythm on the drum became even and his tone firm, indicating a restored sense of inner control. He began to sing with the therapist, at first quietly mouthing single words as he continued to drum. Eventually he stopped drumming, looked up and sang in full voice, "I got a fingerstick; it really hurt, and I feel really mad." He returned to his drumming after singing these words one time.

The improvised song culminated with tremolos on the cymbal and guitar as the therapist and Troy looked at each other, singing, smiling, and furiously playing. There was a deep connection between them at this moment. Troy had transformed an otherwise painful and terrifying experience into one filled with communication, meaning, and purpose. The experience of improvising music expressively imbued him with a sense of his own strength.

Judith[2]

After being diagnosed with non-Hodgkin's Lymphoma, Judith, a creative and successful woman in her forties, began music therapy. In her first sessions, she began by making vocal sounds. The therapist musically responded to these sounds by improvising harmony on the piano that supported and enhanced her musical/emotional expression. He created music that left space for and highlighted Judith's musical expression by using open-voiced harmonies, rubato, and dynamics that mirrored her sounds. Judith often sang one tone, which the therapist put into various harmonic contexts to reflect the emotional content of her expression. The sessions continued in an essentially similar format every week.

Judith created lyrics about her feelings related to her illness, the decisions she faced in choosing doctors and medical procedures, and how to communicate her situation to family and friends. As Judith continued to explore these issues in the music, she began to expand the breadth of the issues she brought to therapy. She sang about life-long issues, including feelings of loneliness and oppression, as well as her perpetual need to act "normal" and pretend that everything was okay. She improvised melodies and lyrics that expressed her deep emotions related to these issues. The therapist continued to support Judith's musical expression in various ways. At times he reflected the rhythmic phrases she created with her lyrics; at other times he created harmonic support that left space for her individual voice. Sometimes the music was used to intensify the emotional content of her expression, and sometimes the music had a distinct contrast to the presented emotion. Occasionally, the therapist made a decision to continue the music after Judith had stopped singing to urge her to continue the process. At other times, the musical choices of the therapist helped Judith to bring her expression to a close. These clinical decisions and interventions were based on Judith's creations, her interaction with and response to the therapist's music over time, and the established therapeutic alliance that allowed for an increasingly deeper understanding and trust between them.

As the sessions progressed and the musical relationship continued to develop, both the therapist and client began to anticipate each other's musical choices. Judith began to take more risks musically by changing her tones and creating melodic fragments as she vocalized. The

---

[2]The name *Judith* is a pseudonym that was chosen with specific intent. Judith is the main character in Bartok's opera, *Bluebeard's Castle*, and she chose this character because the images from this opera, as well as the character's struggle, appear in many of her improvisations.

therapist continued to provide harmony that gave Judith several potential pathways for her melodic ideas. Her vocalizations became more varied and personally expressive. At times Judith cried as she sang about the deep anguish and pain she was feeling. She held long tones, sobbed, growled, or sang in a high falsetto and a low monotone. Often, her lyrics were questions she asked to herself, pondering her feelings and her situation.[3]

A variety of styles were utilized in creating these improvisations. Hymn-like music supported Judith's connection to God and her attempts to accept herself without judgment. Other improvisations grew out of Judith's playfulness and developed into a blues-like style. As time went by, Judith began to sing in a more earthy style, swinging her body and enjoying the syncopated rhythms. Improvisations that expressed hope and joy were created with flowing music that had an uplifting tone and mood. A variety of modes and scales were explored. Often in the midst of a vocal expression, Judith would create a melodic idea that gave the improvisation a sense of form and tonal direction. At other times, the harmony and phrasing created by the therapist helped to lead Judith into creating a melody. These improvised song forms were not decided beforehand, but were created together as both the therapist and client listened to and built on each other's musical ideas. A musical collaboration—a co-active musical relationship with an established sense of mutuality—had developed between therapist and client.

A few months after she began music therapy, Judith's cancer went into a spontaneous regression and became "indolent," though she was poignantly aware that it could start to grow again at anytime. As she created personally meaningful improvisations and faced the painful feelings of her inner conflicts, she described the process as helping her to get on with her life. A veteran of various types of therapy, Judith realized she was beginning to explore her inner life in a new way. As she vocally improvised about traumatic events, she gained insight and strength. She reflected on the topics she sang about—topics that previously she had been unable to openly examine due to their painful nature. She discovered that by being able to embrace the repressed emotions that were surfacing through the music, she was able to live a fuller and richer emotional life. She welcomed the sessions in which she was able to tell her truth and be genuine about all of her difficult life challenges. She also felt exhilarated about her developing relationship to music and her ability to express herself through singing.

The therapist offered Judith the opportunity to audiotape the sessions. Judith decided to play the tapes for significant people in her life and began to share the complex issues that she was facing. Judith felt understood in a deeply meaningful way as her family and friends heard her personal process through musical improvisation. Her feelings of isolation diminished as a result of these experiences. She began to learn the music that was created in the sessions, choosing sections that were meaningful and aesthetically satisfying, and decided to share her music publicly. What had begun as vocal sounds became fully formed songs that she proudly learned and shared with others.

The experience of a life-threatening illness for a 4-year-old boy can be dramatically different from that of a 40-year-old woman. The emotional needs, developmental implications, personal processes, and therapeutic aims of these patients differ greatly. Yet many of the feelings (although experienced and processed in different ways) are common among patients throughout the age

---

[3]For examples of these lyrics, refer to Logis, M., & Turry, A. (1999). Singing my way through it. In J. Hibben (Ed.), *Inside music therapy: Clinical experiences.* Gilsum, NH: Barcelona.

continuum. In addition, the foundation of a clinical approach can be consistent, though the specific application and therapeutic process may vary. Common experiences among patients of any age who undergo treatment for cancer can include feelings of helplessness, isolation, anger, sadness, fear, powerlessness, and confusion. In addition to the emotional components, there are also significant physical effects of treatment that can include noxious side effects from medication, pain, fatigue, nausea, and dramatic changes in appearances. Despite the age or developmental level of the patients, diagnosis, hospitalization, and treatment can strip them of their identity and dignity, and their available resources often become compromised.

Therapeutic Implications of Musical Elements

Improvisation

Improvisation acts as a catalyst in illuminating painful feelings. Improvised song forms help to externalize these intensified feelings and provide a nonintrusive way of offering direction through emotions such as confusion, despair, or turmoil. By recognizing areas of exploration that may have meaning or emotional depth, the therapist can enhance or amplify the client's expression with improvised music.

Improvisation can help to integrate fragmented polarities of the self. Judith found that behind her vocal expressions were a variety of different musical personalities. She spoke about the different qualities and attitudes she heard in her voice as she sang about her life and recognized that her singing voice represented certain aspects of herself. At times her voice sounded like "the frightened child" and at other times the "angry mother." These aspects of herself could be identified and, through musical exploration, become less rigid and more integrated. Exploring these personality aspects through improvised songs allowed Judith to reflect on them, identify them, and eventually sing in a more accepting, less fragmented way. At the end of some of these improvisations, her voice did not sound like one clearly defined aspect of her musical personality or the other—it sounded as if it had elements of both. Thus, connections were made and an integration of previously separated parts of the self took place. This process is enhanced by the song form, as different sections of an improvised song allow for different types of expression, yet it is held together in an overall form.

The mutuality inherent in the musical relationship between therapist and client is an intimate contact that provides the opportunity for self-discovery. "A communicative relationship is established through meaningful musical interactions as therapist . . . and client . . . work together to find the power and significance of various musical elements, styles, and idioms" (A. Turry, 1998, p. 161). A co-active musical moment creates an environment of greater focus and attention for the client *and therapist*. As the therapist created music based on his responses, Troy sensed there was room for his expression—that he was an equal co-creator in the process—and he gained a sense of control over the situation. This feeling of equality and interesponsiveness can be crucial for someone with a debilitating illness who may feel weak, inferior, or out of control of important aspects of his or her life.

In improvisation, there is an intimacy of thinking and anticipating together where the music will go in the future. It is an intimate act to improvise music with another person. This natural and healthy impulse to connect with others can be cultivated to eventually help the client to re-establish meaningful relationships. By staying focused on the present moment and carefully listening and responding to the client's musical expression, the therapist can gain insight and empathy for the client's state of being. This sense of musical attunement can transcend the barriers of loneliness and isolation as well as any physical incapacitation that the client may be experiencing. When clients feel that the therapist is deeply listening and understanding them, their trust in the therapist and in the situation is intensified. Dileo (1997) described this phenomenon as "resonance," which is "the ability of the therapist to empathize as fully as possible with the condition of the client" (p. 126). Judith expressed feeling more connected to others after entering into the improvisatory process.

Form

Every expression inevitably takes on a form (whether tangible or intangible) in which its expressive qualities are realized. The capacity for living in forms is an essential aspect of being human. Within form exist the possibilities for interactive communication and exploration. The creation of song form in the therapeutic setting represents an understandable structure. In this structure, aspects of the client's emotional life can be combined with cognitive processes in ways to further development, provide comfort, or remediate a pathological condition to a greater extent than through the undirected discharge of emotion. Although all musical expression can be considered as form in a broad sense, therapeutic exploration and expression through music often require a coherent and accessible form. Aldridge (1996) writes:

> Creative expression is not the same as cathartic expression. Whereas personal emotive expression may be the first step in the process of healing, the continuing therapeutic process is to give articulation to a broad range of human feelings. . . . When we introduce form and order into the creative act then we promote a higher form of human articulation. This is the process of healing; the escape from emotive fragmentation to the creative act of becoming whole. (p. 18)

This is especially true when working with patients who are coping with the pervasive uncertainty of their illness and prognosis. Specific aesthetic forms, either recurring or those created in the moment, can provide a necessary sense of security, mastery, and predictability essential to achieving a wide range of clinical goals. Song form is a familiar musical bridge that allows the client and therapist to live in the creative moment together.

Through the form of the improvisation and the sensitive combination of the musical elements (i.e., the harmony of the guitar, tonal quality of her voice, the rhythm and tempo of the strum, etc.), the therapist created a structure into which Troy could direct his overpowering emotions. The improvised song structure provided a holding environment for Troy through its repetition of form and words, while simultaneously offering an outlet for his impulses, which were not yet under his control. The structure consisted of clear, repeated phrases that allowed for free playing on the drum, followed by a punctuation on the cymbal at the end of the phrase. This stability in the form was important, given his fragile state. At first, Troy was able only to beat erratically and in a weak manner within the phrases, but the repetitive symmetry of the overall structure (i.e., a phrase followed by the cymbal accent) helped to initially stabilize his general sense of balance, timing, and tempo in the music. Within the phrases themselves, the therapist provided further grounding through her use of meter and clear rhythm. This further helped to increase his awareness of the music and intrinsically organize his beating within the phrases. Through this structure, Troy eventually became more organized and was able to affirm his sense of control and awaken his awareness of and connection to his environment.

> As a child re-engages and begins to live in musical activity, he becomes present in the moment and regains a sense of himself in a specific time and space. A child's natural impulse toward spontaneity and imagination, elements that are inherent to creative musical interaction, can be reinforced as the healing process toward re-integration of the senses, emotions and physiologic functioning commences. (A. E. Turry, 1997, p. 93)

A fluid and creative musical structure can offer possibilities for new discoveries in melody or harmony, contemplation in slower tempi, or a deepening of the expression through dynamic changes. By improvising in a free way, aspects of the self that can trigger differing points of view about one's illness can surface and be explored. Words that a patient may feel unable to communicate to the medical team or their significant caretakers (who have their own feelings and processes with which to contend) can be uttered with safety. Feelings about the illness that previously have been unidentified or avoided can spontaneously surface. In music, these feelings can be supported and enhanced. As a therapist creates a space of receptivity and responsiveness through music, he or she can encourage a client to take risks. Moments of emotional catharsis and also integration become possible.

Singing

Singing can be a particularly powerful event in exploring emotions. Austin (1996), whose clinical practice is built around vocal improvisation, states that "our emotions are mirrored in the way music works. Music gives sound to inner feeling states" (p. 35). She later describes the act of singing as a way to "access one's deepest self. The voice is like a bridge that can connect the mind to the body and heal splits between thinking and feeling" (1998, p. 316).

After becoming more organized and related in his music through rhythm and form, Troy was able to take the next step and sing the words of the improvisation. "It is important for children to sing their songs . . . in order to express the identified feelings and take ownership of the stated feeling" (A. E. Turry, 1999). This step symbolizes the integration of emotional and cognitive processes and further enables the process of "reconstitution" (A. E. Turry, 1997), a process in which the senses, emotions, and ego functions are restored and re-organized after an intense emotional experience.

Austin's (1998) vocal holding technique utilizes two chords in order to "establish a predictable, secure musical container" (p. 316) for the client. Although the harmonic structure underneath many of Judith's improvised melodies was harmonically complex, consisting of a variety of chords and tonal centers that could shift, the structure was usually clearly stated. Instead of two chords, there were two contrasting *series* of chords—chords either related to the tonic (variations or substitutions), or chords in contrast to the tonic. There were also times when both therapist and client utilized the whole tone scale or improvised in an atonal or bi-tonal fashion so that there was no clear tonal center. This made the eventual establishment of a tonal center more significant. Myriad tone combinations were utilized, including harmony that emphasized the quality of specific intervals, inversions and root positions, open and closed voicings, different registers, and a variety of extended tone colors. These harmonic variations created different potential scales/modes to vocally enter and explore. Contrasting registers helped to widen Judith's vocal range and explore her chest or head voice. Open voiced chords in inversions often triggered further introspection for Judith, while chords in root position grounded the music with a stable foundation. The therapist used free and varied tempi to allow for freedom of expression and new directions. Often, during a moment of intense emotion, Judith would sing a new tone that was not in the implied scale or mode. At times this happened simultaneously with new harmony. At other times, one or the other therapeutic partners would lead to the new musical direction, and new tonal centers were created based on the different directions taken. At these times, additional harmonies were included, and a chord progression or harmonic song form developed. Judith described these developments as powerfully aesthetic moments that felt emotionally expressive and satisfying. The music functioned as a container and as an enhancer/motivator to move into uncharted musical/emotional territory. The musical creation itself had an aesthetic shape and direction that helped to "frame raw experience into a whole experience" (Aigen, 1995, p. 241).

Flow

Musical repetition found in songs—short, clear, repeated melodic ideas—helps to anchor the improvisation by giving the music a clear reference point. It helps to order and communicate meaning. By shaping a repeated musical phrase, the therapist can pose a question or create a space in which the client is invited to respond. Musical pauses or silences create space for introspection, moments to ponder what has happened and what might still happen. Rhythm imbues music with energy and momentum; it is a predictable element in time, and the therapist and client relate to it simultaneously. In pulse, there exists a paradoxical sense of being involved in the present, yet aware of where the musical time will be in the future. On one level, music is personally expressive and is a subjective experience, yet ironically, on another level, it has a form in and of itself that provides a more objective experience. These factors contribute to the ability of music to allow for emotions to be addressed indirectly yet with immediacy. Scheff (1979, cited in James & Johnson, 1996) talks of the importance of finding the midpoint between being emotionally overwhelmed by feelings or cognitively distanced from them. He calls this healing midpoint the "aesthetic distance" (p. 312). By entering into the process of improvising within a song form, one can gain a sense of aesthetic balance and process difficult feelings without being overwhelmed by them. Troy was able to use music to gain a sense of mastery over his situation and express his feelings directly and creatively. His physiologic functioning reconstituted, and he was able to integrate his feelings and his thoughts by singing about his experience. Judith was able to experience her feelings and gain a sense of containment over them by creating songs out of her improvisations. She was proud that her expression became something tangible that she could remember and organize as a song. It gave her something to hold onto, something within which she could continue to explore parts of herself. Audio-taping the sessions provided her the "aesthetic distance" to reflect on her feelings and gain a sense of integration and balance. Singing the songs in a predictable way made the feelings expressed in them less frightening.

For many people with cancer, engaging in the creative process of improvising songs can be a key to fostering hope, finding a purpose, and staying connected with those who care about them. In improvisation, the focus is on the moment and being present in the here-and-now, which is important in an environment that is unpredictable and in which dramatic changes can occur suddenly. Active music-making can inspire a sense of empowerment. Even as patients' fears of diminished capacity overwhelm them or they lay immobile in their beds, creating music can instill a feeling of continued growth, creativity, and purpose. In improvisation, the possibility of participating in a meaningful and dynamic interaction remains alive. Music can help to underscore that a patient is more than the illness. Through music, persons with cancer can simultaneously mourn their condition, while celebrating their existing vitality as they tap into their inner life, their imagination, and their potential.

References

Aigen, K. (1995). An aesthetic foundation of clinical theory: An underlying basis of creative music therapy. In C. Kenny (Ed.), *Listening, playing, creating: Essays on the power of sound.* Albany, NY: State University of New York Press.

Aldridge, D. (1996). *Music therapy research and practice in medicine: From out of the silence.* London: Jessica Kingsley.

Austin, D. (1996). The role of improvised music in adult psychodynamic music therapy. *Music Therapy, 14*(1), 29–43.

Austin, D. (1998). When the psyche sings: Transference and countertransference in improvised singing with individual adults. In K. Bruscia (Ed.), *The dynamics of music psychotherapy* (pp. 315–333). Phoenixville, PA: Barcelona.

Broyard, A. (1992). *Intoxicated by my illness.* New York: Clarkson-Potter.

Bruscia, K. (1987). *Improvisational models of music therapy.* Springfield, IL: Charles C. Thomas.

Dileo, C. (1997). Reflections on medical music therapy: Biopsychosocial perspectives of the treatment process. In J. V. Loewy (Ed.), *Music therapy and pediatric pain.* Cherry Hill, NJ: Jeffrey Books.

James, M., & Johnson, D. R. (1996). Drama therapy for the treatment of affective expression in post traumatic stress disorder. In D. Nathanson (Ed.), *Knowing feeling: Affect, script and psychotherapy*. New York: Norton.

Logis, M., & Turry, A. (1999). Singing my way through it: Facing the cancer pain and fear. In J. Hibben (Ed.), *Inside music therapy: Client experiences* (pp. 97–117). Phoenixville, PA: Barcelona.

Needleman, J., & Eisenberg, R. (1987). States of consciousness. In M. Eliade (Ed.), *The encyclopedia of religion* (Vol. 4, pp. 52–59). New York: Macmillan.

Nordoff, P., & Robbins, C. (1971). *Therapy in music for handicapped children*. London: Victor Gollancz, Ltd.

Nordoff, P., & Robbins, C. (1977). *Creative music therapy.* New York: Harper & Row.

Nordoff, P., & Robbins, C. (in press). *Creative music therapy*. Phoenixville, PA: Barcelona.

Robbins, C. M., & Robbins, C. (1991). Self communication in creative music therapy. In K. Bruscia (Ed.), *Case studies in music therapy*. Phoenixville, PA: Barcelona.

Rugenstein, L. (1996). Wilber's spectrum model of transpersonal psychology and its application to music therapy. *Music Therapy, 14*(1), 9–28.

Scheff, T. J. (1979). *Catharsis in healing, ritual, and drama.* Berkeley: University of California Press.

Turry, A. (1998). Transference and countertransference in Nordoff-Robbins music therapy. In K. Bruscia (Ed.), *The dynamics of music psychotherapy*. Phoenixville, PA: Barcelona.

Turry, A. E. (1997). The use of clinical improvisation to alleviate procedural distress in young children. In J. V. Loewy (Ed.), *Music therapy and pediatric pain*. Cherry Hill, NJ: Jeffrey Books.

Turry, A. E. (1999). A song of life: Improvised songs with children with cancer and serious blood disorders. In T. Wigram & J. DeBacker (Eds.), *Clinical applications of music therapy in developmental disability, paediatrics and neurology* (pp. 13–31). London: Jessica Kingsley.

PART IV:
COMBINED APPROACHES

Entrainment, Resonance, and Pain-Related Suffering

Cheryl Dileo, PhD, MT-BC
Joke Bradt, MMT, MT-BC

Theoretical Approach

PAIN IS A MULTIDIMENSIONAL PHENOMENON that results from actual or potential tissue damage and is influenced by a number of variables. A model for these various pain-associated mechanisms is presented in Figure 1. While this categorization is somewhat artificial in that many of the categories overlap, what is important to note is the implied interaction among these variables in the patient's experience of pain. When one considers the number and the individual nature of the variables that come into play, it becomes easier to understand how the experience of pain is unique to each individual. According to McCaffery (1968), pain can be defined only by whatever the person in pain says it is; further, it occurs only when the person who experiences it says it does.

Suffering

Just as pain is a highly complex phenomenon that we are only beginning to comprehend, the concept of suffering may be even less clearly understood. Definitions of suffering abound, yet one thing is apparent: suffering also involves many factors, and each individual's experience of suffering is unique.

Pain and suffering are related phenomena, and these terms are sometimes used interchangeably. However, we are far from a consensus concerning the nature of their relationship as well as the distinctions between them. Thus, for purposes of this chapter, we would like to adopt Turk's approach (Basky et al., 1998), which identifies suffering as a reaction to emotional and physical pain that contains feelings of "uncontrollabillity, helplessness, hopelessness, intolerability, and interminability" (p. 177). Suffering, then, involves people's interpretation of pain (Sullivan, in Basky et al., 1998) wherein their intact state is seen as threatened (Cassell,

Physiological

- Origin of Pain
- Tissue Damage
- Neurological Processing of Pain (e.g., Gate Control Theory)
- Biochemical Reactions (opioids, neurotransmitters)
- Type/Duration

Sensory

- Location in Body
- Intensity
- Qualitative Aspects (rhythm, timbre, repetition, etc.)
- Form/Pattern

Emotional/Affective

- Responses (mood, depression, denial, helplessness, anxiety, fear, stoicism, etc.)
- Expression of Affect
- Influence of Personality Variables
- Frustration

Cognitive

- Level of Awareness
- Thought Processes
- Conceptualizations of Self
- Coping Skills
- Attitudes, Beliefs, Knowledge
- Attention to Pain
- Time Perception
- Locus of Control
- Memories
- Expectancy/Intention
- Perceptions of Losses

Behavioral

- Behavioral Reactions to Pain (crying, wincing, avoidance, passivity, etc.)
- Behaviors Used to Control Pain
- Impairment of Movement
- Communication/Expression of Pain
- Other Behavioral Symptoms (sleep, work attendance, inability to fulfill responsibilities)
- Behavioral Consequences of Pain

Sociocultural

- Perceived Social Support
- Demographics (sex, age, etc.)
- Cultural Background
- Roles and Demands
- Perceived Care
- Environmental Factors

Spiritual/Existential

- Interpretation/Meaning of Pain
- Spiritual Values
- Spiritual Support
- Person's Relationship to Pain

Figure 1. Multidimensional Aspects of Pain. (Adapted from McGuire, 1995)

1991). According to Budd (1993), "Suffering occurs when we assess ourselves in a situation and don't like where we are, where we have been or where we are going, and we can take no actions to close the GAP . . . our bodies reflect this linguistic horizon of paralysis and dissatisfaction" (p. 30).

Although it may be surmised from these definitions that suffering is primarily associated with chronic types of pain, it is the opinion of the current authors that suffering may occur with acute types of pain as well. What is critical is the person's interpretation of the pain experience as beyond his or her own resources for coping that leads to the experience of suffering. As all of the variables listed in Figure 1 come to bear in the person's experience of pain, these same variables also are responsible for and contribute to the individual's interpretation of pain, which may or may not lead to suffering. Price (Basky, 1998) discusses a "path" model of pain wherein the affective appraisal of the experience of pain is the end result of various processes involving stages of sensation and cognition.

The implications of this conceptualization for the treatment of pain-related suffering are as follows:

1. Pain assessment methods need to be comprehensive in scope, identifying as many variables contributing to the experience of pain as possible.
2. Treatment methods used should be multidimensional and capable of addressing these various factors. As sensory, cognitive, affective, sociocultural, spiritual, etc., dimensions are identified and addressed either individually or simultaneously, aspects of the pain experience can be modified.
3. Treatment should be individualized to meet the person's unique experience of pain and/or suffering with emphasis on the most salient variables.
4. Resources for coping should be emphasized in treatment.

Music therapy has been shown to be an effective intervention for pain in a variety of medical patients and clinical situations through both active and receptive methods (Dileo, 1997; Dileo-Maranto, 1993, 1996). Music therapy may function to reduce or eliminate pain in one or more ways, including the following: (a) as a distraction from the pain, (b) as a stimulus for comfort and relaxation, (c) as a conditioned stimulus, (d) as a provider of sensory stimulation (according to the Gate Control Theory), (e) as a means for mood-enhancement, (f) as a mechanism for providing choice and control, (g) as a means for perceived time-compression, (h) as an outlet for self-expression, (i) as a method for cognitive reframing, and (j) as a vehicle for social support.

Entrainment is one among other music therapy approaches that has the potential for addressing multidimensional aspects of pain or pain-related suffering. Entrainment procedures involving music have been described by a variety of authors, including Bason and Celler (1972); Biedermann (1991); Cass-Beggs (1981); Dileo (1997); Eagle and Harsh (1988); Haas, Distenfeld, and Axen (1986); Loewy, MacGregor, Richards, and Rodriguez (1997); McIntosh, Thaut, Rice, and Miller (1994); Prassas, Thaut, McIntosh, and Rice (1997); Rider (1985, 1997); Saperston (1995); Turry (1997); and Thaut, Tian, and Azimi-Sadjadi (1998).

Entrainment is based on several interrelated principles: (a) the iso-principle, which states that after having matched music to the existing mood of a person, the mood can be altered through gradual changes in the music (Altschuler, 1948); (b) the concept of resonance or sympathetic vibration, in which a system capable of vibrating at a certain frequency is acted upon by another system vibrating at the same frequency causing vibration in the former (Backus, 1977); and (c) entrainment, wherein there is a "pull" exerted from one vibrating object to another vibrating in close frequency, thus creating a phase lock (Prassas et al., 1997; Saperston, 1995).

It is important to realize that the principles underlying entrainment as a therapeutic intervention explain to some extent only emotional, sensory, and physical phenomena, and it is clear that experiences of pain and pain-related suffering include but go beyond these factors. Thus, from a theoretical perspective, entrainment can be said to operate similarly in other human domains as well.

Clinical Approach

The use of music entrainment in the treatment of pain or pain-related suffering always involves a process wherein the music and therapeutic relationship both play significant, yet interconnected, roles. This process has been described by Dileo (1997) and Rider (1985, 1997), and stages of the process are presented below. Healing implications for various aspects of the process, according to some of the numerous biopsychosocial factors impinging on pain and suffering, are mentioned in the following sections.

Discovering the Pieces: Assessment

Besides the traditional medical, psychosocial, and musical information gathered during assessment from various sources as well as from the patient, it is often significant whenever possible to use music therapy experiences for assessment as well. Free, musically structured, or theme-based improvisations of the patient alone, the patient with the therapist, or the patient with the group can uncover subtle yet revealing information concerning the way the patient relates to his or her pain, the meaning of the pain, nonverbal characteristics of the pain, as well as evidence of pain-related suffering (i.e., feelings of helplessness, hopelessness, etc.). It is important to recognize that the assessment procedure in and of itself, i.e., just asking questions about the individual's pain, can begin to change the person's perceptions of pain.

Determining a Path: Goal Formulation

Based on the information collected and analyzed during assessment, the therapist and client formulate goals for treatment. In addition, the environment for the entrainment procedure is prepared to create a safe, secure place for the patient and to provide various musical options and appropriate musical instruments. If possible, the music therapy area should be adequately sound-proofed so that people in the vicinity of the area cannot hear/absorb the music of the patient's pain. This is a most important consideration, as will be discussed later in the chapter.

Entrainment is not suitable for every person experiencing pain. It may be most appropriate for patients (a) with high levels of perceived pain; (b) with pain that does not respond consistently or fully to medication; (c) for whom adequate pain medication is not an option because of medical reasons (pregnancy, for example); (d) who have the necessary motivation to engage in a music therapy process; (e) whose belief systems support alternative methods of pain treatment; and (f) who may be experienced pain-related suffering.

Entrainment may be contraindicated for patients (a) who have psychiatric problems, (b) who are medically very fragile, (c) who lack the cognitive ability to understand the process, (d) who have severe hearing problems, and (e) who may have any medical condition that may be exacerbated by entrainment.

Imaging the Pain as Music

Often, patients in pain employ various means to avoid coming into contact with their pain directly. Denial, resistance, and distortion are common reactions to having pain; these reactions may further exacerbate the pain experience. During the assessment phase and following, the patient begins to acquire an awareness of his relationship to the pain and its various manifestations.

This process is continued during this phase by asking the patient to form an auditory image of the pain and to begin to describe the characteristics of the pain musically (e.g., vocally or on instruments). The therapist assists the patient by listening carefully to the description of the pain and suggesting and playing various instruments, timbres, etc., as needed. The therapist also asks the patient specific questions about the pain, including its rhythm, texture, intensity, etc., to make the auditory image as real and consistent with the pain as possible. Thus, there is usually much experimenting with music and sound during this phase. The desired result is identification of musical sounds that match the pain as precisely as possible.

In a second part of this stage, the therapist asks the patient to create an auditory image of musical sounds that can heal the pain or are healing to the patient. The same procedures are used to assist the patient with this goal.

The healing components of this phase include the patient's increased awareness and exploration of the nature and characteristics of the pain. In essence, describing the pain in musical terms marks the beginning of a confrontation with the pain. Also, significant factors in healing are the awarenesses (a) that there *are* sounds that can heal (i.e., the pain is perhaps able to be controlled, have an end, etc., factors associated with pain-related suffering); and (b) these healing sounds have particular characteristics. It is important to discuss these issues and potential insights with the patient at the end of this phase of the process.

Confronting the Pain and Letting Go

Once the sounds of the pain and of healing have been identified by the patient, a musical improvisation is created. The patient is asked to close his or her eyes and sit or recline quietly, giving full attention to the music. The improvisation is usually created by therapist and is experienced by the patient in vivo and is also tape recorded.

The musical improvisation begins with the sounds of the onset of the pain, progressing to a peak of pain intensity for a short period (until the therapist assesses that entrainment has occurred), followed by a gradual diminishing of the pain music and movement into the healing sounds. The improvisation, if it indeed matches the patient's pain, is usually quite powerful for both the patient and therapist. The pain may subside immediately after the entrainment, or it may take some additional time to feel the relief.

There are two important healing components to this phase of the process. The first involves the patient's externalization of the pain through hearing the improvisation. By listening to the sounds of his pain outside of him or herself, the pain becomes concretized and part of the external world, rather than an internal phenomenon for the patient. When external to himself, the patient hears the pain and confronts it directly on an auditory and/or emotional level. This procedure, in general, creates a more realistic appraisal and awareness of the pain, contains the pain within a musical structure, and allows the patient to evaluate the pain from a more objective perspective. Through this and other types of exploration that may result, insight into the pain, into his or her relationship to the pain, and into him or herself results.

The second healing component of this phase involves the therapist's resonance with the patient's pain. By initially listening to the patient's pain, assisting the patient in creating its auditory image, and participating in the musical improvisation of the pain, the music therapist is able to enter directly into the patient's pain and resonate with his or her experience of it in a unique way (and perhaps as no other person can do with the patient). This provides validation for the patient and his or her experience, while also facilitating trust and closeness. Simply put, the therapist has shared the pain experience. Through this resonance, the therapist has played a significant part in shaping the person's experience of pain and suffering.

Continued Application

The patient continues to use the entrainment music tape at home, in music therapy, or in other circumstances at the onset of the pain to provide relief. There is a continuous monitoring of the suitability of the music for the patient's pain as the quality of the pain for the patient will often change. When this occurs, new improvisations are created for the patient. When the procedure is used by the patient at home, he or she is asked to document the frequency of the pain and the amount of pain experienced both before and after using the tape for the therapist's information and evaluation. The healing components of this phase include empowerment, reduced helplessness and hopelessness, improved pain tolerance, and reduced pain and suffering.

Precautions

Based on experience with this very powerful process, several precautions in its use have become evident:

1. This is not an intervention strategy that should be used by inexperienced therapists; special training and supervision are required. In addition, music therapists should have opportunities to "practice" this strategy with nonpatients before beginning to use it in treatment. This procedure cannot be classified as an "activity."

2. Awareness of boundaries is of great concern. The therapist and any other persons that may be involved in the process, particularly during the improvisational sessions, must be consciously aware of where they are with respect to the patient's pain and how the music is affecting or may potentially affect them. The therapist must learn the skill of entering into the patient's pain to achieve resonance and then consciously leaving and returning to his or her own boundaries. Other persons involved in the process and any observers to the process, especially if they are fellow patients, must be instructed in keeping boundaries, i.e., keeping themselves grounded and not allowing themselves to enter into the patient's pain musically, imaginally, cognitively, and/or emotionally. Often, it is suggested that they use an image of being in the room within a glass bubble, safe from absorbing feelings, music, energy etc. It is possible for this process to cause

pain in participants and observers. It is also important, as mentioned previously, that other individuals not be exposed to the pain music inadvertently for the same reasons as cited.

3. The success of this method is proportional to how accurately and specifically the music matches the patient's experience of pain. This technique has been observed to be ineffective when the patient does not allow the full extent of his or her pain to be reflected in the music, for whatever reasons. When the pain is great, the patient needs to be reassured that appropriate safeguards are in place for the therapist, as well as any other participants or observers to the process.

4. At times, the pain-relieving effects of this process will have some delay in the patient, although some relief is often experienced immediately. It may take some time, usually an hour or more, for the patient to experience full relief.

Conclusions

As therapists, it is important to realize that no experience of pain in life is wasted, as therapists can use their own experiences to empathically connect with the patient and the universality of suffering. Music entrainment provides a way for therapists to use themselves as well as the music as healing agents. Entrainment is a powerful tool in therapy and should not be used without advanced training and supervision. With that said, the entrainment approach may offer relief of pain, as well as the suffering that can accompany it. In other words, it may help suffering patients close the "GAP."

References

Altschuler, I. M. (1948). A psychiatrist's experience with music as a therapeutic agent. In D. Schullian & M. Schoen (Eds.), *Music and medicine.* New York: Books for Libraries Press.

Backus, J. (1977). *The acoustical foundations of music* (2nd ed.). New York: W. W. Norton.

Basky, A., Baszenger, I., Bradley, L., Casey, K., Chapman, C. R., Gracely, R., Haythornthwaite, J., Jackson, J., Jensen, M., Keefe, F. J., Liebeskind, J., Logan, H., McGrath, P., McGuire, D. B., Melzack, R., Morris, D., Post, S. G., Price, D., Rouse, F., Spross, J., Sullivan, M., Turk, D. C., Underwood, L., & Zeleznik, C., Fr. (1998). Perspectives on pain-related suffering: Presentations and discussions. *Advances in Mind-Body Medicine, 14*(3), 167–203.

Bason, P. T., & Celler, B. G. (1972). Control of the heart rate by external stimuli. *Nature, 238,* 279–280.

Biedermann, B. R. (1991). *Synchronisation of a music pulse to listener heart rate: The effects of tempo changes.* Unpublished master's thesis, Temple University, Philadelphia.

Budd, M. A. (1993). Human suffering: Road to illness or gateway to learning? *Advances, 9*(3), 28–36.

Cass-Beggs, B. (1981). The need for a musical environment during babyhood. *Journal of the Association for the Care of Children's Health, 1,* 132–134.

Cassell, E. (1991). *The nature of suffering.* New York: Oxford Press.

Dileo, C. (1997). Reflections on medical music therapy: Biopsychosocial aspects of the treatment process. In J. Loewy (Ed.), *Music therapy and pediatric pain* (pp. 125–144). Cherry Hill, NJ: Jeffrey Books.

Dileo-Maranto, C. (1993). Applications of music in medicine. In M. Heal & T. Wigram (Eds.), *Music therapy in health and education* (pp. 153–174). London: Jessica Kingsley.

Dileo-Maranto, C. (1996). Research in music and medicine: The state of the art. In M. Froehlich (Ed.), *Music therapy with hospitalized children: A creative arts child-life approach.* Cherry Hill, NJ: Jeffrey Books.

Eagle, C. T., & Harsh, J. M. (1988). Elements of pain and music: The Aio connection. *Music Therapy,* 7(1), 15–27.

Haas, F., Distenfeld, S., & Axen, K. (1986). Effects of perceived musical rhythm on respiratory pattern. *Applied Physiology, 62,* 1185–1191.

Loewy, J., MacGregor, B., Richards, K., & Rodriguez, J. (1997). In J. V. Loewy (Ed.), *Music therapy and pediatric pain.* Cherry Hill, NJ: Jeffrey Books.

McCaffery, M. (1968). *Nursing practice theories related to cognition, bodily pain, and man–environment interactions.* Los Angeles: University of California.

McGuire, D. B. (1995). The multiple dimensions of cancer pain: A framework for assessment and management. In D. B. McGuire, C. H. Yarboro, & B. R. Ferrell (Eds.), *Cancer pain management* (2nd ed., pp. 1–17). Boston: Jones & Bartlett.

McIntosh, G. C., Thaut, M. H., Rice, R. R., & Miller, R. A. (1994). Stride frequency modulation in Parkinsonian gait using rhythmic auditory stimulation. *Annals of Neurology, 36,* 316.

Prassas, S., Thaut, M., McIntosh, G., & Rice, R. (1997). Effect of auditory rhythmic cuing on gait kinematic parameters of stroke patients. *Gait and Posture, 6,* 218–223.

Rider, M. (1985). Entrainment mechanisms are involved in pain reduction, muscle relaxation and music-mediated imagery. *Journal of Music Therapy, 22*(4), 183–192.

Rider, M. S. (1997). Entrainment music, healing imagery, and the rhythmic language of health and disease. In J. V. Loewy (Ed.), *Music therapy and pediatric pain.* Cherry Hill, NJ: Jeffrey Books.

Saperston, B. (1995). The effects of consistent tempi and physiologically interactive tempi on heart rate and EMG responses. In T. Wigram, B. Saperston, & R. West (Eds.), *The art and science of music therapy: A handbook* (pp. 58–82). Switzerland: Hardwood Academic.

Thaut, M., Tian, B., & Azimi-Sadjadi, M. R. (1998). Rhythmic finger tapping to cosine-wave modulated metronome sequences: Evidence of subliminal entrainment. *Human Movement Science, 17,* 839–863.

Turry, A. E. (1997). The use of clinical improvisation to alleviate procedural distress in young children. In J. V. Loewy (Ed.), *Music therapy and pediatric pain.* Cherry Hill, NJ: Jeffrey Books.

18

The Use of Music Psychotherapy in the Treatment of Pediatric Pain

Joanne Loewy, DA, MT-BC

THIS CHAPTER PRESENTS an overview of the pediatric population and highlights specific goals in working within a medical model. The focus of the assessment and treatment interventions will address the needs of children (infants through teenagers) who experience acute, chronic, and/or procedural pain. The reader will gain insight concerning how to incorporate music therapy into a medical treatment plan, thereby enhancing team cohesion while also attending to the emotional parameters that accompany the experience of having pain. The model incorporating the integration of mind and body in the treatment of pain will derive from a music psychotherapy orientation. To this end, issues of transference and countertransference will be addressed.

Pediatric Music Therapy

Working with children who are hospitalized presents unique clinical challenges for the music therapist. The first of these is the broad range of illnesses that one encounters on a daily basis. A music therapy session might involve a one-time assessment of a child admitted for the ruling out of a series of possible illnesses, and who is discharged within a day or two. Another session might be the continuation of a three+ month music therapy plan involving a child who is nearing the end of life. For this child, the final stay will involve a poignant closure and bereavement process that encapsulates years of music therapy sessions amidst frequent admissions and discharges. It is this broad spectrum from life to death and everything in between that presents the music therapist with constant shifts in clinical applications.

Since disease has the capacity to affect every kind of person, experience with a variety of populations has its advantages. Understanding how an autistic child can cope with asthma or how a diabetic teenager with attention deficit disorder can be taught to manage insulin can be a delicate matter. The involvement of music therapy as part of the treatment regimen is best implemented by a therapist who has both an understanding of child development as well as experience with children who have special needs.

Treating children for any ailment must take into account a larger system. The family is the binding frame which typically shapes the way a child perceives his or her own growth. In this respect, working with a pediatric population is complicated. The music therapist may include the parents or siblings. Unlike other settings, the therapist has access to the child's family, and the hospital room serves as a temporary living space in which significant issues emerge. The therapist considers how the child is internalizing the illness not only from a physical perspective, but also from cognitive, emotional, and spiritual vantage points. Assessing family parameters as well as the child's perception of how his or her family is affected is a unique and important part of pediatric music therapy.

Whether a child is newly diagnosed or returning for recurring chronic symptoms, anxiety is always a component of the pediatric setting. Especially for infants and toddlers, being in an unfamiliar space can throw off eating and sleeping schedules. Conscious and unconscious parental anxiety can translate into fear, which can further compound the feelings associated with being ill.

THEORETICAL APPROACH IN MUSIC PSYCHOTHERAPY

A relationship that develops within a musical context seems to hold its own therapeutic process. Yet, the history and development of music psychotherapy treatment is best grounded in a psychological school of thought. Indeed, the models of psychotherapy to which a therapist subscribes will be evident and reflected in the work itself. The musical interventions that a music psychotherapist makes are rooted in the way he or she is thinking about the ego and how behaviors manifest themselves both in and out of the musical relationship. It would be difficult, for example, for me to encourage a patient to release through drumming if I were not convinced that an instinctual impulse, the id content, could not help in letting go of tensions being blocked by the ego.

The principles of psychotherapy that have been incorporated into my work in music therapy stem from the blending of three schools: Anna Freud's theory of ego development, Jean Piaget's constructs of intellectual development, and Fritz Perls' Gestalt therapy.

Ann Freud's teachings about identification and introjection are central to the way in which a child experiencing pain can assimilate the traumas he or she has to undertake while hospitalized. As a child uses music to actively play out an unpleasant experience, he or she learns to incorporate frightening experiences which may then be carefully discharged as the process of transformation occurs. The anxiety relating to a past experience can be understood and realized as a coping mechanism that can help an ill child prepare for the future. Building ego strength and integration through musical activities that empower the child can assist in defense building and can enhance endurance for painful procedures that may be a necessary part of hospitalization. When a child is provided with the opportunity to introject through story song or improvisational play, the ego integration is strengthened.

Instincts and defenses are integrated unconsciously, but at times are mediated by the process of thinking. Jean Piaget's development of the evolving stages of thought in a child is based on his years of observing children. This very act, observation, is central to the act of understanding and feeling another being's music of the body. By music, I am referring to a person's rhythm of breath, patterns of speech, phrasing, pitch of sentences expressed, as well as dance of his or her every movement. Each of us is a musical being, even without musical instruments. If we listen carefully, we can feel the music of a person's being. I have developed a knack for guessing a child's favorite kind of music. It comes from intuiting through careful observation.

Piaget has contributed to cognitive psychology in a significant way. In understanding the thoughts of children, it is helpful to think of metaphoric play and symbols that develop during the sensorimotor period. A child develops symbolic functioning through imitation. Repetition and imitation provide children with great safety in thought and feeling. Music naturally provides for these kinds of experiences. Music can synthesize the child's ability to translate feelings into a meaning that is realized through verbal and nonverbal expression. Musical play can assist in a child's confirmation of a conception of reality through thought and play. Piaget's model includes motoric play and extends to concrete and formal operational thinking. Because children's levels of thinking and learning are constantly changing, it is important to have a theory of thought development and an awareness of how concepts of the mind can interact with perceptions of the body. This is critically important in the treatment of infants, babies, and teenagers who experience pain.

Gestalt therapy was developed first by Fritz Perls in the 1940s. In the music therapy experience, the moment of play is critical to the expression of feelings in the here and now. Gestalt implies a configuration of the whole. Each independent part of a person is related to every other part and has greatest meaning as an entire whole. Therefore, to hear a teenager with abdominal pain blow relaxed, long breaths through a recorder, but notice his right foot willfully but maybe unconsciously shaking, provides an interesting challenge. The goal of the music therapist in a Gestalt context would be to illuminate the relatedness of these alienated aspects of presentation and integrate them on a conscious level. How can the music and the music psychotherapist help integrate the parts of the individual that contribute to the hospitalization? Awareness is important, and music can provide a nonconfrontational means of opening channels of self-acceptance and creative mechanisms for change, in part and in whole.

Clinical Applications

The daily experiences provided by music therapists vary based on the needs of the child. Routinely, patients are referred by doctors, nurses, social workers, and child life specialists for specific needs or treatment goals. Sessions could be grouped into three categories: (1) day-to-day individual and group music psychotherapy, (2) specific consults that address a particular medical/psychosocial need, and (3) procedural music therapy.

The day-to-day music psychotherapy sessions can be broad, addressing general fears or coping needs. However, often a particular referral is made to assist the team in assessing what may be the physical or emotional status of a patient. For instance, social work may refer an infant with a broken limb or head injury and the parent (who could be on hold by the city's protective services agency) to music therapy with a recommendation to assess mother-infant bonding. A general referral from a doctor might include assisting a teenager who will be in isolation for several months (resulting from an infectious disease such as tuberculosis) with self-expression using musical improvisation that can address increasing and apparent anger or rage.

Often, a patient is referred because he has stopped eating or has had discomfort due to constipation or gas pain. Perhaps a child has been unable to sleep. Staff have increasingly recognized the importance of music therapy in addressing these important physical and emotional needs. Musical mastery experiences involving esteem building and musical empowerment activities have motivated patients who have shut down their intake ("I'm not hungry"). Music-making can aid in the recovery of an appetite, helping the body to remember that the taking in of food (as in the taking in of music) can be a pleasant experience.

Music therapy has increased a patient's ability to void. Drumming, in particular, has enhanced the flow and release of energy, beginning from outside of the body and affecting movement and eventual release from inside of the body. As patients actively structure and control their own body's ability to create rhythms for sustained periods, the body responds and rids itself of waste.

Sleeping and the ability to rest is essential to recovery. Children of all ages, but particularly young children (infants and toddlers), are often reluctant to sleep without a parent nearby. As well, children approaching the end of their life may equate sleep with death and are willful of staying awake; they fear if they go to sleep, they may not awaken. A meaningful lullaby, catered to the need and desire of a dying child, can assist the transition from life to death in ways that are difficult to describe.

Music, specifically lullabies, are irreplaceable in creating a containing atmosphere of trust and safety. The use of song and lullaby can serve as a transitional object (Winnicott, 1953) for young children and toddlers, amidst medical crises and unfamiliar surroundings. Lullabies nurture and soothe the parent who is unconsciously translating fear and tension to her baby by bouncing or breathing too rapidly. A song of kin (learned by the music therapist and offered to the parent) can nurture the nervous father and calm him subtly in a direct, nonaccusatory way, so that he, in turn, may transmit safety and calm to his toddler, who may have been awake for an entire night prior to a music therapy session.

Specific music therapy consults include referrals for pain (acute or chronic), asthma and breathing enhancement, or sedation prior to medical testing. The experiences provided for a patient in pain (assessed to have a 3+ pain score) will be addressed later in this chapter. Consults may include a routine involvement (providing musical sedation for a series of tests throughout several days), or a one-time, prolonged session, such as surgery. In this case, the therapist may begin with a patient in the holding area and follow him or her through to the operating room and stay until the anesthesia has taken effect.

Asthma and breathing consults typically include the use of live music, imagery or visualization, wind playing, and clinical improvisation, all of which address the depth of breath in the body and the rate and control of breath a patient can achieve within an active musical context. Music relaxation techniques enable patients to be aware of how they breathe, and clinical improvisation seeks to help them realize how feelings and emotions can impact the way in which they breathe.

Sedation consults involve the use of music therapy instead of, or as a complement to, pharmacological agents prior to medical testing or surgery. In medical tests, such as EEGs, MRIs, scans, endoscopies, etc., music therapy may serve as a primary means of sedation (most often conscious sedation) prior to and/or during a test. In surgery (before, during, and after), music therapy may assist in enhancing the body's natural receptors for sedation more effectively, rapidly, and comfortably. At times, patients' blood pressures have been too high for anesthesia to be administered safely. Music therapy, particularly with the use of entrainment to slow the rate of respiration, can serve to decrease blood pressure and help the patient to feel relaxed.

A pilot study of 3 surgeons and 10 pediatric surgery residents found their biggest emotional concern related to their young patients' last memory prior to surgery. As one surgeon said, "I just imagine she'll hold this horrific vision of us [surgeons, anesthesiologists] hovering over her face, laying down estranged by a mask, and unsettled by what is unfamiliar." Music therapy is used in the holding area prior to surgery, in escorting the child from the holding area to the operating room, and in the operating room until the anesthesia has taken effect. This has been an appreciated service at Beth Israel Medical Center in New York City. Postsurgery consults can be useful as well, assisting in awareness/reorientation and in pain management.

The third kind of music therapy sessions includes procedural pain treatment. These sessions include accompanying the medical team in minor surgical procedures that can cause physical pain and emotional duress, such as venipunctures (IV insertions, blood drawings, etc.), taps, biopsies, and procedures of all kinds. Most often these sessions are best thought of as group sessions, as they involve doctors, nurses, technicians, and, when deemed important by the child and/or treatment team, parents. Procedural music therapy sessions have been instrumental in helping the general, entire scope of treatment for a child.

Being "stuck" with a needle can elicit fear in children of all ages. Holding a child down evokes feelings of distrust and harm that can linger throughout the hospital stay and can haunt treatment implementation for years to come. McGrath and Craig (1989) noted that children with cancer (a disease plagued with suffering, including pain, nausea, and restricted activity), report needle procedures to be the worst part of their illness.

It seems children may sense their own lack of control, as well as a disrespect of their bodies by medical staff, during needle procedures. This can bring forth feelings of helplessness and fear. There is a sense from most clinicians performing such procedures that it "needs to get done," and it is "going to get done." Venipuncture, as I first observed at various hospitals, was done to children, rather than with them. The term *medical rape* came into my mind. There was no respect for the children and their unique needs, and direct communication and eye contact were minimal.

An important use of music therapy in treating procedural pain has been to create a safe environment for both children and staff. Doctors and nurses have reported that having their names (e.g., "Dr. Smith is wiping, is wiping . . .") sung before and during a procedure enhanced their own feelings of trust and safety, not only with regard to how children perceived them but also within their own actual performance of the procedure as well.

The applications of music therapy with a pediatric population as described above may involve music as medicine or music in medicine (Dileo-Maranto, 1991). The integration of these two applications may serve the needs of the child and family most effectively. In this way, the approach to music therapy with a baby, child, or teenager facing an illness of any magnitude involves a full orientation to psychosocial parameters and a complete physiological understanding of the illness as well. Both of these separately and interrelatedly are important in ascertaining the most essential piece of treatment planning: how the child experiences the illness and treatment on a concrete level.

Barr (in McGrath and Craig, 1989) notes:

> The tendency to ignore the child patient and to rely on an informant (however well informed) deprives the clinician of the child's understanding and report of the symptoms

and the opportunity to provide potent treatment directly to the child . . . family therapists have long described families in which parents are inappropriately overinvolved. (p. 829)

Indeed, how a child thinks about a disease, whether rational or not, is one of the most crucial aspects that influences how he or she feels and ultimately how slowly or quickly treatments may or may not take effect. The perspective that serves most useful in the application of medical music therapy in pediatrics involves how the music, in conjunction with psychotherapeutic clinical inferences, integrates the mind and body. It is critical to realize that it is not the music alone that evokes change. The therapist contextualizes musical interventions in a psychotherapeutic framework, and the music psychotherapy goal involves knowledge of the patient's history, ego orientation, and psychological functioning. The work always involves a balance of ascertaining how the mind affects the body and how the body affects the mind. Music psychotherapy can bridge the way these two systems interface. This becomes extraordinarily important when we consider the assessing and treating of a child in pain.

Assessing the Emotional and Physical Parameters of Pain

The International Association for the Study of Pain defines pain as the sensory and emotional experience associated with actual or potential tissue damage. Pain is the only vital sign that includes an emotional experience as part of its definition.

As soon as a child is referred to music therapy for a pain consult, the assessment process begins. The referral, whether written or spoken, is central to the process of assessment. Most often, a referral will include a diagnosis and a qualitative or quantitative description of the pain as well as the source (location in the body). At times a doctor or nurse will offer a description of how a patient or family is coping with the pain.

Knowing whether the pain is chronic or acute offers valuable information. Using music therapy to treat pain that is recurrent and of an unknown origin, in contrast to pain that is the result of a procedure, requires completely different treatment strategies and clinical challenges.

Chronic pain generally is categorized as that which persists beyond the usual time for healing or in the absence of an obvious injury. Diseases such as hemophilia, sickle cell anemia, and arthritis produce frequent painful crises that may last from several days to several weeks. Children can also have chronic pain that is caused primarily by psychological factors.

Acute pain is more common than chronic pain and is caused by damaged tissue involving a noxious stimulus. Children's perceptions about acute pain, as in chronic pain, are influenced by situational, emotional, and familial factors. Acute pain can be caused by physical accidents, or as the result of a procedure or corrective surgery.

The source and location of pain is essential to a referral. Equally important is the child's clinical context as described by a referring clinician. The way in which a child's pain episode is shared formally (in a written referral form), or informally (verbal referral-in rounds), provides an impression of how a child's pain is perceived or interpreted by others. The number of complaints, availability or presence of a parent, and quality of a patient's cry are key aspects of the pain experience that are directly or indirectly translated through a referral.

It is best if the music therapist can resist reading the patient's chart until after the music therapy assessment session has occurred. In this way, the therapist's own intuition and findings may uncover new material and offer insight into treatment challenges that may not yet have been discovered.

During the music therapy pain assessment, the challenge is to understand and feel the pain of the patient as well as it can be defined by him or her. The location, temperature, intensity, and degree of absorption or denial of pain within the body, as well as the rhythm and color of the pain as it occurs, is useful for the therapist to sense. It is helpful to inquire about the times the pain becomes most intense, or about the patient's most painful experience of all time. How has the patient dealt with the pain in the past? Does he or she like to be alone or around others when having pain? Who and what has been helpful or unhelpful during painful episodes? With children, it is also essential to explore what they think is the source of their pain. At times, their answers depict fantasies that direct the work into establishing truth or alleviating guilt (e.g., "This pain is the result of something I did wrong"). At other times, the imagination can help the child tune into his or her body more accurately. This can assist the doctor in determining the root or source of the pain, rather than simply knowing that it "hurt."

Patients should be encouraged to play or direct the therapist to musically improvise the sound that the pain is making inside their bodies. The music of the physical discomfort can provide the therapist with clues on how to address physical aspects of the tension. The sound of pain when played alone by the patient or when framed harmonically or rhythmically by the therapist provides hints about the amount of support or space the patient needs to have.

A full pain assessment in working with patients in any kind of pain must address the pain episode itself and, in particular, the moments prior to deciding when and how the patient came to the hospital. This poignant time will provide a snapshot of how pain and crises or sudden traumas are addressed within the family. Listening to the stories involving a patient's history with pain will offer invaluable information about potential prolific and undetected pain associations.

In my practice, I have seen occasional, unexpected sources of pain. One 16-year-old male had abdominal pain of an unknown etiology that we learned, through weeks of music therapy sessions, was the result of sexual molestation from years prior. Another 8-year-old girl's severe pain was discovered to be caused by an emotional withholding about her recent diagnosis of leukemia (typically unpainful) in an attempt to protect her parents.

Most hospitals and medical settings have instituted procedures for pain measurement. The scales available for children are becoming increasingly more creative. They include verbal self-reports, a photographic scale of facial expressions, color scales, ladder scales, interviews, visual analog scales, pain thermometer pictures, poker chip scales, etc. The common purpose of these measurements is to obtain objective information about children's subjective pain experiences (McGrath, 1990). One commonly instituted pain assessment tool is the Wong-Baker Faces Scale (Figure 1).

The implementation of projective scales that include color assessments as part of the pain description is a useful option. Stewart (1977), Eland (1982), and Jeans and Gordon (1981) have devised projective color tools. Interestingly, the color red has been found to be the most common color children use to reflect pain. There have been reports that these assessments, although more qualitative than quantitative in nature, do reflect the process of how pain is experienced and provide a more explicit understanding of how children internalize discomfort. DiLeo (1977) compared children's drawings with their conversations about pain and found expressivity to be more direct through drawings than through discussion. It is recommended that music therapists

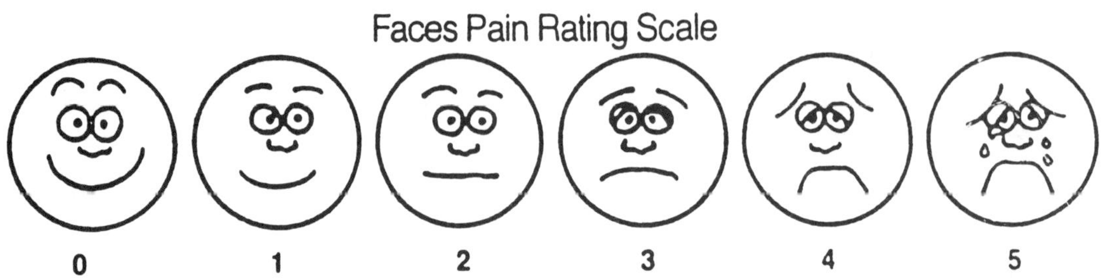

Explain to the person that each face is for a person who feels happy because he has no pain (hurt) or sad because he has some or a lot of pain. **Face 0** is very happy because he doesn't hurt at all. **Face 1** hurts just a little bit. **Face 2** hurts a little more. **Face 3** hurts even more. **Face 4** hurts a whole lot. **Face 5** hurts as much as you can imagine, although you don't have to be crying to feel this bad. Ask the person to choose the face that best describes how he is feeling.

Rating scale is recommended for persons age 3 years and older.

Figure 1. Wong-Baker Faces Scale (Wong & Baker, 1988; reprinted from Beth Israel Medical Center's Flow Sheet).

use both qualitative and quantitative measurements to assess the status of a child's pain both pre- and posttreatment.

The following tool was developed for a music therapy and venipuncture pain study at Beth Israel (Loewy, MacGregor, Richards, & Rodriguez, 1997) and has been useful in both assessing and evaluating patients in chronic and acute pain, as well as in procedural pain. The illustration (Figure 2) was completed by a 17-year-old with sickle cell anemia prior to a music therapy session. For the left figure, she selected red and confined the pain to the areas colored. She described her pain as "burning hot—like someone is stabbing me over and over again right in my joints." Her numeric rating was a 10. After a 30-minute pain intervention, which included vibrational gong work and d'jimbe African drumming, she selected blue for the figure on the right and commented that the pain had diminished and "felt cooler—there is more flow. I don't feel it as much." The scale postsession went to a 3.

The Attia Scale (Attia, Amiel-Tison, Mayer, Shnider, & Barrier, 1987; Figure 3) is useful for assessing pain in infants and babies. There has been some controversy in the past concerning whether babies experience pain. Current research reveals that the neuroanatomic apparatus for conducting nociceptive impulses from the periphery to the sensory cortex is intact even in the newborn infant. (Anand & Hickey, 1987). Human infants do have the anatomic and functional components required for appreciation of painful stimuli (Gilles, Shankle, & Dooling, 1983). In treating infants who are experiencing pain, often much of the work is filtered through the parent, as it is imperative to address the parent-child dyad as a unit.

In a music therapy assessment, the patient and therapist decide together what instruments and type of music will address the physical elements of pain. The emotional issues resulting from the pain are also assessed and addressed in treatment.

Patient chose red crayon. Patient chose blue crayon.

Figure 2. Qualitative Color Pain Scale (Child).

CATEGORY	0	1	2
Sleep during preceeding hour	None	Short naps: between 5 and 10 minutes	Longer naps: >10 minutes
Facial expression of pain	Marked, constant	Less marked, intermittent	Calm, relief
Quality of cry	Screaming, painful, high pitched	Modulated, i.e., can be distracted by normal sound	No cry
Spontaneous motor activity	Thrashing around, incessant agitation	Moderate agitation	Normal
Spontaneous excitability and responsiveness to ambient stimulation	Tremulous, clonic movement, spontaneous Moro reflexes	Excessive reactivity (to any stimulation)	Quiet
Constant and excessive flexion of fingers and toes	Very pronounced, marked & constant	Less marked, intermittent	Absent
Sucking	Absent or disorganized sucking	Intermittent (3 or 4) & stops with crying	Strong, rhythmic with pacifying affect
Global evaluation of tone	Strong hypertonicity	Moderate hypertonicity	Normal for the age
Consolability	None after 2 minutes	Quiet after 1 minute of effort	Calm before 1 minute
Sociability (eye contact) Response to voice, smile, real interest in face	Absent	Difficult to obtain	Easy and prolonged

Figure 3. Attia Behavioral Pain Scale (Attia et al., 1987; reprinted from Children's Hospital of Philadelphia Pain Manual).

When the pain experience is denied or even healthily defended against, a conscious or unconscious rage can diminish the body's ability to cope. In the playing of music, the patient uses the body to physically create a dynamic expression. The energy tendencies and needs of the patient experiencing pain often become transparent. The music therapy assessment moves the patient beyond a quantifiable rating. The therapist can see and hear how the patient expresses him/herself physically and dynamically. The way to treat the pain is carefully discerned. The rhythm of a patient's speech is critical. The way a variety of instruments are played and range of dynamic expression that occurs when the patient plays alone and with the therapist can provide important information for treatment. In general, the majority of pain sessions include either the full extreme of the forte or piano dynamics. The person in pain wants to yell, drum, kick or cry, and to be joined or listened to while doing so. This experience might begin as a call and response. The safety and order of this might build the trust, which then leads to drum rolls and free expression of range. Another person in pain might need soft nurturance and integrative breath work. Inhaling to the point of the pain and exhaling on a toned "Ah" may provide a gradual air flow and enhance relaxation. A song of the patient's choice sung slowly with no vibrato and carefully attuned to the patient's breath rhythm may be mesmerizing and can help induce a sleep response, allowing the patient to let go of the holding onto the pain (consciously or unconsciously).

The following section offers interventions that are broad and represent a range of musical interventions that have been useful in the author's practice. They are meant to be thought of as options and ideas, rather than prescriptive solutions. The context and uniqueness of each and every experience of pain must take into account the energy that emerges between patient and therapist. This is the single most important factor in deciding which route to pursue as the discomfort and associated issues unravel. The interventions applied may be straightforward and obvious (such as breathing, use of a wind instrument) for a screaming teen with abdominal pain who has been hyperventilating and yelling all morning. More often, however, the intervention and clues as to how music should be suggested involves a wide host of variables (both physical and emotional) and a limit of time, due to frequent tests, visitors, and the general lack of meter that exists within a hospital environment.

Pain Intervention

As mentioned previously, pain is not considered a phenomenon that is solely physically based. Thus, how a person perceives his or her own ability to heal can impact how pain is addressed.

Following a musical warm-up, a greeting of structure in which the therapist provides a song and atmosphere of openness and safety, open-ended inquiries that relate to how the patient is feeling both physically (pain scale) and emotionally can be addressed. The assessment questions and musical opportunities should offer insight into how the patient has addressed his or her needs thus far. What is significant to realize is that patients (especially children) do not necessarily say what they feel. In other words, the content of a patient's discussion can be the polar opposite of what is experienced in the thematic expression of his or her music. How can the music connect the mind and the body? This is an essential qualifier. At the route of a pain crisis is a balloon waiting to pop—a person so angry that he or she may simply need to release and yell or cry, but instead, he or she may be holding on or holding back. Many times, children in terrible pain often hide their feelings, protecting those around them. This is a common prototype that becomes evident, especially in young boys. I call it "the quiet soldier" (Loewy, 1999).

There is the opposite scenario of a child whose pain is mild but increases suddenly, every so often. The issue of secondary gains (McGrath, 1990) can be at play here, especially in young children who may not know how else to receive attention of such great magnitude from a parent or sibling.

Still another child may be experiencing terrible pain and, in focusing on it, exacerbates the sensation of its existence. Like fire, it spreads throughout the body, and nothing is helping to dissipate it. A vibrational sound bath with the gong might be the perfect remedy for this instance. Toning and encouraging this patient to use his or her voice on a particular note with a specific vowel might soothe and balance the flow of energy. In this way, a painful fire might shift into a steady stream of vibration that cools and stabilizes the pain.

There are many scenarios. Pain scales that shift from 10 to 1 in the presence of family, medical staff, and in the wake of constant, gentle prodding of the patient who can find 100 different reasons to resist music therapy. In the first months of working with patients in pain, the hardest part was walking into the patients' rooms. Having been part of so many transformative experiences, there is rarely a time today that patients will refuse my attempt to work with their pain through music. Perhaps they sense opportunity and confidence in the way that music therapy is offered, although no promises are made. In its presentation, it is important that music therapy be appropriately described. Too often, alternative options explored with patients were, at best, called "fun" or "diversional." The way music therapy can be offered is with the rationale that it will address the pain directly through specific interventions.

The following five treatment options were developed in my clinical practice at Beth Israel Medical Center. These experiences include techniques that have been implemented successfully with patients in pain. The techniques and their refinements have been explored within clinical supervision groups involving medical residents, nurses, and music therapy interns. In this way, the experiences were tested and modified through the years. Experiential rounds for medical staff provide opportunities for feeling and understanding the effects of music therapy techniques that they will inevitably encounter during the day. By experiencing the treatment, referrals broaden, and patients experiencing pain are identified more readily for music therapy.

I. Vibration/Toning

The sound of the body gongs resonate at particular points (head, abdomen, lower body). The gongs can be used to enhance blood flow and can increase the current of energy in the body in many ways. Often patients in pain will have the upper or lower part of their bed raised, and they may be holding onto the region of the body that is in pain. This can confine the flow and be vaso-constricting. By encouraging patients to level their body flat, the gong's vibration can enhance connections from one region of the body to the next. The warm-up to this work involves breath-relaxation (in through the nose, out through the mouth slowly) and a brief tightening and releasing of each part of the body from the toes up to the head.

Encouraging the patient to tone (sing or vocalize) on the 3rd or 5th of the basic resounding tonic of the gong tone (or other vibrational instrument such as a tone bar, chrutie box, or Suzuki chimes) can enhance the feeling of balance or shift in energy and awaken a new area of need within the body. In my work, I have identified specific vowel sounds that seem to open resonant chambers within various regions of the body (Figure 4).

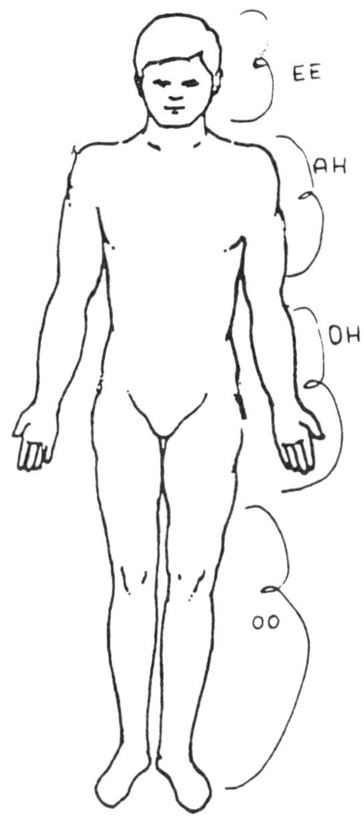

Figure 4. Qualitative Pain Scale (Adult).

Sometimes the gong helps move the pain out of the body. The sound of the gong can become tinny or limited when played above a painful region of the body. The goal is to create a steady pure vibrational flow which will stay consistent in tone when played from head to toe or around (circular) the entire body. The specific techniques that have developed from my work include: (a) ironing—motioning the gong quickly in one region, creating a vibrato effect that can smoothen an area that's cramped or "tied up in a ball"; (b) balancing—moving the vibration from one side of the body to the other; (c) moving—consistently pulling the sound slowly and systematically from top to bottom or bottom to top; and (d) color/visualization (Bradway, 1997)—using the air in synchrony with the gong, tracing where and how the air is inhaled and exhaled, supporting and deepening the breath by visualizing specific colors that carry the air and vibration to where the point of pain is and nourishing that spot.

II. Sedation

Painful episodes can tire the body, causing a cycle of inward battles in which children overexert themselves trying to fight off the pain. This can shut off healthy signals that, in turn, block blood flow or restrict or cramp muscles. Music, especially chanting, can enhance the relaxation response and help children to lose consciousness or fall asleep, letting go of the pain. Entraining a simple familiar melody to the meter of a patient's breath, and eventually recontextualizing the theme in a 6/8 holding meter can provide a holding that soothes and induces a sleep response. Slowing the breath down through music is a natural process. The final moments that carry the child from light sleep to deep sleep involve lulling tones that are simple single-toned whole notes, 3rds, or 5ths. This creates a feeling of safety and trust contained within a blanket of tone.

III. Integration

Integration is an effective way of describing what many practitioners might think of as distraction. The notion is that if children are not looking at or thinking about the pain, then they won't notice it as much. Perhaps in the case of playing a computer game, or watching television, *distraction* would be an appropriate term. In creating music, however, there is evidence that there is more than a refocusing occurring in the body. Theories suggest that music and pain are processed along the same neural pathways (Eagle & Harsh, 1988).

This could mean that engaging in music may turn off the pain signal, redirecting the pathway into a music signal response. Integration means that two or more systems of the body are working together at the same time, causing synergy. The rhythmic patterns set up by a patient playing the tongue drum may be in meter with the way that the patient is singing; this integrates movement (physical action) and thoughts (cognitive intention), which can shut off a pain response. A slow breath recorder piece that is played in harmony with a harmonic theme can integrate breath (physical respiration) with theme (emotional expression). These examples reflect how music can integrate systems of the mind and body. When thoughts and feelings are activated and connected consciously to biophysical responses of the body, the pain response can lessen or be eliminated.

IV. Release

The term *release* is synonymous with the words *vent, clear, free,* or *undo.* Although there is evidence that relaxation (Varni, Gilbert, & Dietrich, 1981) and hypnosis (Olness & MacDonald, 1981) are useful in treating pain, there has been little, if any, exploration of the actual physical expression of pain as a means of diminishing it. Indeed, simply screaming might actually increase the perception of pain, reinforcing the lack of control a patient has, not to mention the fact that exerting vocal energy may tire the body physically and emotionally. Yet, releasing the experience of pain in the presence of a music therapist who can frame and encourage primal discharge has been shown to be effective in many instances. The most common way I have used release in my work with children has been in the instances of acute pain, such as during an acute sickle cell crisis and with children suffering from abdominal pain (of unknown origin).

During an assessment, themes of anger can emerge. Perhaps a child has had the "maximum dose"of pain medication and still has not perceived any reduction in pain. Or perhaps there is an important event that is being missed at school, which can evoke issues of helplessness or lack of control in the body. There might be an energy of anger in the content of what the patient is saying that is not being realized or expressed in the music that he or she is presenting. In instances such as these, African drumming is a viable option with the goals of expressivity, tension release, and, most importantly, alleviation of pain. The technique of release is different with each patient, and how the therapist organizes the process depends upon the need or thematic development of the situation. It usually begins with both the patient and therapist playing a basic beat together, each on separate d'jimbe drums.

The immediate contact of the hand to the drum is central to the process. A mallet removes the direct force of energy that needs to be exerted by the patient. As the drumming continues, an African chant, a rap, a call and answer, or wordless toning may be encouraged. Careful attunement to the patient's investment in the experience and the physical changes (such as color in the face, breath rate, heart rate, body language) will provide information on how the drumming is experienced. At some point, the synergy between patient and therapist increases, as does often the basic meter of the beat. There can be solo interludes established between beats 4 and 1 by the therapist improvising on beats 2 and 3. Eventually, a peak or long roll (constant alternating hands) is experienced together and held for an extended time. A vocal AHHHH is recommended and can be encouraged by the therapist at this point.

V. Comfort/Soothing

The patient that needs to be consoled is often difficult to read. Although there may be 20 relatives surrounding his or her bed, dozens of flower arrangements, and gifts of all kinds throughout the room, the patient may be experiencing a level 10 pain but will tell you that "everything is okay."

Once the visitors are convinced to take a break, the patient may become quiet. It may almost feel like resistance, but in a moment's willingness to check out the possibilities of a variety of experiences, it may become apparent that there doesn't have to be any activity. The patient has accepted your entry and is relieved to have the visitors gone. At this point, what this patient may truly desire is the sound of a warm voice offering a favorite spiritual from his or her church, or a lullaby that his or her mother is unable to sing at this time. Another option is a baroque or classical piece played on the guitar or Celtic harp. Perhaps a wordless tune or an a capella theme warmed by the ocean drum or chimes will provide a moment's serenity.

As the body is reminded to relax through familiar or soothing sounds of comfort, the patient may cry. He or she may want the music to continue or may reposture the body to a position that reflects a need to talk. It is important to provide options and inquire about the pain and the amount of time a patient would like the therapist's musical offering or company. Even the gift of silence, which in itself is a powerful part of music, can truly assure a patient that the therapist is listening.

Countertransference in the Music Psychotherapy Pain Session

Absorption

One of the most difficult tasks of working with people who are in pain is to learn how to be sensitive to their experience of pain without absorbing it. Creating a healthy buffer means that the pain can be understood or felt momentarily for the purpose of deciding the most effective intervention, rather than empathizing to the point of over-attachment and internalization.

The music therapist must take caution to keep a steady stream of space and separateness when involved in this work. Because the activity of music-making involves the therapist's connecting with another person's energy while they are experiencing pain, the pain can be physically and dynamically transferred through the music. The therapist must constantly breathe and create an imaginary buffer to ensure that the pain or elements of the condition are not transferred.

Blocking

At times it may be uncomfortable to address physical tension or unpleasant issues musically or verbally. The therapist may be seeking to move the patient's music into a particular mode because the therapist fears the intensity or rage of that which the patient is needing to let go. The therapist may block out the opportunity for a patient to release, because the therapist may lack the energy resources to take the patient to that point.

Fixing the Pain

When a pain session occurs, it is the therapist's intention (and most usually the patient's as well) to help reduce the pain experienced. Often a therapist will spend long periods of time and a great deal of energy seeking to alleviate a child's pain during a crisis. Children, in general, typically display approval-seeking behavior; they want to be liked and respected by both peers and adults. Additionally, a child in pain has the need to believe that the pain will indeed go away. If a therapist becomes overly eager to treat the pain, the patient's true experience may be overlooked. There are times when all the music and techniques have been offered, and still there is no pain relief. The patient should not feel compelled to shift from reporting the honest fact that the pain still exists to protect the therapist's or doctor's feelings.

Fix-it tendencies are subtle. Merely the way a practitioner asks about pain, that is, "How are you feeling?" versus "Are you feeling better?" may lead a patient to answer and report the pain in varying ways. The first question is open and provides for a full range of responses. The second is leading and pushes the patient to say that things are better, so the doctor can move on to the next patient, or the music therapist knows that the soothing song just offered did the trick. In both cases, the child rewarded the clinician, and the pain experience was overlooked. The inquiry of a patient's pain scale is important and ideally should be asked before and after a session. Yet, it should be asked very matter-of-factly, and at a separate time from the music therapy experience—on the way out of the room, rather than right before the closing theme, for instance.

Conclusion

This chapter provided an overview of pediatric music psychotherapy with a specific focus on ways to work with pain from a mind-body perspective. Throughout each section, I have tried to illuminate the value of consistently viewing pain as a physical and emotional parameter that requires a complete assessment, as well as family consultation and multidisciplinary treatment planning.

The essential role that music psychotherapy can take in pain assessment and treatment is only in its infancy in being understood and recognized. The techniques presented in this chapter are part of a creative process that stem first from my own experience as a patient, chronically ill, in a hospital bed for three months; and second, from the fascination of how music and its life energy continuously are able to nurture, heal, and activate people suffering from the most complicated ailments. Music therapy, as the integrating force that connects all of our systems internally and synchronizes our thoughts and emotions externally, safely continues to ignite the power we have within ourselves to heal.

References

Anand, K. S., & Hickey, P. R. (1987). Pain and its effects in the human neonate and fetus. *New England Journal of Medicine, 317,* 1321.

Attia, J., Amiel-Tison, C., Mayer, N. N., Shnider, S. M., & Barrier, G. (1987). Measurement of postoperative pain and narcotic administration in infants using a new clinical scoring system. *Anesthesiology, 67,* A532.

Barr, R. G. (1989). Pain in children. In P. D. Wall & R. Melzack (Eds.), *Textbook of pain* (2nd ed., pp. 568–589). London: Churchill Livingstone.

Bradway, D. (1997). *An integrated approach to music therapy: Advanced pranic healing.* Unpublished master's thesis, York University.

DiLeo, J. H. (1977). *Child development: Analysis and synthesis.* New York: Brunner/Mazel.

Dileo-Maranto, C. (1991). A classification model for music and medicine. In C. Dileo-Maranto (Ed.), *Applications of music in medicine* (pp. 1–6). Washington, DC: National Association for Music Therapy, Inc.

Eagle, C., & Harsh, J. (1988). Elements of pain and music: The Aio connection. *Music Therapy, 7,* 15–27.

Eland, J. M. (1982). Minimizing injection pain associated with pre kindergarten immunizations. *Issues in Comprehensive Pediatric Nursing, 5,* 361–372.

Gilles, F. H., Shankle, W., & Dooling, E. (1983). Myelinated tracts: Growth patterns. In F. H. Gilles, A. Leviton, & E. C. Dooling (Eds.), *The developing human brain* (pp. 118–182). Boston: Wright & Co.

Jeans, M. E., & Gordon, D. J. (1981). An investigation of the developmental characteristics of the concept of pain. *Pain* (Suppl.1), S11.

Loewy, J. V. (1999). The quiet soldier: Pain and sickle-cell anemia. In J. Hibben (Ed.), *Inside music therapy: Client experiences* (pp. 69–76). Gilsum, NH: Barcelona.

Loewy, J. V., MacGregor, B., Richards, K., & Rodriguez, J. (1997). Music therapy pediatric pain management: Assessing and attending to the sounds of hurt, fear, and anxiety. In J. V. Loewy, (Ed.), *Music therapy and pediatric pain* (pp. 45–56). Cherry Hill, NJ: Jeffrey Books.

McGrath, P. (1990). *Pain in children: Nature, assessment and treatment.* New York: Guilford Press.

McGrath, P., & Craig, K. (1989). Developmental and psychological factors in children's pain. In *Acute pain in children: The pediatric clinics of North America* (Vol. 36, No. 4, pp. 823–836). Philadelphia: W. B. Saunders.

Olness, K., & MacDonald, J. (1981). Self-hypnosis and biofeedback in the management of juvenile migraine. *Journal of Development & Behavioral Pediatrics, 2*(4), 168–170.

Stewart, M. L. (1977). Measurement of clinical pain. In A. K. Jacox (Ed.), *Pain: A sourcebook for nurses and other health professionals* (pp. 107–136). Boston: Little Brown.

Varni, J. W., Gilbert, A., & Dietrich, S. L. (1981). Behavioral medicine in pain and analgesia management for the hemophilic child with factor VIII inhibitor. *Pain, 11*(1), 121–126.

Wong, D., & Baker, C. (1988). Pain in children: Comparison of assessment scales. *Pediatric Nursing, 14*(1), 9–17.

Winnicott, D. W. (1953). Transitional objects and transitional phenomena: A study of the first not-me possession. *International Journal of Psychoanalysis, 34,* 89–97.

CONTRIBUTORS

DAVID ALDRIDGE, B.Ed., B.Phil., Ph.D., has the Chair for Qualitative Research in Medicine in the Faculty of Medicine at the University of Witten Herdecke, Germany. He teaches music therapy students about professional aspects of clinical communication and is responsible for organizing research and research support services. He publishes an illustrated German music therapy book series called *KAIROS* that brings various clinical aspects of practice and research together. His research interests are concerned with the broad spectrum of creative arts therapies. His newest project is as a graphic artist preparing a series of print installations with a composer of modern music.

GUDRUN ALDRIDGE, Dipl. Mus., Dr. Phil., is Lecturer in Music Therapy at the University of Witten Herdecke, Germany. She is also a music therapist at the same institute and supervises students in training. Her work has specialized predominantly in psychosomatic problems with adult patients. She is currently preparing a book together with David Aldridge about a qualitative research approach to the development of melody that will be published by Jessica Kingsley Publishers in the year 2000.

JOKE BRADT, MMT, MT-BC, received her Master of Music Therapy degree from Temple University, Philadelphia. As a doctoral student in the Department of Health Studies, she is currently researching the effect of music entrainment on pain in pediatric postsurgical patients. She is a visiting professor in the music therapy programs at the College of Science and Art, campus Lemmensinstituut in Leuven, Belgium, and at the College of Arnhem and Nijmegen in Nijmegen, The Netherlands. She gives several music therapy lectures and workshops in Belgium every year.

CHARLES BUTLER, MD, PhD, FACS, FACC, FACCP, spent over 10 years as Director of Cardiac Surgery at Bronson Medical Center, Kalamazoo, Michigan, with an academic appointment through Michigan State University. Previous academic teaching appointments were at Harvard University, the Mayo Clinic, the Medical College of Alabama, and the University of Utah. Dr. Butler's Ph.D. is in biophysics. He has spent over 10 years studying the effects of low frequency sound on human beings. He has authored many books, chapters, and articles.

CHERYL DILEO, PhD, MT-BC, is Professor of Music Therapy at Temple University in Philadelphia. She received her bachelor's and master's degrees in music therapy from Loyola University of the South, and her Ph.D. from Louisiana State University. She is the Immediate Past-President of the World Federation of Music Therapy, Past-President of the National

Association for Music Therapy, Inc., and has served in many leadership positions for these and other organizations during the past 25 years. She is the author/editor of 9 books and over 70 chapters and articles on music therapy; her specialties include medical music therapy, professional ethics, and music therapy education and training. She is a consulting editor for the *Journal of Music Therapy, The International Journal of Arts Medicine,* and *The Arts in Psychotherapy*. She is a frequent international lecturer having taught in 17 countries on 5 continents. In 1995, she received the *Merit Award* from the National Association for Music Therapy, Inc.

JANE EDWARDS, M.Mus., RMT, is the Lecturer in Music Therapy at the School of Music, the University of Queensland, Brisbane, Australia. She is also a part-time doctoral student in the Department of Paediatrics and Child Health in the Faculty of Medicine investigating research methods appropriate to pediatric music therapy. She has a Master of Music degree from the University of Melbourne, where she was supervised by Denise Erdonmez Grocke. Her undergraduate studies in music therapy were also completed there, and she has been a registered practitioner in music therapy since 1986.

ELLEN GRIGGS-DRANE, MM, MT-BC, is Assistant Professor of Music Therapy at Western Michigan University and Coordinator of Clinical Experiences for the WMU Music Therapy Clinic. Developing and researching treatment protocols using musical wind instruments in the treatment of asthma, cystic fibrosis, and COPD is one of her areas of expertise.

ROBERTA WIGLE JUSTICE, MM, MT-BC, FAMI, is a music therapist with 25 years of clinical experience in inpatient, outpatient, and partial hospital programs. She has published articles on music therapy in psychiatry and eating disorders. She is currently in private practice in music therapy and Guided Imagery and Music in Ann Arbor, Michigan.

ROSEANN KASAYKA, DA, MT-BC, FAMI, received her Doctor of Arts degree from New York University and has been a Fellow of the Association for Music and Imagery since 1988. Currently, she is the Vice-President of Dementia Services and Healing Arts Therapies at Heather Hill Hospital, Health and Care Center in Chardon, Ohio. Roseann maintains a private practice in Guided Imagery and Music in Chicago, Illinois, and in Cleveland, Ohio.

JOANNE VICTORIA LOEWY, DA, MT-BC, directs the Music Therapy Program at Beth Israel Medical Center in New York City. She also consults at Children's Hospital of Philadelphia and to institute medical music therapy programs in hospitals throughout the country. Joanne received her doctorate from New York University, where she serves as adjunct faculty. She edited the text, *Music Therapy and Pediatric Pain,* and has written articles and presented nationally and internationally on pain, sedation, and asthma. Dr. Loewy has served on the editorial boards for *Music Therapy* and the *Journal of Music Therapy*. This year, she presented at the American Psychiatric Association's annual conference.

DAVID RAMSEY, MA, ACMT, is currently working at Beth Abraham Health Services in the Bronx, New York, as a music therapy supervisor. He is a part-time faculty member at New York University, where he is also completing his Doctor of Arts degree in Music Therapy. As the former Executive Director of the American Association for Music Therapy, he served on the transition team during the formation of the American Music Therapy Association. He is currently innvolved in music therapy research with neurologically impaired adults.

ALAN D. REITMAN, PhD, MT-BC, is Adjunct Assistant Professor of Music Therapy at the University of Miami. He completed his undergraduate and graduate education at Temple University in Philadelphia, where he earned a double major in music therapy and music education and a doctorate in psychoeducational processes. He has worked as a music therapist for over 15 years and has extensive clinical experience with a variety of client populations. Dr. Reitman has developed several models of music therapy for work with a variety of clients, including a music video intervention for adolescents, and a music-assisted treatment for musicians with performance anxiety. He is an active presenter at workshops and conferences around the country. He is a member of the editorial board of *Music Therapy Perspectives,* and currently serves as President of the Florida Association for Music Therapy.

BARBARA REUER, PhD, MT-BC, is Past-President of the National Association for Music Therapy, and Founder and Director of Music Works of California, a contractual and consulting agency based in San Diego, California. Her music therapy practice includes direct services to children with "special needs"; oncology and hospice patients; and substance abuse, cancer, and bereavement support groups. Major areas of Dr. Reuer's current professional involvement are in music therapy program and job development in San Diego County, including an international music therapy internship training program. In addition to her clinical work, she provides workshops and seminars (wellness, community building, stress management) nationally and internationally for health care professionals, educators, and corporate clients. She has authored several articles in professional publications and co-authored several books. Dr. Reuer was one of the recipients of an Administration on Aging grant through San Diego State University Center on Aging, *Best Practice in Music Therapy Utilizing Group Percussion Strategies for Promoting Volunteerism in the Well Older Adult.*

MARK RIDER, PhD, RMT, is a clinical psychologist and music therapist at the Behavioral Medicine Clinic in Grapevine, Texas. He is the innovator of the entrainment imagery improvisational techniques and the homeodynamic theory of psychoneuroimmunology, recently published by MMB Press in his book, *The Rhythmic Language of Health and Disease.*

RUTHANN RITCHIE, MT-BC, received her B.A. in Music Performance from the University of Evansville, her B.S. in Music Therapy from Augsburg College, Minneapolis, and her M.M. in Organ/Church Music from the University of Colorado in Boulder. She is currently employed as a music therapist in hospice and home care at the Hubert H. Humphrey Cancer Center of the North Memorial Medical Center in Minneapolis. She is also a professional freelance harpist.

KAY ROSKAM, PhD, MT-BC, is Director of the Music Therapy Program at Chapman University, Orange, California. She is the author of *Feeling the Sound: The Influence of Music on Behavior* and is the President-Elect of the American Music Therapy Association.

BRUCE SAPERSTON, PhD, MT-BC, is an Associate Professor of Music and Head of the Department of Music at Utah State University, where he was Director of Music Therapy from 1987–1997. Dr. Saperston holds a B.A. in Music from the University of North Texas, a master's degree and Ph.D. in Special Education from the University of Texas at Austin, and is a Board-Certified Music Therapist. He is internationally renowned as a clinician, researcher, and educator, was a member of the Editorial Committee of the *Journal of Music Therapy*, and has served on the International Scientific Committee for the World Congress of Music Therapy and the National Research Committee of the National Association for Music Therapy. His publications include clinical articles, research, and a book he jointly edited, entitled, *The Art and Science of Music Therapy: A Handbook*, which documents international music therapy practices. Dr. Saperston currently serves on the Disciplinary Board of the Certification Board for Music Therapists. He received the Betty Isern Howery Award of Recognition for Outstanding Contributions to the Western Region and Field of Music Therapy in 1997 and was issued a U.S. Patent for his concept of Physiologically Interactive music.

BENEDIKTE B. SCHEIBY, MA (Music Therapy), MA (Music Educatión), CMT, DpMtp, is a Music Therapy Supervisor at Beth Abraham Health Services. She specializes in Analytical Music Therapy, is a certified trainer in Analytical Music Therapy, and is a trained bioenergetic body psychotherapist. She has worked as a music therapy clinician, educator, and researcher since 1980. For 10 years she served as Professor in Aalborg University's Music Therapy Program. Currently, she has a private practice treating a wide variety of clients. She serves as Adjunct Faculty in the Music Therapy Program at New York University and in the Art Therapy Program at Pratt Institute. She has published a book and a variety of articles in English, German, and Danish.

FRED J. SCHWARTZ, MD, practices anesthesiology and MusicMedicine, and is involved in music research at Piedmont Hospital in Atlanta, Georgia. He also does music production for pregnancy, newborns, and children with Transitions Music in Atlanta. He is a member of the International Society for Music in Medicine, International Society of Prenatal and Perinatal Psychology and Medicine, International Society for Prenatal Development, American Music Therapy Association, The National Academy of Recording Arts and Sciences, the American Society of Anesthesiology, and the American Society of Regional Anesthesia.

CONCETTA M. TOMAINO, DA, MT-BC, is the Director of Music Therapy at the Institute for Music and Neurologic Function, Beth Abraham Health Services, New York. She is Past-President of the American Association for Music Therapy and presently serves on the Certification Board for Music Therapy. She was presented with an Award of Accomplishment by the Music Therapists for Peace at the United Nations in 1999, and received a "Touchstone Award" from Women in Music, recognizing her visionary spirit and pioneering mission of service to the music industry. Dr. Tomaino serves on the Advisory Board of the Research Center in Alternative and Complementary Medicine in Rehabilitation at the Kessler Institute and also serves on the editorial boards of several professional journals. She is an adjunct clinical supervisor at the New York University graduate program in music therapy.

ALAN TURRY, MA, MT-BC, NRMT, is Co-Director of the Nordoff-Robbins Center for Music Therapy at New York University. He oversees the clinical training program at NRCMT and teaches clinical improvisation at New York University. He holds an M.A. from NYU and is a certified instructor in NRMT. He has lectured internationally about the use of improvisation in both clinical work and supervision. His publications include journal articles as well as a recent chapter on transference and countertransference in NRMT. Alan is a doctoral candidate in music therapy at NYU.

ANN E. TURRY, MA, CMT, NRMT, holds a master's degree in music therapy from New York University and advanced clinical certification from the Nordoff-Robbins Center for Music Therapy at New York University. She worked at Tomorrow Children's Institute for five years on a pediatric oncology/hematology unit and has presented and published internationally on the use of clinical improvisation with children with cancer. Ann is a co-founder/director of Creative Music Therapy Studio in New York City and also works at the Nordoff-Robbins Center for Music Therapy at NYU. She is a doctoral candidate in music therapy at NYU.